FEMALE OCCUPATIONS

Women's Employment 1850—1950

Margaret Ward

3 8014 07002 2261

First published 2008
© Margaret Ward, 2008

All rights reserved. No reproduction
permitted without the prior permission
of the publisher:

COUNTRYSIDE BOOKS
3 Catherine Road
Newbury, Berkshire

To view our complete range of books,
please visit us at
www.countrysidebooks.co.uk

ISBN 978 1 84674 097 8

STAFFS. LIBRARY AND INFORMATION SERVICES	
3 8014 07002 2261	
HJ	19-Dec-2008
33l.40941	£12.99
LICH	

Designed by Peter Davies, Nautilus Design
Produced through MRM Associates Ltd., Reading
Printed by Cambridge University Press

*All material for the manufacture of this book
was sourced from sustainable forests*

Introduction

*'Gone forever is the helpless woman
in a world of endless opportunity for energy and wit.'*
(Ignatius Phayre, 'War time service for women',
Windsor Magazine 1915)

Interest in the working lives of our female ancestors has increased tremendously over recent years. This book sets out to demonstrate the range and diversity of women's work spanning the last two centuries – from bumboat women and nailmakers to doctors and civil servants – and to suggest ways of finding out more about what often seems to be a 'hidden history'.

There has been a great ebb and flow in women's employment during this time and a strange ambivalence about it too, equal to Lord Nelson lifting his telescope to his blind eye before declaring, 'I see no ships'. Time and again, with great surprise, commentators and politicians have discovered . . . that women work. This collection of over 300 trades, industries and occupations followed by women in the 19th and 20th centuries is a tribute to our hard-working female ancestors.

In the 19th century, the labour of working class women and children carried forward the Industrial Revolution. They were neat, light workers for the mills and machinery, whose 'nimble fingers' were an asset in this new working world. They toiled in mines and collieries, forged iron chains, made bricks, packed explosives, and much, much more.

Above all, they provided cheap labour. Throughout the 19th and most of the 20th century all women workers were paid less than the men who worked alongside them. The Equal Pay Act was only passed in 1970, followed by the 1984 amendment act that laid down equal pay for work of equal value, though even today cases arise where women are working for lower rates than men.

It was a problem that affected professional women too. When they were trying in the late 19th century to break through the barriers preventing them becoming fully accredited members of professional associations, the fear expressed by male colleagues was that admitting women would lead to lower rates of pay, and lower status, for all.

The persistence shown by women who wanted to become doctors, lawyers, accountants, etc. was remarkable, as were the lengths professional bodies of the late 19th and early 20th centuries went to in order to keep them out. It took legislation, beginning with the Sex Disqualification Removal Act 1919, to force the issue to its logical conclusion.

Yet women running a business were not new. By late Victorian times they are everywhere you look – owning or managing shops, pubs, hotels, private schools and academies, brickworks, factories . . . the list goes on – just browse through any contemporary trades directory. They were to be found in traditional male roles, too, such as the blacksmith or the miller, and by the later 19th century they had their own practices as accountants, dentists, doctors. Middle class women were beginning to demand a role in life outside the home, while working class women were discovering how to use political and trade union activity to their advantage.

The two world wars brought great charges. Women had long been involved in dirty, strenuous occupations – but those were working class women and now articulate middle class girls had discovered that they, too, could weld metal, pack explosives and drive heavy vehicles.

It is hard nowadays to comprehend how large a part class played in Victorian times and beyond, yet it is essential to grasp the differences when considering our female ancestors. The choices for working class girls on leaving school were restricted to a degree that seems unbelievable today. The majority of young girls in the second half of the 19th century and up to the 1920s and 1930s found their choice of 'what to do after school' boiled down to becoming a servant, a shop assistant, or a factory hand; often following in the footsteps of their mother or sisters. An ambition beyond that was seen as 'getting above yourself'.

Domestic service was one of the major employers of female labour. Being able to afford a servant was a matter of social status for the middle classes and was not lightly given up. The number of female servants was consistently well over a million from 1861 to the Second World War, peaking in the 1890s. A distaste for domestic service, given an alternative, was apparent in working women during and after the First World War but the long years of the Depression drove many back into it. By the end of the Second World War, however, that world had gone for good. That lack of choice for girls was partly down to their education. Until they were educated beyond the need to be good wives and mothers, they could not take part in the 'white blouse' revolution in offices, banks and the Civil Service, but from the late 1800s state education began, slowly, to make a difference.

By the end of the 19th century middle class girls were
seeking new opportunities in education and employment.

Yet middle class girls, too, faced obstacles in a choice of work. Educated they might be, but a girl would still need a little steel in her character to force her way into a profession and stay there, no matter how bored she might be with nothing to do. The middle class ideal was that a woman should not work outside the home. Even where she managed to find a good job, a 'marriage bar' existed in most professions, offices, banks, the Civil Service, teaching, nursing, etc., until the 1960s or so – if a woman married she lost her job, or was expected to bow out gracefully. To some extent this was a problem solved by part-time working, which was a wartime practice that continued after the 1940s because it filled a need, being popular with married women and a convenient and flexible alternative for employers – about one in five women were working part-time in the 1950s. However, it proved a bit of a cul-de-sac for any woman wanting promotion or to follow a career.

Some working class women had always worked from home of course, as outworkers, an option used by industries such as dressmaking in all its forms, strawplaiting, lacemaking, glovemaking, weaving and many more. Although this could give women independence and sometimes a good wage, in too many cases it was a recipe for sweated labour, with starvation wages and insecurity thrown in.

The entries in this book concentrate on the period from the 1840s to the end of the Second World War, drawing on trends and experiences beyond those dates. It has not been possible to represent every occupation followed by women – in fact, it would have been simpler to list all the jobs they did *not* do – and especially in wartime they were present in every sphere of industry and commerce. There is, of course, much more to be discovered, as the books, websites and museums mentioned in individual entries will show. To save repetition, the ideas in the 'Finding Out More' chapter are intended to be used with all the occupations.

A woman welder in the Second World War.

This book is concerned with industries and groups of workers. However, every occupation had its own vocabulary of job titles and processes. If you are puzzled by an odd occupation and don't know where to start, Colin Waters' *Dictionary of Old Trades, Titles and Occupations* (Countryside Books, 2008) may be of help.

I would like to thank all my friends who have contributed photographs and stories for these working women. Most of the illustrations and quotes are from my own collection, including *Girl's Own Paper*, *Windsor Magazine*, *Harmsworth Magazine*, *Strand Magazine*, *Illustrated London News*, *Punch*, *Living London*, *Good News*, *Cassell's Family Magazine*, *Cassell's Household Guide*, *Home Notes* and others.

The great majority of our female ancestors worked, but they didn't always admit it to census enumerators or registrars, or even to their own family. I hope that reading about these possible occupations will move you to consider what the women in your own family may have done.

Margaret Ward

■ ACCOUNTANT

The demand for accountants soared as new businesses and industries were created in the 19th century. There was nothing to stop women working as accountants, and they are recorded as such in the census (e.g. in 1881 Amelia Barrett, 47 years old, of Islington, or Isabella Brown, 29 years old, of Lambeth). The 'world's first professional body of accountants' – the Institute of Chartered Accountants of Scotland (ICAS) – was awarded its royal charter in 1854; the first professional body in England, the Institute of Accountants in London, was formed in 1870 and in 1880 the Institute of Chartered Accountants in England and Wales (ICAEW) was also established by royal charter. However, there was determined resistance to admitting women as members, which it was thought would 'lower the status of the profession'.

Mary Harris Smith (1847–1934) was obviously born with a love of figures and had worked as an accountant for some time before her first attempt to gain membership at the age of 41. By 1888 she had her own business in London and that year she applied to join the ICAEW but was refused admission because she was a woman. In 1889 and 1891 she was similarly turned down by the Society of Incorporated Accountants and Auditors (SIAA, formed in 1885, merged with the ICAEW in 1957) – in the 1891 census she is recorded as a 'practising accountant'. Nearly 20 years later, in 1918, the SIAA changed their rules to allow the admission of women and voted to admit Mary Harris Smith as an Honorary Fellow. Mary, by now aged 72, renewed her application to the ICAEW and in 1919 became the first, and only, female chartered accountant in the world.

Although the professional gates were open, relatively few women followed in Mary Harris Smith's footsteps (they still formed only 4% of the workforce by 1980).

After 1870 several professional societies were formed: a history and index can be found on the website of the ICAEW, which also has a searchable database of 'Accountancy Ancestors' – 'Who was who in accountancy 1874–1965' – which includes obituaries and photographs (Library and Information Service, Chartered Accountants' Hall, PO Box 433, Moorgate Place, London EC2P 2BJ; telephone: 020 7920 8620; www.icaew.co.uk).

The Guildhall Library has a useful leaflet guide to the records it holds relating to the ICAEW and the bodies that predated it; or consult *Chartered Accountants in England and Wales: A Guide to Historical Records*, Wendy Habgood (Manchester University Press, 1994). The website of ICAS is at www.icas.org.uk.

■ Actress, music hall artiste

In 1802 the *Lady's Magazine* had warned: 'The stage is a dangerous situation for a young woman of a lively temper and personal accomplishments.' Over a century later, Noel Coward's advice to Mrs Worthington not to put her daughter on the stage echoed the sentiment – the theatre was no place for a nice girl. Actresses were sought after, admired and envied, but very often they were outside the pale of respectable society and were sometimes considered little better than prostitutes.

The Victorian actress could only learn her trade by practice. Some, like Dame Ellen Terry (1848–1928), were the children of actors and appeared on stage from infancy but, as Charles Booth summarised in the 1880s: 'The chief methods of obtaining engagements are (1) by advertising, (2) through an agent, (3) applying directly to the management.' At the time, rates of pay could be anything from £1 10s to £4 or £5 a week, depending on the theatre and the actress's place in the stage hierarchy: she might just be a 'walking woman' with little or nothing to say. Young actresses with promise might get the chance to understudy a part, or sometimes more established actors took pupils for paid tuition. Not until the establishment of the Academy of Dramatic Art in 1904 (the prefix 'Royal' was added in 1920) was there a school where the techniques of stage acting could be taught, but the profession remained one where chance could play as large a part as hard graft and experience in the making of a 'star'.

An actress of the 19th century would have found employment within the 'stock company system', where she worked at a particular theatre performing a repertory of plays, which would be repeated in sequence. Subsequently that system gave way to touring companies or 'long runs', where the company of actors performed one play either at different locations or for a long period in one theatre.

The 'stock company' routine was revived in the early 1900s as 'repertory theatre' or 'rep' and was a good training ground for young actresses.

Violet Cameron (Violet Lydia Thompson, 1862–1919), centre, with Minnie Byron and other members of the cast of The Mascotte *at the Royal Comedy Theatre in 1881. She made her first stage appearance at the age of eight and was a popular performer in operettas, plays and music hall, but became notorious for a series of scandalous love affairs.*

Wendy Hiller (1912–2003), who became a highly respected stage and film actress, went into rep at Manchester straight from school in the 1920s and, like many others, gained experience of the theatre as an assistant stage manager before working as an understudy and taking walk-on parts; her big break came in the 1930s with the lead in *Love on the Dole*, taken to London and then to New York. Since the 1910s more opportunities had been opening up for stage actresses in the rapidly expanding film industry, followed by radio and television, and many actresses moved from one medium to another. There were also women who went into management, such as Annie Horniman, who ran a repertory company after she bought the Gaiety Theatre in Manchester, from 1908 to 1917, and was influential in expanding the opportunities for actors in the early 20th century.

It can be difficult to categorise some individuals – were they actresses, dancers, singers, comediennes, or a combination of all four? The other side of the coin to 'legitimate' theatre was the music hall, beloved of the working classes. There had for some time been unlicensed 'free and easies' – small theatres, often in rooms attached to pubs, that put on short musical plays (burlettas), pantomimes and bills of variety including singers, dancers, speciality acts and comedians, but by the second half of the 19th century music hall was incredibly popular and had moved into the mainstream; there were literally hundreds of halls in London and provincial towns and cities by the 1870s. The last music hall to be purpose-built was the Chiswick Empire, in 1913, a 'Palace of Variety'.

'The great difference between an actor in a theatre and a music hall "artiste" is that whereas the first has his part provided for him, the second has to depend upon his own individual efforts and abilities,' Charles Booth decided. 'Music hall artistes bring their own company and their own piece and the manager of the hall has nothing to do but mount it in the matter of scenery.'

The stars were household names in their day – women like Vesta Tilley, Marie Lloyd, Bessie Bellwood, Jenny Hill and Nellie Power were some of those whose catch-phrases and songs were common currency. They were larger-than-life characters and they had to be, to make an immediate impression on an audience in a noisy, hot atmosphere where 'turn' followed 'turn' and the audience was free to move about – and walk out – at any time. But they were only the well-paid tip of the iceberg and the great majority of performers existed on low wages and uncertain contracts, and lived and died in poverty.

Tracing a woman who worked in the theatre is not easy. It was frequently a peripatetic and uncertain life, the use of stage names was very common, and actresses frequently lied about their age! See *My Ancestor Worked in the Theatre*, Alan Ruston (Society of Genealogists, 2005), for helpful information on research. The Theatre Museum collections, at Covent Garden until August 2007, have been moved to the Victoria and Albert Museum but see their website (www.peopleplayuk.org.uk) for a wealth of information on people from the worlds of theatre, music hall, pantomime, circus, dance etc. The National Archives has a leaflet on *Sources for the History of Film, Television and the Performing Arts* available there and elsewhere. An article entitled 'Under the spotlight' by Nicola Lisle (*Ancestors* magazine, June 2007) will also be helpful.

There is advice on tracing music hall and variety artistes at www.hissboo. co.uk/musichall_artistes.shtml. The website of the Scottish Music Hall Society (www.freeweb.com/scottishmusichallsociety/informationwanted. htm) has a page where people post queries on past artistes. See also **ballet dancer; film, television and radio; 'principal boy'.**

■ ACTUARY

Dorothy Beatrice Spiers (née Davis, 1897–1977) was the first qualified woman actuary, a graduate of Newnham College, Cambridge who gained her degree in mathematics in 1918. She worked for the Guardian Insurance Company and studied for the examinations in her spare time, achieving qualification as a Fellow of the Institute of Actuaries in 1923. By 1960, there were still only eleven female fellows of the Institute.

It is a highly skilled, and highly paid, profession requiring advanced and accurate statistical and problem-solving abilities, usually in the world of insurance, pensions forecasts etc. And it required dedication from women like Dorothy, who refused initial offers of marriage from her future husband because she would not be deflected from her ambition. The first woman to try to break into the profession had been an American, Alice Hussey, in 1895, but the Institute sheltered behind its constitution until the First World War, when the increasing numbers of women filling posts in insurance offices began to bring pressure for change.

The Institute of Actuaries (Oxford, OX1 2AW) has responsibility for England and Wales, while the Faculty of Actuaries (Edinburgh, EH1 3PP) acts in Scotland (the website www.actuaries.org.uk is for both of them). The Worshipful Company of Actuaries was granted its charter in 1979.

■ AERATED WATER BOTTLER

Carbonated drinks (using carbon dioxide dissolved under pressure) had been available since the end of the 18th century and were in growing demand throughout the Victorian period; fizzy soft drinks and water were popular in particular with the Temperance movement as alternatives to alcohol. Manufacturers can be found all over the country – Hull, for instance, had over 20 factories producing ginger beer, lemonade, etc by the 1890s. Women were employed in the bottling plants and this could be hazardous work.

In 1900 the *Harmsworth Magazine* published an article by W.J. Wintle that appeared under the skull-festooned title of 'Daring Death to Live: The most dangerous trades in the world'. It included the women who filled glass bottles with aerated water or soft drinks for R. White & Sons at their Camberwell factory. To protect the women from flying glass, 'All the bottlers, wirers, and labellers wear masks of strong wire gauze, while their arms

A wire mask and woollen gauntlets protect a woman filling bottles with aerated water. (Harmsworth Magazine, 1900)

are protected with full length gauntlets, so constructed as to cover the palm of the hand and the space between the thumb and fourth finger. It has been found by experience that a knitted woollen gauntlet of thick texture answers much better than one of leather or india-rubber. The bottling machines are so arranged that the bottle is contained in a very strong wire cage during the process of filling.' The most dangerous point, however, was when the newly-filled bottle was taken out of the machine by hand.

■ AERONAUT

Name for a Victorian **balloonist**, or sometimes a trapeze artist in the circus (see **circus performer**).

■ AGRICULTURAL LABOURER

Agriculture was historically a major employer of female labour, before domestic service and factory work became more important in the 19th century. By the 1880s there was a feeling in many rural areas that working in the fields ('goin' a-field') was not suitable work for women, although they continued to play an important part in the farming year throughout the 19th and early 20th centuries.

This is one of those occupations where female involvement could vary quite considerably depending on the part of the country; there was always more work for women in arable counties, for instance. In rural areas where women could find other work (such as straw plaiting, lacemaking, glovemaking etc), they tended not to work in the fields, but, if the male labourers' wages were low and there was no other way for the women to supplement them, they would do so. In Hertfordshire, for example, where straw plaiting provided a good income for women (see **straw plaiter**), there was very little farm work done by them except at haytime and harvest.

In the early spring they might go out stonepicking – removing large stones from the fields by hand, usually on new acreage or before ploughing – and then follow the plough, gathering up roots and invasive weeds such as couchgrass before the new crops were sown: 'The cold clods of earth numb the fingers as they search for the roots and weeds. The damp clay chills the feet through thick-nailed boots, and the back grows stiff with stooping' (wrote Richard Jefferies in 'Women in the field', *Graphic*, 1875). As the crops grew, women would be employed to hoe between the young plants to keep weeds down, and then to pull turnips, swedes, potatoes, etc., or pick fruit and vegetables such as strawberries or peas. In the 1930s, in Lincolnshire, women were employed by the day or by the amount of crops

Women working on the land at the beginning of the 20th century, clearing the fields for the plough.

gathered – if it rained the work was muddy and wet: 'The women were kitted out with wellingtons and trousers and had hessian sacks tied round their middle with binder twine.'

In some areas women helped with the sheepshearing: 'They handle the wool, cut away and throw out the dirty and knotty parts, and then roll up the fleece, the cut side outwards, ending with the neck, which serves to bind the parcel round. After all the washing and squeezing and paring away, it is a dirty business at best, as any one will say who has unfolded a fleece in the mill.' (*Once a Week*, 1860)

If at no other times, country women would usually be out at haymaking and harvest. In June when the hay was ready it had to be cut, then spread out over the ground to dry ('tedding') and turned several times. It was then raked up and gathered into ricks in the farmyard for winter feed. This was one area where haymaking machinery gradually superseded some of the traditionally female tasks.

At harvest time, usually in August, women would be out in the fields in the early morning, often with children in tow, to work all day following the reapers to gather the crop. This is generally represented as an enjoyable country romp, but the reality was hard, back-breaking work. Richard Jefferies described the scene: 'Through the blazing heat of the long summer day, till night, and sometimes under the pale light of the harvest-moon this labour continues. Its effects are visible in the thin frame, the bony wrist, the skinny arm showing the sinews, the rounded shoulders and the stoop, the wrinkles and lines upon the sunburnt faces. Many women labour thus while still suckling their infants; and at night carry home heavy bundles of gleanings upon their heads.'

During the winter months, female part-time labour would not generally be wanted by the farmer. When a woman's full-time occupation was as an agricultural labourer, however, even during these slow months, she would be employed about the farm. In 1882 Theresa Brown, just 22 years old and soon to be married, died at her home in Watlington, Buckinghamshire, following an accident. She had been recorded in the 1881 census as an 'ag lab', 'working at field work', and in November 1882 her hand was crushed in the oilcake crushing mill at the Model House Farm, Shirburn; despite amputation of the hand and wrist, lockjaw set in and she died a few days later, 'after great suffering'.

Because of the seasonal nature of so much female agricultural work it is rarely documented. Village histories may be useful for discovering the local rhythms of life, as may local museums. *Labouring Life in the Victorian Countryside*, Pamela Horn (Alan Sutton, 1995) is helpful for the background. The Museum of English Rural Life at Reading has a great deal of information about country matters in general; its website has online catalogues, a bibliographical database etc (the museum is at the University of Reading, Redlands Road, Reading RGI 5EX; telephone: 0118 378 8660; www.ruralhistory.org). Read *My Ancestor Was an Agricultural Labourer*, Ian Waller (Society of Genealogists, 2007) for advice and sources. See also **bondager; farm servant; gangworker.**

■ AIR TRANSPORT AUXILIARY (ATA)

The **ATA was** the brainchild of Gerard d'Erlanger, director of British Airways in the 1930s, when, with war looming, he convinced the government that there would be a need for experienced pilots – who would not be eligible for the RAF by reason of age or perhaps disability – to run an air taxi/despatch service. The ATA remained a civilian air service throughout the war, although it was gradually taken over from BA by the Ministry of Aircraft Production, and was disbanded at the end of the war.

The first intake of male pilots were in place by September 1939. By the time women were recruited for the ATA at the beginning of 1940, ferrying aircraft from factory to aerodrome had become the main task and a desperately important one as the Battle of Britain was fought. Women were not initially welcomed, and it was largely the lobbying of Pauline Gower that swayed the Air Ministry. Miss Gower herself had over 2,000 flying hours under her belt and was a commissioner in the Civil Air Guard; she was made commander of the female ATA intake and became a highly respected officer for the duration of the war.

On 1 January 1940 the 'First Eight' officially began duties at the de Havilland works at Hatfield, ferrying Tiger Moths – Winifred Crossley, Margaret Cunnison, Margaret Fairweather, Mona Friedlander, Joan Hughes, Gabrielle Patterson, Rosemary Rees and Marion Wilberforce. All were experienced flyers. By 1942 there were 14 ferry pools in the ATA, and 22 by 1945 – Cosford, Hamble and Hatfield were all-female, while personnel were mixed elsewhere.

At first the women were restricted to non-operational planes, but the drain on personnel was such that by the summer of 1941 they were cleared to fly Hurricanes and Spitfires. Eventually all types of aircraft were included in their rosters, even the heavy four-engined bombers and, by the end of the war, the Meteor jet. In the summer of 1943 they were granted equal pay with their male counterparts, and in late 1944 were cleared to fly to the Continent. The intakes included foreign volunteers, including many from the USA.

The ATA also had female ground staff – some 900 out of a workforce of 2,000 – who worked in offices and training schools, as well as on maintenance of aircraft and armaments.

The uniform was dark blue, with a blue forage cap; brass buttons inscribed 'ATA'; and insignia of gold wings with 'ATA' in the centre. The pilots flew with no radios, no navigational instruments and no armaments, risking attack by enemy fighters as well as our own anti-aircraft batteries. The risks were well illustrated by the loss of one of the world's leading female pilots, Amy Mollison, née Johnson, in 1941. She is thought to have lost her bearings in bad weather over the Thames Estuary and was drowned when her plane went down. Though these women were non-combatants, they faced death every time they took off. Twenty women died in the service.

Personnel files for the ATA are held by the RAF Museum at Hendon (www.rafmuseum.org.uk), but are only available to the women themselves or their next of kin. Background information can be found on the internet: there is a history of the service at www.airtransportaux.org, which is dedicated to the American women pilots but covers the English side as well; a history and list of 'incidents and casualties' at www.fleetairarmarchive. net; a range of photographs at www.bamuseum.com; and a history and photographs at www.raf.mod.uk/history. The National Archives has some records for the organisational side of the service. The ATA Association can be contacted via Wing Commander Eric Viles, 40 Goldcrest Road, Chipping Sodbury, Bristol BS17 6XG.

There have been several books about, and by, the women who flew, including *Brief Glory*, the official ATA history published in 1946, and the most recent, *The Spitfire Women of World War II*, by Giles Whittell (Harper Press, 2007). All the websites given above have good booklists for further reading.

▪ ALMERIC PAGET MILITARY MASSAGE CORPS

Founded by Mr and Mrs Almeric Paget in 1914 (and originally called just the Almeric Paget Massage Corps), the APMMC provided over 100 trained **masseuses** to military hospitals in this country during the First World War and also supported an out-patients department in London. The success of these early physiotherapists in treating wounded servicemen was so great that the Corps was recognised by the War Office as the official body for the employment of masseurs and masseuses for military hospitals for the duration of the war, and in 1916 the word 'Military' was added to the title (in 1919 abbreviated to the Military Massage Service). Corps members served both in the UK and overseas (from 1917) – by 1919 there were some 2,000 in the service.

See www.familyrecords.gov.uk/focuson/womeninuniform/almeric_profile.htm for more details, and a profile of the service of Ethel Jones, a nursing sister in the Corps; for general information see the Women's

Work Collection of the Imperial War Museum; and pension records may be available at The National Archives. The names of members of the Corps may be found in the contemporary issues of the journal of the Society of Trained Masseuses. See **physiotherapist**.

■ ALMONER, LADY

The office of almoner is an ancient one, deriving from the Christian tradition of the Church and King distributing charity to the poor, but it is the 'lady almoner' we are concerned with here. It was a post that was 'female' from its inception. In 1895 Mary Stewart was appointed as almoner at the Royal Free Hospital in London, the first of her kind and something of an experiment, paid for by the Charity Organisation Society (COS – today the Family Welfare Association – which since the 1870s had been using 'assessors' in a similar role).

Large hospitals such as the Royal Free were facing the problem of being too popular for their own good – out-patient departments were becoming grossly overcrowded by people who could be equally well treated at a dispensary or at home, while the perennial task of separating those who could and should pay for their treatment from those who were entitled to free treatment was not being addressed. The almoner made sure that better-off patients paid the cost of their treatment, and that poorer patients could continue their treatment or convalescence when they left the hospital. She could offer financial assistance to those who needed it, arrange care for children, advise on cleanliness, cooking and nursing in the home, and any social problems, find work for those who lost their jobs because of illness, arrange apprenticeships for young men and women, liaise with the NSPCC in cases of child cruelty, and so on – it comes as no surprise to know that her job was eventually superseded by that of the social worker.

They were few in number, each hospital making its own decision as to whether it was financially worthwhile, and when the Hospital Almoners' Association was formed in 1903 it had only 13 members. Demand by hospitals continued to increase during and after the First World War, and in 1920 it was given to the Hospital Almoners' Association to organise the profession and the Institute of Hospital Almoners to set the examinations. In 1945 the two were combined into the Institute of Almoners (which became the Institute of Medical Social Workers in 1964). After 1948 and the coming of the National Health Service, the financial aspect of their work ceased but the almoner's department was still to be found in hospitals for some years, dealing now with social problems, discharge of patients, etc.

As hospital employees, records of almoners, where they still exist, will be found with hospital archives. Some charities also employed almoners, for the same kind of work as those in hospitals – in effect, assessing whether applicants were eligible for help, visiting, and advising on the best use of resources. The records of the Institute of Medical Social Workers 1895 to 1971 are held at the University of Warwick, Modern Records Centre – see their subject guide 'History of Social Work' for sources (www2.warwick. ac.uk/services/library/mrc).

■ APOTHECARY

When Elizabeth Garrett was beginning her attempt to storm the medical establishment in the 1860s, she gained the diploma of the Society of Apothecaries in 1865 as a way of getting her name onto the Medical Register. The Society had been granted its charter in 1617; the word apothecary was derived from the Latin *apotheca*, a place where wine, spices and herbs were stored, and reflected the profession's origins as those who made up and sold drugs and gave medical advice, like today's community pharmacists. In 1704 a long-running battle with the Royal College of Physicians was settled in court with the agreement that apothecaries be allowed to prescribe and dispense medicines. A century later, in 1815, the Society became responsible for regulation by licence of all those allowed 'to practise medicine', restricting membership to those who gained the Licentiateship (LSA; from 1907 the Licence in Medicine and Surgery, LMSSA) by an apprenticeship of five years, or, from the 1850s, attending lectures and examination. Some apothecaries also qualified as surgeons, and the origins of our general practitioners lie with this profession.

However, for hopeful women doctors in the 1860s, the interest primarily lay in the fact that the Society's examinations were open to 'all persons' and, under threat of legal action by Elizabeth Garrett's father, they were forced to admit that this included any woman who had fulfilled the same conditions as a man. Gaining the qualification enabled her to open a dispensary for women in London and take the first step to full registration as a doctor. The Society hurriedly bolted the stable door by changing their rules to exclude women, which was the situation until after the First World War.

The Society of Apothecaries has been involved in much of the development of the medical profession: see **doctor; midwife; pharmacist**. The Society's website (www.apothecaries.org) has details of its archives, but many have been microfilmed and are freely available at the Guildhall Library.

■ ARCHAEOLOGIST

W omen were active in archaeology from the late 1800s, quickly taking advantage of the new opportunities to obtain a higher education once they were allowed into universities, despite the difficulties put in their way by the male academic hierarchy – as late as 1939, when the highly respected archaeologist Dorothy Garrod (1892–1968) was elected to the Disney Chair at Cambridge University, women were not accepted as full members of the university or allowed to attend public awards ceremonies, and still got their certificates by post; it would not be until 1948 that they were allowed to officially graduate (see the Newnham College website, www.newn.cam. ac.uk, for biographical details of their distinguished female alumni).

Sometimes archaeology, travel and adventure seem to have formed a potent mix for women. Gertrude Bell (1868–1926) led a colourful life after graduating from Lady Margaret Hall, Oxford (the first woman to get a First in Modern History at Oxford), spending a considerable time in Iraq and founding the National Museum in Baghdad after the First World War; her remarkable times are described in *Desert Queen: The Extraordinary Life of Gertrude Bell* by Janet Wallach (see also http://wingsworldquest.org). Katherine Routledge was another pioneer, one of the first female graduates from Oxford and the first woman archaeologist to work in Polynesia. She led the Mana Expedition to Easter Island 1913–1915 and performed the first excavations of the famous stone figures: see *Among Stone Giants: The Life of Katherine Routledge and her Remarkable Expedition to Easter Island*, Jo Anne Van Tilburg (Scribner, 2003). Few in number, the women who followed this profession made their mark, such as Margaret Taylor (1881–1963), who was elected a Fellow of the Society of Antiquaries in 1925 and was secretary of the Society for the Promotion of Roman Studies from 1923 to 1954 and president in 1955.

■ ARCHITECT

The designing and construction, or restoration, of buildings has always been a prestigious occupation, and today the use of the word 'architect' is protected by law and can only be assumed by those who have followed the course of training recognised by the Royal Institute of British Architects (RIBA) and the Architects Registration Board. By the 1920s associateship or fellowship was open to both men and women, although as usual the profession had put up a strong resistance to the entry of female candidates.

Ethel Mary Charles is believed to have been the first qualified woman architect in England (though others may have been working in the field before that, as with **accountants**). Following a period under articles with the firms of Sir Ernest George & Peto and Mr Walter Cave, she sat her final examinations in 1898 and was elected an Associate Member of RIBA in that December. She had a particular interest in Gothic and domestic architecture, and was registered as practising in York Street Chamber, London.

By the 1920s there were several female architect partnerships, such as that of Norah Aiton and Betty Scott in Derby, and in 1928 Elisabeth Whitworth Scott won the competition for a design for the new Shakespeare Memorial Theatre at Stratford-upon-Avon, a prestigious award that brought the work of women architects into the public eye. In the 1930s the proportion of women among the students at the School of Architecture of the Architectural Association was one in five, but during the Second World War it increased to about one in two. 'By now it is generally recognised that women are well fitted for this important and exacting profession, and on completing their training they are employed, whether by Government departments or local authorities, or in private practice, on the same terms as their male colleagues,' said *The Times* in September 1943. Women were thought to have something extra to contribute to the planning and reconstruction of a post-war world; during the war the usual five year course of study was compressed into three and a half years so that young women could get at least as far as their intermediate examinations before they became eligible for call-up at the age of 20.

The website of the Royal Institute of British Architects, London W1N 6AD (www.architecture.com) has a biographical database of architects and a searchable catalogue; their library is open to the public by appointment. A 'Dictionary of Scottish Architects 1840–1940' can be found at www.codexgeo. co.uk/dsa/, which includes pioneers such as Edith Burnet Hughes (1888–1971), who had her own practice in Glasgow in the 1920s but was refused admittance to RIBA. The book *Women and Planning: Creating Gendered Realities*, Clara Greed (Routledge, 1994) names many women working in architecture, planning and surveying in the 19th and early 20th centuries.

■ Artificial flower maker

A glance at any fashion plate of the 19th and early 20th centuries, when hats and dresses were enhanced with elaborate adornments, makes it clear why the art of artificial flower making employed hundreds of girls and women.

The best quality artificial flowers – intended for the most fashionable creations – were prepared in small factories, but it was also work done at home. In 1896 in *Home Life* a wholesale dealer explained that the Franco-Prussian War of 1870 had boosted the British industry because previously the majority of artificial flowers had come from France or Germany. 'Cutters who cut the leaves, petals, etc, with a stamp cutter start at 7s a week, gradually rising to 14s; there is very little skill required, so the wages are not very high. Shaders, viz, those who dip the various parts in the dye, shade and strip them, earn better money, theirs rising to 25s. From these we come to the leaf makers; here we require skill, and a girl who is sharp and has good taste will take an average of £1 per week, whilst during the busy season, by working overtime, as much as 35s is earned.' Skilled workers in the 'mounting and making' departments earned 35s to £2 a week. The work was not without its dangers – the dyes used for colouring contained arsenic.

The flowers were made of materials such as silk, cotton, taffeta or organdy, and it was a job that required nimble fingers, the smaller pieces having to be manoeuvred using tweezers. Petals, blossoms, buds, leaves and stalks all had to be cut out, the petals and leaves curved and shaped to match Nature. The whole creation was wired and glued together, dyes were used to colour the materials, and feathers and other decorative features added – including artificial fruit and small stuffed birds! Flowers were also used for wreaths and bouquets, cake decoration and home furnishings.

At the bottom end of the market were the coloured paper flowers made for the poor by the poor. Women who made paper flowers in the winter may have been engaged in making and hawking fire-stove ornaments in summer – these were made of coloured paper and tinsel, with streamers and rosettes, and were bought by the working class to ornament their hearth in summer when the stove fire was out.

■ ARTIST

'Never has the position of woman in the field of English art been so strong as it is today,' wrote Arthur Fish in the *Harmsworth Magazine* in 1900. 'There, as in other branches of work, she is competing closely with men; in some instances equalling him; in a few, outdistancing him . . .'. Yet, he mused, 'It is curious that in spite of the fact that women students carry off a large percentage of the prizes from the Academy Schools each year, and that women artists contribute largely to the success of the annual exhibitions at Burlington House, the members [of the Royal Academy (RA)] continue to fail to recognise the right of women to be represented in the Academy itself.' Without that recognition from the RA, women could not be regarded as truly professional artists. Despite the fact that the Academy had been started in 1768 with the backing of two female artists, Angelica Kauffmann and Mary Moser, no woman had ever been elected to membership.

The woman whose career Mr Fish chose to illustrate his point was Elizabeth Thompson (1846–1933), who when she married Sir William Butler became Lady Butler and who was recognised as one of the finest painters of battle scenes of the 19th century. She had a phenomenal public success with her paintings *The Roll Call* in 1874 and *The 28th Regiment at Quatre Bras* in 1875, but her four attempts to be accepted as a member by the RA failed. The fourth, and last, time was in 1879, when she was beaten in the voting, by two votes, in favour of Hubert von Herkomer. See *Lady Butler, Battle Artist 1846–1933*, Paul Usherwood and Jenny Spencer-Smith (Alan Sutton, 1987), for more on this remarkable artist. Only in 1922 was a woman accepted as an Associate Member (Annie Swynnerton), and the first female Academician was Laura Knight in 1936. This sidelining of even the best of female artists is perhaps the reason why for so long there was a common belief that there were 'no women painters' in the Victorian period.

For girls interested in serious training as an artist, there were a number of well-known schools by the early 1900s, most of them with a majority of female students. The famous Newlyn School in Cornwall, for instance, took about 30 students at a time, of whom two-thirds would usually be women – Mrs Stanhope Forbes took a personal interest in them and made sure that their lodgings in cottages in the village had her approval – while the Bushey School of Animal and Figure Painting was by 1910 under the direction of the artist Lucy Kemp-Welch. Schools of art were also opened by colleges and universities all over the country, offering examination courses for those who wanted to go on to teach. Some women set up on their own account and offered tuition in drawing or painting in their own homes. There was also work in illustrating books, newspapers and magazines – see **illustrator**.

An internet gateway to art libraries and archives is provided by Goldsmiths College at http://libweb.gold.ac.uk/subgates/artlibgate. php, while the website of the National Art Library at the Victoria and Albert Museum has a page on 'Finding information about artists' with a bibliography and links (www.vam.ac.uk/nal/findinginfo/info_artists/ index.html). There are several books with short biographical entries for artists, such as the *Dictionary of Victorian Painters* by Christopher Wood (Antique Collectors Club, 1971). For a general background see *Women Artists in 19th Century France and England*, Charlotte Yeldham (Taylor & Francis, 1984).

■ AUCTIONEER

The **auctioneer organises** the salerooms, assesses items for sale, and controls the auction itself. In a specialist auction house it is a job that requires experience and expertise in fine arts, and, in general, confidence and quick wits are essential.

A shortage of men in the London auction rooms during the First World War gave Evelyn Barlow the chance to conduct sales at Sotheby's in July 1917. She was the sister of Sir Montague Barlow, MP, senior partner of Sotherby, Wilkinson & Hodge, and her 'career' seems to have been brief. In 1940, a similar situation brought Mrs Helen Naddick to the rostrum at Bonham's, the family business (she too was a sister – of Leonard Bonham, who had been called up) but in her case it did indeed lead to several years in auctioneering. In 1956 she was asked if a girl could make a career in the salerooms and replied that opportunities were limited but she saw no objection. It was not until 20 years later, however, that Sotheby's and Phillips' both appointed young women as career auctioneers.

Outside the big specialist salerooms there were women acting as auctioneers, though often because of the absence of men in wartime – a woman was conducting the weekly cattle sales at Mansfield in 1917; an 'exceptionally successful' woman was employed in 1919 by Messrs Harmer, Rooke & Co, stamp dealers of Fleet Street; and a woman who carried on after the death of her husband had a successful business in Wandsworth Road in the early 1920s. They were enough of a rarity to be reported in local newspapers. Women also worked in salerooms in other capacities, such as clerk or secretary (in 1891, for example, Eleanor Smith, 36 years old and living in the St George's Hanover Square area, was working as a 'Secretary to Exchange & Sale Room'). There are also close connections between auctioneers and estate agents; in fact, working as a clerk for three years or more was one way by the 1930s to enter the profession, allowing entrance to the examinations of the Auctioneers' and Estate Agents' Institute of the United Kingdom. Otherwise, it was by serving three years (usually) in articles with a practising auctioneer, and paying a premium, from 100 guineas to 500 guineas.

■ AUXILIARY TERRITORIAL SERVICE (ATS)

The ATS was formed in September 1938 under Dame Helen Gwynne-Vaughan. Initially the Service worked with the Army and the RAF, but their duties revolved solely around the Army after the **Women's Auxiliary Air Force** was formed in 1939. Their uniform was army khaki – 'not a becoming colour'.

By the time war was declared in September 1939 the ATS was in action – in fact, the declaration of war was transmitted by an ATS wireless operator. In the spring of 1940 part of the Women's Transport Service (FANY) – see **First Aid Nursing Yeomanry** – was incorporated into the Service (members were allowed to keep their 'FANY' shoulder flashes). In April 1941 the ATS was brought under the Army Act, meaning that its members were accepted as part of the Armed Forces, although they were assured by the Secretary of State that 'the Service will remain a women's service under the general direction of women'. The women received two-thirds of the pay of a man of the equivalent rank.

Although volunteers were sufficient to man the Service at first, by 1942 conscription had become necessary to replace men needed for active service. The ATS filled a wide range of duties for the Army. At first they were accepted only as cooks, clerks, orderlies, storeswomen and drivers, but by December 1943 there were over a thousand categories of employment open to them. The ATS numbered some 212,000 women at its height. They filled 80 trades, including armourers, draughtswomen, fitters, welders and wireless operators, as well as fulfilling the usual clerical, catering, driving and orderly work. They could be found attached to the Royal Army Ordnance Corps, the Royal Corps of Signals, and the Royal Army Pay Corps. Some with engineering qualifications worked with the Royal Electrical and Mechanical Engineers. Much of the Army Blood Transfusion Service was run by the ATS, including the 'bleeding teams', that went round the country collecting blood.

After 1941 they also served in mixed ack-ack batteries with the Anti-Aircraft Command – the first ATS Searchlight Troop was formed in July 1942. They did not man the guns (well, not officially, anyway) but worked alongside the Royal Artillery as instrument operators, plotters and radiolocation operators. At the end of 1944 mixed batteries were sent to France for the first time. *The Girls Behind the Guns: With the ATS in World War II*, Dorothy Brewer Kerr (Robert Hale, 1990) describes life in the batteries by a woman who was there.

Any ATS auxiliary aged between 19 and 40 was liable for service overseas and the first girls had been posted to France in the spring of 1940 with the British Expeditionary Force – just in time for the Fall of France. They were evacuated with the Army, but stayed manning vital switchboards to the last possible moment as the Germans entered Paris. Junior Commander Mary Carter was awarded the MBE for her part in bringing out 24 ATS girls, plus one female French liaison officer they smuggled out in a spare ATS uniform. Wherever the Army went, the ATS went too. Hundreds were sent out to the Middle East, for instance, providing support during the North Africa Campaign and earning themselves the Africa Star medal. Sgt Janet Fitzgerald was one of four girls sent to the West Indies to recruit local girls for an ATS unit to be based out there to work with British troops.

New recruits to the ATS, attached to the Beds and Herts Regiment, at Folkestone in 1939. The only named member is Hilda Suckling, second right in the middle row. (Maureen Jones)

The ATS became a regular Army corps on 1 February 1949, and was renamed the Women's Royal Army Corps (WRAC) – it was disbanded in 1992.

ATS personnel records are held by the Ministry of Defence and will only be released to the women themselves or proven next of kin, for a fee: Army Personnel Centre, Historical Disclosures, Mailpoint 400, Kentigern House, 65 Brown Street, Glasgow G2 8EX (telephone: 0141 224 3030; e-mail: apc_historical_disclosures@dial.pipex.com).

There is some background information at www.atsremembered.pwp. blueyonder.co.uk, and the Imperial War Museum has an information sheet on 'The Auxiliary Territorial Service in the Second World War', which gives guidance on research sources. The contents of the WRAC Museum at Guildford, which closed in the 1990s, are now at the National Army Museum (Royal Hospital Road, Chelsea, London SW3 4HT; www.national-army-museum.ac.uk). See also *The Women's Royal Army Corps*, Shelford Bidwell (Leo Cooper, 1977).

■ BABY-FARMER

The Victorian **baby-farmer** can be seen as the ancestor of today's childminder, in that she took in other women's young children and babies for a fee, usually so that they could be free go to work – these were often unmarried mothers or widows of the poorer classes, who had little alternative if they were to keep out of the workhouse. The arrangement could be ongoing (i.e. the children were left there permanently or semi-permanently) rather than day-to-day and was a legitimate business, but unfortunately was open to great abuse.

There were no controls on the women who ran the 'farms' and terrible cases of neglect and cruelty came to light in the later 19th century, with stories of babies being sold under the guise of 'fostering'; even worse, some baby-farmers were found to be 'disposing of' unwanted babies. A series of crimes in the 1860s and 1870s led to calls for the registration of houses where child care was carried on (Infant Life Protection Act 1872), but the problem of how to regulate the system so that the good childminder or foster mother was not penalised along with the bad went on until well into the 20th century. In 1883 a day care crèche was opened in Croydon and for many campaigners this pointed the way to the future – a safe place where working mothers could leave their children during the day, on payment of a small fee. It was not until 1948 that compulsory registration for childminders was brought in.

Unfortunately, it is the names of the criminal baby-farmers that are recorded, and there are sadly many reports in the newspapers of the second half of the 19th century when cases of cruelty or murder were brought to light, often by the vigilance of doctors, registrars of births and deaths, coroners or, latterly, the NSPCC.

■ BAKER

Making **bread on** a commercial basis was hard work, particularly before powered machinery such as dough mixers and easier to manage gas ovens became available from the end of the 19th century. The day began in the early hours, as bread had to be made ready for the morning trade, and large quantities of dough had to be kneaded by hand, knocked up and set to bake; the oven would have been heated overnight and the baker worked in a hot, dusty environment.

However, a look at any trade directory will show that it was common for women to run baker's shops – they may have employed a journeyman baker or apprentices to carry out the heavier work, or done the baking themselves, particularly of lighter breads, cakes and confectionery. The baking industry website (www.bakeryinfo.co.uk) and that of the Federation of Bakers (www.bakersfederation.org.uk/baking_home.aspx) have background information on baking and bread, as does the Worshipful Company of Bakers' website (www.bakers.co.uk/about-beginning.php.4).

■ BALLET DANCER

The term 'ballet dancer' or 'ballet girl' was widely used in the mid-1800s for dancers we would more probably identify as chorus girls. In the summer some might appear in the *corps de ballet* in a 'proper' ballet, while in the winter they would be in the chorus line in a pantomime – usually as a fairy.

The ballet proper was dominated by foreign dancers and when Charles Booth investigated in the 1880s, he found that English girls were thought to be unwilling to work hard enough in training. If young and pretty they could be in the 'front eight' of the chorus, but age and lack of agility and ability would place them in the middle and back rows (the front row might command a wage of 30–35 shillings, more at panto time, the middle row getting roughly half that and the back row a meagre 12s 6d to 18s; out of that the girls had to provide their own tights and shoes).

The Empire Theatre in Leicester Square was opened in 1884 as a venue for ballet and variety and put on 'grand musical spectaculars', becoming in 1887 the Empire Theatre of Varieties. If dancers managed to be accepted into the *corps de ballet* at the Alhambra or Empire, they would have fairly steady employment through the year, but most girls could only find work at pantomime time or if they went on tour round the provinces. Otherwise, Booth recorded, 'they live with their parents (who are usually of the working class), or turn dressmakers or needlewomen, or have recourse to less reputable modes of obtaining a livelihood'. In fact, the link between ballet dancers and prostitution was one often noted at the time.

The great sea change that took ballet from the working classes to the middle classes began when a popular Danish dancer appeared at the Empire in 1897. Adeline Genée (1878–1970) was to be billed in America in the 1900s as 'The World's Greatest Dancer', and was made a Dame of the British Empire in 1950. Dividing her time between London, New York and Australia, over the next couple of decades she used her popularity to revive classic productions, and by 1920 was involved in the creation of the Association of Teachers of Operatic Dancing of Great Britain (which received its Royal Charter in 1935 and was renamed the Royal Academy of Dancing in 1936). Her place at the pinnacle of British dance was taken by another legend, Dame Margot Fonteyn, by 1939 the star of the Royal Ballet.

The website of the Royal Academy of Dancing is at www.rad.org.uk. See **actress** for ideas on theatrical research. There are many books on the great stars and companies; for a more local view see, for instance, *Ballet in Leicester Square*, Ivor Guest (Dance Books, 1992).

■ BALLOONIST, AERONAUT

In the 1800s the ascent of a woman in a balloon, frequently at night and accompanied by fireworks, was the high spot of many a fête or other outdoor entertainment. Madame Sophie Blanchard, a Frenchwoman, who made her first ascent in 1805, was among the pioneers of this new form of entertainment (as opposed to the serious aeronauts whose aim was to further the study of manned flight). In 1819 she appeared at the Tivoli Gardens in Paris, as *The World of Adventure* described in the 1890s: 'Suddenly, the explosion of a bombshell gave the signal for the ascent. The glow of Bengal lights arose among the trees as the band struck up; and Madame Blanchard, seated in her little car, sailed slowly up out of the glare into the blackness of the heavens above. Hanging from the carriage was an illuminated star; a shower of golden flame burst forth from the fireworks with which the car itself was decorated; and rained among the spectators. The applause of course, was furious; and amid it Madame Blanchard stooped and lit a bomb of silver which, suspended from a parachute, descended with supernatural majesty to the gardens below.'

Unfortunately, all those pyrotechnics so close to a gas-filled balloon were highly dangerous – the balloon caught fire and Madame Blanchard fell to her death.

English aeronauts were appearing in the provinces, too. In 1838 Mrs Graham was advertising herself as 'The Only English Female Aeronaut' when she made her first ascent from a field 'adjoining the Gas-Works, Shrewsbury', while as late as 1890 the *Lancaster Gazette* reported that 'Miss Cissie Kent made a successful balloon ascent and parachute descent at High Wycombe on Wednesday afternoon. . . . The balloon rose to a height of 5,000 ft, when the parachute was detached, and Miss Kent descended safely into a barley field, a mile distant'.

■ BANK CLERK

'While on duty at the Bank of England a cashier never knows a restful moment. What with counting sovereigns, taking care not to make an error, and keeping a look-out for forgeries, his task must be the most worrying known to mortal man,' thought C. Duncan Lewis in 1902 (*Living London*). The 1911 census shows that out of over 40,000 bank employees, only 500 were women.

No wonder, then, that even when the banks desperately needed staff to fill the posts left by men called up for military service during the First World War, the *Bankers Magazine* was still worried about the ability of women to cope: 'It is probably impossible to employ them on heavy tills or in offices subject to periodic rushes, where the physical and nerve strain would be beyond the endurance of a normal woman.' Where they were taken on as counter staff, as at Lloyds Bank, women were reminded to dress soberly in dark colours.

Janet Courtney was Oxford-educated in Philosophy, German and Greek, but when she became the first woman to be employed by the Bank of England in 1894, she was segregated to a separate office and thought capable only of sorting cheques into piles. Anne Tulloch was the first woman employed at Midland Bank's headquarters in 1907, but only to translate French and German newspapers for the senior managers. The First World War proved the catalyst for change, albeit slowly, and then increasing mechanisation from the 1920s brought more opportunities for women, whose 'nimble fingers' proved particularly adaptable to the new adding machines. The first woman bank manager in Britain was Hilda Harding, working for Barclays, in 1958.

To trace any woman bank employee, you would need to know the bank and branch where she worked, and there have been many amalgamations and takeovers in the banking world since the 19th century. *British Banking: A Guide to Historical Records*, Alison Turton and John Orbell (Aldershot, 2001) is a good place to start.

■ BARBER, LADY

In October 1899 the *Pall Mall Gazette* carried an enthusiastic article entitled 'The Woman Barber: Her Qualifications and the Development of her Art in London': 'The lady barber is no new thing, but she is new in the sense of modern development. Some of us, whose memories can go back a good few years, can remember a little barber's shop, somewhere off Holborn, where, if the good man was not in, his buxom wife would herself operate upon customers with razor and shaving brush. The female barber too is and was by no means unknown in Paris. But it is in its organised form as a recognised calling for women that it presents features of novelty. The Lady Barbers Association – the original one, mark you! – which is the peg upon which these words of introduction have been hung, has existed for eleven years. Its present address is 65 Chancery Lane, and its latest proprietor Mme St Quentin, who has been in possession since June last. She is a charming and accomplished lady – learned in the mysteries of hypnotic influence, and has even views on Buddha'.

The writer was correct that it was not a new trade and examples can be found in earlier decades – Elizabeth Briggs in the 1880s at Hampstead, for instance, a 54-year-old widow. Unfortunately, by the early 1900s, lady barbers were suffering from a certain scepticism about their trade, perhaps not surprisingly as many of them also offered 'vibro-massage', 'face massage', and just 'massage', not to mention **chiropody**.

■ BARK PEELER

Between May and July bark peeling occupied women in rural areas, right up to the 1930s in some cases (such as in the Wyre Forest in the West Midlands; see the website www.search.revolutionaryplayers.org. uk for a photograph from Bewdley Museum). The bark was stripped from trees or branches when the sap was rising, cleaned of any lichen, then dried in the open air and sent off to tanneries – the tannin in the bark of oak, chestnut, willow, larch and other trees was used for the curing of hides in the leather industry. It was casual employment that came at a lean time in the year for many labourers' families. It may be known by different names in places – in Norfolk, for instance, it was known as 'barsel' time in the 19th century. An article on *The English Bark Trade 1660–1830* is online at www.bahs.org.uk.

■ Barmaid

There have been 'serving wenches' for centuries but the barmaid as we know her made her appearance in the 19th century, the earliest in large town and city pubs where trade was brisk or where there was no publican's wife or daughter to serve behind the bar counter. Barmaids were also employed in hotels and at railway station buffets, and in the bars of clubs, music halls and theatres. In 1886, for the *Girl's Own Paper*, Anne Beale described the 'subterranean hostelries' of the London underground railway, where young women 'spent long days in a small, dark, close vault' serving food and alcohol to travellers, mostly men, 'who look on her who waits on them as a recipient for coarse compliment or feeble jest'. She went on, 'In some places, the atmosphere is clearer than in others . . . but everywhere the young women stand the livelong day imbibing the very unpleasantly-combined odours of sulphur, smoke and alcohol.'

Evidence given before the Royal Commission on Labour in 1891 showed that hours were particularly long in pubs and railway bars – up to 100 hours a week. Girls might start in employment at any age from 15 onwards and larger establishments would give opportunities for promotion to a senior, or first, barmaid, or perhaps manageress. Wages in 1891 for a hotel barmaid, for example, might start at 10 to 12 shillings, plus board and lodging, rising to 15 shillings, and then to 18 to 38 shillings for manageresses. See **publican** for possible background sources.

■ Basketmaker

Basketmaking was an important rural craft practised all over the country, the product being in great demand for a variety of containers from heavy industrial and laundry baskets to shopping bags, to crab and lobster pots. The basic process was that the young willow shoots (osiers) were boiled to soften them, and either peeled or left 'natural' for different effects, then dried and finally soaked before use to make them pliable. In some areas women worked on certain parts of the process, usually the preparation, while in others they actually made the baskets. The craft of weaving cane seats for chairs was also important.

Willows could be grown on suitable land anywhere in the country, though much of the raw material was imported before the early 19th century; some areas such as the Somerset Levels were particularly heavily cropped. There was a concentration of basketweaving around industrial towns and ports, and in areas where market gardening was important, such as Bedfordshire and the Vale of Evesham. In 1891 there were some 14,000 basketmakers listed in the census, and about one fifth were women, who worked particularly on smaller, lighter baskets and those requiring some intricacy of weaving. From the turn of the century, foreign competition and increased use of containers made from cardboard or paper meant that the industry gradually declined in importance, although it has never completely died out.

Re-caning chair seats was an associated craft to basketmaking, sometimes carried out door to door, as here in Buckinghamshire in the 1940s.

The Basket Makers Company had traditionally controlled apprenticeship and the admittance of freemen (see www.basketmakersco.org; the Company admitted widows who were carrying on their husband's business). The many techniques and designs of basketmakers are covered in *Baskets and Basketry*, Dorothy Wright (Batsford, 1964); and see the website www.craftsintheenglishcountryside.org.uk for some background on the industry. Museums with basketmaking or chair-seating interest are listed on the website of the Basketmakers' Association (www.basketassoc.org/pages/museums.php).

■ BATHING MACHINE ATTENDANT

It was not 'done' in the late 18th and 19th centuries for a woman to appear on the beach in what amounted to a state of undress, so bathing machines were invented. From these contraptions, little dressing rooms on wheels, the bather could emerge unseen and slide into the surf. Some machines were 'parked' at the water's edge, but there were also early ones that floated. A horse usually pulled the machine down to the water, and into it, but the 'floating bath-rooms' most enjoyed by the ladies were probably those that required them to be carried out to the machine in the arms of a strong man. Bathing machines could still be found on Britain's beaches into the 20th century, when they were finally pensioned off as sheds or chicken huts.

Proprietors of bathing machines jealously controlled certain patches of the beach, and employed women to 'man' the machines themselves. The women – usually into their mature years – who controlled the machines, and who helped ladies to dress, undress and bathe, were also known as 'dippers'. They would distribute cards advertising their services, making their living from fees and tips, and could be found anywhere around the coast where sea bathing was popular. Martha Gunn was perhaps the most famous dipper and worked the Brighton beach from about 1750 to 1814 – she died in 1815 at the age of 89. She was said to have been 'stout and rather ugly' and her face adorned souvenir toby jugs as her fame spread. At Bognor, Mary Wheatland worked till she was in her seventies and is said to have saved 34 people from drowning during her career. As late as 1881, Ann Fox, a 36-year-old widow, was working as an attendant at Ramsgate in Kent.

■ BEERHOUSE KEEPER

A beerhouse differed from an inn or a public house in that the proprietor was allowed only to sell beer, not wine or spirits, a deliberate distinction created by the government in 1830 to try to discourage the drinking of spirits such as gin. Brewing was traditionally a female household occupation, and many beerhouses were run by women, often widows, who also brewed their own beer. The legal situation regarding application for Excise certificates etc changed through the 19th and 20th centuries, but in general a beerhouse was run in a room in the woman's own home and could be 'on' (selling beer indoors, as in a normal bar) or 'off' (only selling beer for consumption off the premises, sometimes also called an 'outside'). Beerhouse keepers did not have to apply for a licence from the local magistrates, only an Excise certificate, so they do not appear in the licensing sessions records (although after 1869 they had to get a 'certificate of permission' from the Justices). See also **publican**.

■ BESOM MAKER

A besom is a type of broom (typically the witch's broomstick). Besom making was a rural industry, often carried out by men but in some areas women made them, working from home. In the 1800s women living in the Finsthwaite area, near Lake Windermere, were expected to make several dozen a day – using birch cuttings, bound with strips of elm bark, willow, briar or wire onto a handle of ash, lime or hazel – for a grand halfpenny a dozen (www.fellsanddales.org.uk).

■ BETWEEN MAID, 'TWEENY

The 'tweeny was usually a very young servant girl who helped both the housemaid and the cook. In the morning, therefore, she might be cleaning and polishing or carrying coals and shining boots and shoes, while later in the day she would be down in the kitchen washing up pots and pans, polishing the copper utensils, preparing vegetables, laying the table for kitchen meals and clearing away.

If her fellow servants were hard on her, the little girl's life could be miserable. 'Her duties are difficult to define, as they are so numerous and varied; indeed, every mistress should watch that her little maid is not overworked,' *Everywoman's Encyclopedia* of 1911 advised, when a between maid might be paid from £8 to £14 a year. 'The girl is usually allowed to go out in the afternoon and evening every alternate Sunday, and one afternoon or evening every week, with one week's holiday every year.' A woman who started as a 'tweeny in 1940 at Gedding Hall in Suffolk recalled that she 'worked from 6.30 am to 10.30 pm and had to scrub the kitchen floor daily (including my day off!)'. She was paid 7s 6d a month (*Suffolk Within Living Memory*, Suffolk Federation of WIs, Countryside Books, 1994).

■ BIBLE WOMAN

She was a working class woman paid a small amount to work in her own neighbourhood (having been given some instruction in poor law and hygiene) visiting the homes of the poor to give them practical help and advice, and to talk about the Bible and Christianity. She might also be called a 'mission woman'.

The idea for this embryonic social worker is credited to Miss Ellen Ranyard (1809–1879), who set up the Bible and Domestic Female Mission in London in 1857 (which became the Ranyard Mission in 1917; see also **nurse, Ranyard**), and who wanted to offer working class women 'self-help' and give them the knowledge to better themselves. By 1867 there were over 200 bible women in London, and the idea had spread to other UK cities – the Dublin Bible Woman Mission was established in 1861, for instance.

The term 'bible woman' was also used abroad for women who worked amongst their own people for European and American missionaries as interpreters, teachers and bible readers.

■ BILLIARDS/SNOOKER PLAYER

The game of billiards was often linked to gambling and a dissolute (male) lifestyle, so much so that in the mid-18th century it was actually declared unlawful in public houses, and it is not a sport that is commonly linked to professional women players before recent years. However, professional players there were. They included Ruth Harrison, who held the women's professional snooker title from 1934, Agnes Morris, professional champion in 1949, and Thelma Carpenter, champion professional billiards player 1940 to 1950 and the first woman to be invited to commentate on the game for the BBC. You can see a two-minute film of Agnes Morris and Ruth Harrison at www.screenonline.org.uk – *Cue for Ladies* (1948).

Women sometimes popped up elsewhere too – 'There was a billiard saloon in Oxford Street where, some fifteen years ago [1874], a girl officiated as marker, and did her work carefully and well,' noted the *English Illustrated Magazine* in 1889.

■ BLACKSMITH

'The smith, a mighty man is he' – Henry Wadsworth Longfellow's poem *The Village Blacksmith* crystallised the brawny figure of the blacksmith in popular culture and the idea that the smith might be a woman seems laughable. However, it would be wrong to dismiss it out of hand.

The village blacksmith usually performed two main functions – as a farrier shoeing horses, and as a smith working black metal, i.e. iron, to

After their sons joined the Army during the First World War, Mrs Emmeline Saunders of Essex 'gave her husband active and efficient help in his business, and learned to shoe a horse as satisfactorily as she could mend a fire.'

make and mend tools and agricultural implements, wheel trims, nails, locks, bolts, pots and pans and so on. It was work vital to life in both town and country before the railway and, particularly, the internal combustion engine destroyed its importance by the 1950s.

A female blacksmith sometimes crops up in medieval literature, but she was an evil soul who bore the responsibility of having made the nails for Christ's crucifixion (her husband having feigned illness to avoid the task). One who attracted rather a better press was Mary Ann Hinman of Melton Mowbray, who in the 1850s worked in her father William's forge and 'excelled in the shoeing department, which she managed with admirable tact and skill, and might often be seen, with leather apron and muscular arms, leading or riding a high-bred hunter home through the streets to its stable'. Mary Ann was only eighteen when she died in 1858 after a short illness, so we can only guess at how her career might have developed.

Female blacksmiths appear quite often in census returns and in trade directories, yet are seldom credited with having actually worked as smiths themselves. Admittedly, many of them were the widows of blacksmiths who had taken over the business after their husband's demise: in Hinxworth, Hertfordshire in 1851 Ann Briant was recorded in the census as 'Blacksmith employing 6 men' and, aged 78, was head of a business that included four sons, a grandson and a lodger. Few probably wielded the hammer (especially at Ann's age), but women were quite capable of working at a forge – as not only Mary Ann Hinman but also the **chainmakers** of the Midlands could testify. As could the unnamed woman blacksmith at Witham in Essex in 1917, who was reported as keeping the business going while her three brothers served in the Army (at night she worked in munitions), or Mrs Emmeline Saunders, also of Essex, who was photographed helping her husband at the forge.

Entry into the trade was for centuries by apprenticeship and, as with other crafts, women could apply for admittance to the guild in the place of a male family member who had died. Women also took on apprentices: in 1900 a 15-year-old boy was apprenticed for six years to Ann Cluer, blacksmith of Burton Lazars (*Leicestershire and Rutland Within Living Memory*, Leicestershire and Rutland Federation of WIs, Countryside Books, 1994). The Worshipful Company of Blacksmiths (City of London) has a website at www.blacksmithscompany.org. An American website (www.appaltree.net) has useful information about blacksmithing techniques. Try also *The Village Blacksmith*, Ronald Webber (David and Charles, 1973) or *The Village Blacksmith*, Jocelyn Bailey (Shire Publications, 1985) for background.

■ BLANKETMAKER

Woollen blankets, rugs, and such 19th-century necessities as horse collar cloths were all woven by a substantially female workforce. See **wool spinners and weavers**.

■ BLEACHER

Cotton and linen cloth, grey and brown in its natural state, went to the bleachworks to be whitened before it could be used, either as it was or as a base for dyeing; some bleachworks specialised in certain items, such as lace and hosiery bleachers in Nottingham, while others were integral parts of dyeworks. Cloth meant for papermaking also had to be bleached before use, so that printworks often had a bleaching department.

In the 19th century some linen was bleached in the open air, particularly in Scotland and Ireland, while in chemical bleaching chloride of lime was used. In either case, the cloth had to be finished by being steamed in hot stoves, and this was often a female occupation, before further 'chemicking and souring' treatments using carbonic acid gas. Because the bleachers worked to order, once a process had been started they continued until the batch of cloth was complete, which might be 24 hours or more. Cases were cited of young girls sometimes staying overnight at the works, sleeping for a few hours on makeshift beds in a storeroom. Working from 18 to 20 hours a day was common.

The cloth was steamed in a 'kier', an iron container that acted as a kind of pressure cooker, and the room in which this work was done was extremely hot, sometimes reaching 180 degrees Fahrenheit. The workers called it the 'wasting room' and it was not uncommon for women to be carried out, overcome by the heat and humidity. All would leave with their clothes saturated with sweat. In Parliament in 1856 William Cobbett reported seeing rooms where 'the temperature [was] frequently so high that the nails in the floor became heated and blistered, that burnt the feet of those who were employed in these rooms and who were therefore obliged to wear slippers'.

In the 1850s and early 1860s attempts were made (finally successfully) to get a Bleaching and Dyeing Works Bill through Parliament, which would bring the works under the Factory Inspectorate and limit the hours of women and children. The employment of women in bleaching works became less common, but women were still working in the bleaching and dyeing factories into the 20th century. See also **dyeworks**.

■ BOARDING HOUSE KEEPER, LANDLADY

A woman taking in paying guests ('PGs'), short or long term, who provided meals (or at least breakfast) as well as accommodation. In seaside resorts, increasingly popular from the mid-19th century, she would concentrate on the holiday trade, and the best-known resorts such as Brighton, Blackpool, Scarborough etc had hundreds of boarding houses, many of them large and prosperous, with their own small army of servants. In towns and cities, she would take in working people who needed a room near to their employment – as for example, Martha Morris, a 50-year-old widow, who in 1881 was running a boarding house in the St Pancras area of London and whose 'PGs' were six young men, clerks by trade, whose origins were in Norfolk, Germany and New York. Some landladies specialised in guests who travelled for a living – salesmen, perhaps – or most notably there were the famed 'theatrical landladies', who took in touring actors and music hall acts. (*Exit Through the Fireplace: The Great Days of Rep*, Kate Dunn (John Murray, 1998) has a chapter on landladies.)

Local directories would be useful aids, and museums in seaside resorts may well have more information on this essential local industry. Boarding houses thrived until after the Second World War, when in the 1950s and 1960s holiday camps and foreign travel started to threaten the traditional British seaside holiday, and young working people began to share rooms or flats and look after themselves rather than live in as 'PGs'. For a flavour of the seaside boarding house, try *The Blackpool Landlady*, John Walton (Manchester University Press, 1978).

■ BOBBIN MILL WORKER

The Lake District was a centre for the manufacture of the wooden bobbins used by the cotton and woollen mills of Manchester and Ireland. The wood was turned by men and the bobbins finished and decorated by women. In Longtown, Cumbria in the 1920s the girls earned about 12s a week, which was paid to them fortnightly; every evening they came home covered in sawdust (*Cumbria Within Living Memory*, Cumbria Federation of WIs, Countryside Books, 1994). In the 1880s it was estimated that over 30 million cotton reels were made each week.

■ BOBBIN-NET MAKER

See lacemaker (bobbin-net).

■ BONDAGER

Female bondagers were once commonly found working on farms, but by the mid-19th century had virtually disappeared except in Northumberland and other northern and remote areas. The farmer hired a 'hind', a male labourer whose terms of employment required him to provide a bondager (sometimes more than one), who assisted him in his work. The hind took her on at a hiring fair, or she might be his daughter or another relative, and he fed and housed her and paid her wages (unless she was his family) – about 8d a day in the 1860s, or £12 a year. The bondager only worked outside and might undertake any task except ploughing and ditching, and had to do her master's bidding. The bondager and the **gangworker** had much in common, often working in the fields with other bondagers under a male supervisor. Arthur Munby's notes on the system in 1863 are quoted in full in *Labouring Life in the Victorian Countryside*, Pamela Horn (Alan Sutton, 1995). See **agricultural labourer**.

■ BOOKBINDER, BOOKFOLDER

In 1871 there were nearly as many women employed in bookbinding as there were men (7,557 against 7,917) and 40 years later they outnumbered their male counterparts. That women had long had an important role in the craft is shown by the existence as early as 1814 of a Friendly Female Bookbinders Society.

In the 1870s the *Labour News* reported: 'Girls and women are employed in the following branches of the bookbinding trade:- folding, sewing, collating (placing the sheets in alphabetical order), arranging the plates, laying-on gold on covers, head-banding, covering magazines etc.

The number of folders and sewers far exceeds that of the workers in any other branch. In laying on the gold, and in covering magazines, men were formerly exclusively employed, and the introduction of women is a recent innovation. Girls are usually apprenticed to the trade at 14 years of age for two years, but without formal indentures; and they are paid a small amount during apprenticeship. The earnings by piecework and time-work in all branches vary from 7s to 25s per week, but the average may be taken at 11s a week. The usual price for folding is a penny for 100 sheets, but in some shops only three farthings per 100 is paid. Great quickness of hand is required in folding and sewing. In collating, considerable care and intelligence are necessary and the worker is fined for the smallest error. Care and economy must be exercised in laying on the gold leaf. Head-banding is a branch of the work not much in demand now, excepting for expensive bibles, or for some other books in the most costly kind of binding.'

When pages had been printed, folded and collated, the loose sheets were made into a book by being stitched on a sewing press, one woman being able to sew 2,000 to 3,000 sheets a day (1840).

A lot of folding work was also distributed to be done in the women's homes, thus evading the limitations on hours imposed by the Factory Act, especially at peak publication times such as Christmas. The majority of bookbinding firms were in London but they could be found in towns all over the country, and particularly in Manchester. Some 'firms' were very small, such as that of Mary Bellamy, a widow in Oxford, a 'bookbinder and stationer', who worked with her three sons in 1851 and by 1861 was employing seven men, five women and three boys.

Bookbinding in its finest form was also a part of the Arts and Crafts movement of the late 19th century and there were a number of women producing fine artistic work, including Sarah Prideaux, Katherine Adams and Sybil Pie – see *Women Bookbinders 1880–1920* by Marianne Tidcombe (British Library, 1996). See also **printer**.

■ BOOK-KEEPER

During the late 19th and early 20th century, book-keeping came to be seen as something women could do, largely due to the efforts of the accountancy profession to distance itself from the mere upkeep of financial ledgers and order books. All manner of firms, shops and factories will have employed book-keepers in their offices – such as Martha Cook, aged 29 and a 'female clerk and book keeper' at Lambeth in 1881. See also **accountant**.

■ BOOT AND SHOE STITCHER

Stitching the uppers on a boot or shoe, a process known as 'closing', was traditionally women's work (they could also be called machinists or fitters). It was done by shoemakers' wives in small family workshops, and increasingly by outworkers and in factories for mass production in places such as Northampton (especially), Leicester, Stafford, Norwich, Bristol and so on. The uppers and their linings were sewn together by hand or using machines. Women also inserted the eyelet-holes for laces, or button-holes, and fastened the 'tongue'. This completed the upper, which then went on to be fastened to the sole. Women also cleaned, coloured, polished and packed boots and shoes.

In Northamptonshire boot and shoe making was the dominant occupation from the mid-1800s to the 1930s, becoming increasingly mechanised and going through periods of severe depression. See www. northamptonshire-history.org.uk/shoemaking for background and links. Northampton Museum and Art Gallery, Guildhall Road, Northampton NN1 1D has 'the world's largest collection of boots and shoes', which will give a good idea of the work being done at any one time. Information can be found around the country; for instance for K Shoes, a major industry in Kendal since the 1850s, at www.cumbriaindustries.org.uk/kshoes.htm (or see *K Shoes: The First 150 Years 1842–1992*, Spencer Crookenden, 1992); or for Clarks shoes at the Shoe Museum, Street, Somerset, which has material from the company archives (*C.& J. Clark 1825–1975*, C. & J. Clark' 1976). For a general background to the processes see *Shoemaking*, Julie Swann (Shire Publications, 1976).

■ BOXMAKER

A huge variety of boxes were made up either in factories or as a home industry, predominantly by female workers – everything from boxes for collars, ties and other pieces of clothing to boxes for cigars, soap, sweets and foodstuffs. While the work in the factories was fairly well paid, outworkers at home were paid a pittance and had to involve every available member of the family in order to make a living wage. When made by hand, it was simple work involving folding and pasting the paper and cardboard. Another branch of the industry was paper bag making.

Matchboxes for instance, like matches, were produced initially in home workshops before being increasingly made and packed in factories from the late 19th century, with women and children working long hours for little more than starvation rates. The materials were distributed by a middleman, or 'sweater', though the women had to pay for their own paste and twine.

'First there's the wood shavings,' explained a Bethnal Green mother of three small children to a *Daily News* reporter in 1871, 'they're already creased for bending into shape when they come to us. They form the match-box, and are made ready for shaping by machines which are worked by boys . . . one of these shavings makes the outer part of the match-box, and this

Making hat boxes for a silk hat manufacturer: 'I'm able to make a very decent living for a poor widow.'

other shaving which you see is just a trifle less size, it makes the inner part. Then there's a bit of coloured paper, like this, which has to be pasted on the inner half to make it look tasty like; and there's this label, with the maker's name we work for, has to be pasted on the outer box. The sand-paper comes next, and is pasted at the bottom like this. The sand-paper is the nastiest part of box-work.' Three-year-old Freddy's bleeding fingers were exhibited as proof of this. Once pasted together, the boxes were spread out to dry around the room in which the family lived and slept. 'We're paid twopence-halfpenny a gross for our work, and very glad we are to get it.' In the 1920s and 1930s women who worked at the Morelands Matches factory in Gloucestershire were still finding their fingers bled from the sandpaper on the sides of the boxes (and outworkers were still glueing the boxes together).

Another example of the variety of work was given by the widow interviewed for *Living London* in the early 1900s who made hat boxes for a firm of silk hat manufacturers: 'The box is supplied with an outside covering of white glazed paper which is stuck together with paste, but the body and the bottom of the box are sewn together with thread. "I have to find the paste, and the needle and thread, and when I've finished a gross I get half-a-crown. I don't grumble at the pay, for when I can get the work I'm able to make a very decent living for a poor widow. It's only when we're slack I don't like it, for then I have to go out charing and such work is a little beyond my strength."'

■ BRAIDER

see **net maker.**

■ BRASSWORKER

Within the term 'brassworking' is included a huge range of processes – including brass-founding, cabinet, bell and general brass-founding, plumber's brass-founding, rolled brass, wire, tubes, and so on. And amongst these there were some tasks that were seen as particularly 'female'. One was the soldering of brass and copper tubing, of the kind used in brass bedsteads, curtain rods, gas fittings etc: 'Brass tubing is made from sheet metal, by cutting up the sheet into oblong strips, and bending these round a central core . . . The two opposite edges of the brass are made to lap one over the other, and are in that state soldered together.' (*Penny Magazine*, 1844)

Another female task was lacquering finished bronze or brass pieces produced by casting or founding. The *Penny Magazine* described the finishing process for some of the articles produced in the Birmingham factories, from statues to bells, cannon, chandeliers, vases, lamps and railings. The item was heated to get rid of any grease, 'pickled' in dilute acid and brushed well with a wire brush, dipped into 'aquafortis, by which means it speedily acquires a clear bright yellow colour, wholly free from specks and stains', washed in water, dried in hot sawdust, burnished, and then lacquered. 'Lacquer is a liquid composed of spirit of wine, gum-lac, turmeric, saffron, and one or two other ingredients. The brass-work is made clean and hot, and is in that state coated with a layer of the lacquer, either by dipping or brushing. A subsequent drying finishes the process.'

In 1855 women solderers in Birmingham were earning 10s to 12s a week, and lacquerers 8s to 10s. In 1871 nearly 4,000 women were employed in lacquering, burnishing, final polishing and wrapping up goods.

■ BREWER

The old name for a female brewer was a brewster and it was a time-honoured women's occupation in the home and on the farm. Once, nearly every inn brewed its own beer – and female servants and owners would have been concerned with this – but throughout the 19th and 20th centuries the spread of large-scale and increasingly industrialised breweries, initially based predominantly in London but later also in Burton on Trent and other towns such as Hertford, and in Edinburgh for the Scottish market, meant that hundreds of small breweries were taken over or went out of business. However, women can be found who took on a thriving business from either a father or a deceased husband: Elizabeth Taylor, for instance, in 1881 was a 52-year-old widow at Aldsworth in Gloucestershire: 'Brewer and Wine and Spirit Merchant and Farmer employing 6 men on 67 acres of land'. Women would not normally be found as employees of the breweries, except during wartime, when they took on jobs such as malting in the place of men called up for the services.

Because there have been so many takeovers and amalgamations in the brewery world, *The Brewing Industry: A Guide to Historical Records*, Lesley Richmond and Alison Turton (Manchester University Press, 1990) is a good start to tracking down individual companies, and *Researching Brewery and*

Publican Ancestors, Simon Fowler (Federation of Family History Societies, 2003) an essential aid to research. The Scottish Brewing Archive is held by the University of Glasgow (www.archives.gla.ac.uk/sba/default.html). See also **beerhouse keeper.**

■ BRICKMAKER

The demand for bricks was insatiable in the 19th century and beyond, and every town – and most villages – had a brickfield nearby, though the scale of production varied, particularly as industrial machinery took over many of the processes on the large fields. Brickmakers had a reputation for drunkenness and brutality and the brickfields could be barren, dispiriting wastes – as Dickens described in *Bleak House.*

Women were employed usually as part of a 'gang', and were often family members under the direction of the 'moulder' or foreman, who was paid for the work and who doled out a share to those under him. Women had no part in the industrialised brickfields, but had long been involved in the handmaking process, which went something like this (though details would vary in different parts of the country). The employment was seasonal. During the autumn and winter the clay was dug out and left to weather in frost and snow. Then in the spring the work would start by the clay being ground in a pug-mill, and brought in blocks to the moulder standing ready at his hut or 'stool', which sheltered him from sun or rain. Working at the moulder's side was the 'walk-flatter', and this was usually the woman's job – she rough-shaped the lumps of clay for him so that he could fill the brick moulds, which were first coated with sand. The raw bricks were emptied onto boards, and wheeled off to be stacked up to dry out. When they were completely dry, they were fired in a kiln.

Entire families were involved in the process – making up to a thousand bricks in a week – and the work done by children and women in the brickfields became a focus of concern by the 1870s, when George Smith wrote *The Cry of the Children from the Brickyards of England.* The Factories Act (Brick and Tile Yards) then brought women and children under the scope of the Factory Inspectors and their employment in the fields soon waned.

Researching brickmaking ancestors can begin with David Cufley's Brickmakers Index and bibliography of related books, described at www.davidrcufley.btinternet.co.uk. Village histories or museums will often have information on local brickfields and working conditions, e.g. the Somerset Brick and Tile Museum, East Quay, Bridgwater TA6 4AE (www. somerset.gov.uk/museums).

■ BRONZER

Advances in colour printing (chromo-lithography) in the late 19th and early 20th centuries enabled labels, postcards, trade cards, pictures etc to be printed with edgings and raised areas in simulated gold or silver. This technique was called 'bronzing' and was usually done by women. Finely powdered bronze (or aluminium in the case of silver) could be applied to previously varnished areas, to which it would stick. Unfortunately the varnish was highly toxic; the women were supposed to drink a pint of milk a day, or take castor oil, to counteract the effects but rarely did. Bronzers also worked in the metal industry, like Emma Amor, a 57-year-old widow, and Mary Ann Ashford, aged 14, who were fender bronzers in Birmingham in 1881.

■ BRUSHMAKER

Women were prominent in the brushmaking industry throughout the 19th and into the 20th centuries but it was a centuries-old craft – overseen by the Society of Brushmakers – and there was protracted resistance to allowing women equal pay with men for doing the same job. Page's of Norwich were a large brushmaking firm who set up a new factory in Wymondham in the 1880s with the intention of employing low-paid local women. In 1891 the women joined the Amalgamated Society of Brushmakers and went out on strike because they were being paid less than the Norwich workers. It was not until 1917 that women's contribution in the trade was officially recognised, with the setting up of the Brushmaking Industry Trades Board and the National Society of Brushmakers (Working Class Movement Library; www.wcml.org.uk).

In 1883 work in a brush factory was described in an article in *Cassell's Family Magazine*. From the cutting of wood for the brush-backs, to the finished article, thirteen workers contributed to the making of a nail brush. The majority of women were employed on drawing – fastening the bristles into the brush-back. 'It is quite possible to carry on this operation outside

'Drawing' a nail brush – fastening the bristles into the back of the brush (1883).

the factory walls, and, as a matter of fact, many married women once engaged therein take out work and employ themselves at it in their own homes. The cost of fitting up a bench is very small, and the increase of the family income by this use of trained fingers is often considerable.'

In the early 1800s, baleen – hair from a whale's throat – was often used for brushes, though bristles might be of hog's hair or badger's hair or that of some other animal. Cheaper imports of bass (made from the bark of a tree) made brushes themselves cheaper and gave a great boost to the industry in the later 19th century; no wires had to be used for bass, the bristles were simply stuck into the heads with pitch. There was a huge range available, some 80 different varieties of brush coming out of one factory, 'from carpet brooms to brewers' brushes; from oil brushes to jewellers'; from hair to hat brushes to those of the chimney sweep.' See also **besom maker.**

■ BUMBOAT WOMAN

Bumboats were the small craft that plied between the harbourside and ships lying at anchor, carrying supplies for sale to the ships' crews, and sometimes passengers as well. They were often rowed by women. At Devonport in 1881 Mary Holland, the wife of a waterman, was recorded as a bumboat woman.

W.S. Gilbert immortalised Poll Pineapple (Little Buttercup), a bumboat woman, in *HMS Pinafore* in 1878 but they were certainly common for a century and more before that in ports such as Portsmouth or Plymouth, or on the Thames. Poll sang of carrying 'apples and cakes, and fowls and beer', and an 1811 dictionary calls the bumboats 'floating chandler's shops'.

A popular sideline was smuggling illicit goods onto shore, and in 1761 an act required all bumboats to be registered by the Trinity Corporation and gave the Corporation's officers power to search and detain any boat they suspected of having goods on board that were stolen or 'unlawfully obtained' – in the first 40 years of the act's existence there were over 2,500 convictions. There were dangers from passengers too, as an incident in 1802 in Plymouth showed. A bumboat woman was 'crossing the passage' with several passengers in her boat, when a drunken customs officer tried to search her intimately for hidden 'bladders of liquor'. A sergeant from the East Devon Regiment told him to stop and was run through with a sword for his trouble.

■ BURNISHER, BUFFER

A woman who worked on finished pieces of metal, jewellery etc. to put on the final shine. With reference to the electroplating trade in the 1870s, it was said: 'Women and girls are largely employed as "burnishers", with blunt-pointed steel tools, or as "buffers" for polishing forks and spoons by rouge [a granular mixture, oxide of iron, used to bring up the shine]. When this is done by steam-power turning bobbins, a great deal of dust is given off. The inhalation of rouge is apt to cause bronchial irritation and a peculiar oppression in the breathing.'

Earlier, in mid-century, reference is made to burnishing by using 'blood-stone', a hard, smooth Derbyshire stone used on gold and silver – 'fixed in a handle, and held in such a manner as to give considerable power of pressure on the work, it is first moistened to prevent it becoming too hot, and is nibbed rather forcibly over every part of the article which is to be burnished, by which a surface of exquisite brilliance is produced'. See **electroplate worker; goldsmith; jewellery worker; pottery worker.**

■ BUS CONDUCTOR

There may have been one or two women working on rural bus routes in the early 1900s, particularly for family firms, but this was one of the jobs for which women volunteered during the First World War. 'I have heard

A woman conductor on a Glasgow tramway: the female conductor became a commonplace during the First World War.

that some clever people are laughing at us, saying that we only undertake this sort of job for the sake of the uniform (navy blue cloth, with a coat of semi-military cut, a short skirt, and an Anzac hat of the same colour),' wrote one new female conductor for the *War Illustrated* in 1916, 'but a uniform isn't much of an attraction to a woman who cares about dress after she has worn it for a few weeks on a motor-bus.'

The routine was to arrive at the yard in the morning, sign on and get the box containing the tickets, the punching machine and the bag for small change. At night they had to account for tickets sold and hand over the cash. They became familiarly known as 'clippies', from the method of clipping tickets in the punching machine. They had to know all the fares and the routes, learn how to stand on a moving bus without holding on while operating the ticket machine and giving change, keep an eye on passengers, operate the bell that communicated with the driver, and cope with drunks. Into the 1920s, buses still had open staircases at the back, and often also open upper decks.

Some companies kept women on after the war and the clippie became a commonplace. Come the Second World War, women again became essential to keeping the buses running. During the previous war it had sometimes been dangerous work, particularly at night, but in the 1940s the threat from aerial bombardment was tremendous in some areas. The East Kent Company, for instance, ran its buses in a state of permanent emergency over the Dover road; at least fifteen conductors and conductresses were killed by German bombs and machine-gun fire.

As to bus drivers – Dolores Rennie was the first woman to obtain a London bus driver's certificate, in April 1944, but she was not allowed to drive passengers on the public road, only ferry buses between depots and manoeuvre them in garages.

Tracing an individual will not be easy because of the many bus companies that could be found in nearly every large town until routes and services were regulated by the Road Traffic Act 1930, but once a company is known it is possible to find photographs of bus types, routes and sometimes staff, this being a subject that, like the old steam railways, has a devoted following. Identifying a uniform or badge might help – see the website http://stephen1071.fotopic.net for a useful photographic archive. The Omnibus Society's website has links to other useful resources (www. omnibussoc.org), and the London Transport Museum (www.ltmuseum. co.uk) has interesting online photographs showing female conductors' uniforms.

■ BUTCHER

Female butcher's shops are quite commonly found in trade directories – such as those of Margaret Briercliffe, Ann Fairclough, Isabella Harper, Mary Kearsley, Ann Lord, Peggy Parkinson and Fanny Tempest at Bolton in 1853. As with bakeries, they may have employed a man to do the heaviest work, or they may simply have served at the counter or overseen the business. There is no reason to think, however, that this was not a job that women could do – the work carried out on farms at pig-killing time demonstrates their abilities in coping with carcasses and meat products. Certainly as the

19th century wore on, the actual slaughtering would probably be done by a slaughterman, especially in a town or city.

■ BUTTONMAKER

There is a phrase 'Not worth a button' that refers to something worthless but, in the days before the zip fastener came into general use after the First World War, buttons were big business, not least because they were subject to fashion and absolutely essential to the clothing trade. In some areas buttonmaking, like lacemaking and strawplaiting, was an early 19th century home industry that supported many families otherwise dependent upon an agricultural labourer's wage. This was certainly the case in Dorset, where Abraham Case introduced buttonmaking into Shaftesbury in the 17th century. By the beginning of the 19th century it was a major industry throughout the county. From a very young age, perhaps five or six years, a child would be taught the craft, earning little or nothing at first but soon becoming proficient enough to add to the family income. The children worked with their mothers and older female relatives, some women becoming so fast at the job that they could produce up to 12 dozen buttons in a day, giving them a wage far above that which they could earn in agricultural work, which was the only alternative employment for them in this rural county.

The early 19th century saw this home industry at its peak, with over 4,000 people employed. Buttonmaking as a craft was intricate and time-consuming, with some women so skilled that they could produce buttons that were almost works of art. Early examples used sheep horn as the base, covered with cloth and then embroidered with waxed thread. Later, the use of wire rings as a base allowed even more intricate designs to be introduced. However, as the lacemakers were also discovering in the 19th century, machines could make comparable products far more quickly and far more cheaply for the new mass market that was opening up. By the 1850s the Dorset button industry was collapsing and despite attempts at revival in the early 20th century, it became a treasured craft rather than a livelihood.

In Birmingham and the industrial North the story was very different. Buttonmaking by hand was also a source of livelihood here (and elsewhere throughout the country in a smaller way). But Birmingham was also the home of the factories that could soon produce thousands of buttons each week, employing mostly female workers, and it was already an important local industry by the early 1800s. Buttons could be made of a wide variety of materials – pearl, horn, shell, bone, wood, glass, porcelain, gold, silver, plated copper, white metal, pinchbeck, steel, japanned tin, ivory, tortoiseshell, jet, leather and more. Different manufacturers specialised in certain types of buttons, so that mother-of-pearl buttons would be made in a different factory from those of horn or wood. At the end of the process, buttons were sewn onto cards or papers and packed into boxes for delivery.

By the 1870s, female workers outnumbered men in the industry, many of them girls in their teens. Wages were paid, as they always had been, by piecework and 'working from 8 am to 6 pm an average woman can earn 8s to 10s a week, while the more skilful make 14s to 20s; children 1s 6d to 2s'. Many of the factories were small and some of the processes were unhealthy for the workers – 'the shop is generally heated by steam-pipes and there is a good deal of gaslight . . . the atmosphere is far from fresh and there is much noise and vibration from the presses. . . . The dust that is given off in pearl button making is very considerable, and not only induces by inhalation a tendency to respiratory disease and phthisis, but, according to German scientific observers, a special kind of bone inflammation or osteitis, which attacks the thighs and arms.' (*Industrial Classes*, 1876.)

The great variety of hand-made buttons that were native to Dorset can be seen at the Dorset County Museum (High West Street, Dorchester DT1 1XA; www.dorsetcountymuseum.org). Buttons are highly collectable and all things 'button', including examples of workmanship and techniques, can be found online at the website of the British Button Society (www.britishbuttonsociety.org); or see *Buttons*, Alan and Gillian Meredith (Shire Publications).

■ CANAL BOATWOMAN

Women were ever-present on the canals, living on the narrow boats alongside their husbands and taking their share of the work, though as unpaid helpers – 'You want to be at Mark Lane sometimes, and see the good wife, when her boat is tethered to a wharf, and when she is supposed to be resting, turn up, alert and businesslike, ready to receive orders for the return journey to Birmingham, Nottingham, Stoke, Wolverhampton, Derby, or elsewhere,' wrote Desmond Young in the early 1900s (*Living London*).

During the Second World War a Boatwomen Training Scheme brought a number of young women onto the canals to replace men called up for the services. It was the idea of Daphne March, who began using the family narrow boat to transport supplies for a flour mill at Worcester; she was joined by Eily (Kit) Gayford and Molly Traill, who devised the scheme in the summer of 1941. It was launched in February 1942 and was taken over by the government in the spring of 1944 – up till then there was little publicity and most contacts were made by word of mouth.

The Grand Union Canal Carrying Company was the first to give the women a try. They had a brief period of training and then had to go out and prove themselves, working 18 to 20 hour days and doing all the work themselves, including loading and unloading cargoes that might be coal, grain, munitions, aircraft and machine parts, cement, steel etc, and travelling in areas that could come under aerial attack, such as Coventry and the London docks. They were paid £3 a week, had to find their own clothing (ex-naval ratings' trousers, usually, jerseys and overalls) and were given no extra rations – peanut butter sandwiches and large mugs of cocoa played a large role in their diet.

Some of the women wrote about their experiences, including *Idle Women*, Susan Woolfitt (1947) – the Inland Waterways badge they wore with its 'IW' initials gave them this unjustified nickname. The website www.btinternet.com/~doug.small/wtwomen.htm ('Women on the wartime canals') is an excellent introduction, with excerpts from books and articles. The National Waterways Museum is at Llanthony Warehouse, Gloucester Docks, Gloucester GL1 2EH (www.nwm.org.uk).

■ CANDLEMAKER

Candlemaking, or 'tallow chandlery', was allied to soapmaking, both historically using byproducts from the slaughterhouses and tanneries. By 1850 new 'chemical processes' were changing the traditional industry – spermaceti (from whales), stearine (a purer extract, chemically treated tallow) and paraffin wax, which would be the principal ingredient from the 1890s onwards. By the 1870s only a few hundred women were employed in the candle factories, mostly 'to attend to the moulds, set the wicks, cut the ends of the candles, and so forth. The females principally work in the night-light department, forming the cylinders, cutting them into rings (by machinery), putting the bottoms in, and gumming the labels on. The work is simple, and free from any unhealthy surroundings'.

The industry was hard hit by the increased use of gas lighting, and then by electric lighting. When candles represented the only source of lighting in homes and workplaces there were many factories and small tallow chandleries all over the country (the Worshipful Company of Tallow Chandlers has a website at www.tallowchandlers.org). The most famous firm of candlemakers is probably Price's, which had two factories in London and one in Liverpool by the 1850s – see their website (www.prices-candles.co.uk/history/HISTORYdetails.htm) for background information on candlemaking.

■ CARPET MAKER

In the 1750s Thomas Whitty of Axminster designed the first loom large enough to allow the weaving of a carpet and he is rightly acknowledged as the pioneer whose business spearheaded the development of the British carpet industry. However, it was Whitty's five daughters and sister who together learned how to use the loom and actually produced the first Axminster carpet in 1755, and female weavers continued to be an important part of the industry into the 20th century. Women were also employed in the factories for jobs such as picking waste from the finished carpet lengths. Axminster celebrated its 250th anniversary of carpet making in 2005; see the website of the Axminster Carpet company (www.axminster-carpets.co.uk; 'How a carpet is made') for an insight into the techniques that made it famous. Other manufacturers are also still household names, such as Brinson's, Wilton, Tomkinsons and Thomas Bosworth.

Kidderminster was the premier carpet-weaving centre and there is an excellent online exhibition entitled 'Made in Kidderminster: the history of the carpet industry' that is essential viewing for anyone with carpet making ancestors, no matter which part of the country they came from (www.search. revolutionaryplayers.org.uk/engine/resource/exhibition/standard/default. asp?resource=4429); it has many illustrations and a good bibliography too. The industry was also important in other areas, such as Durham, and in Scotland in Glasgow (Elderslie) from the 1860s and Lasswade and Bonnyrigg, near Kilmarnock, from the 1830s. The website www.carpetinfo.co.uk ('All about carpets') has a timeline of carpet history and the inventions that refined the looms on which the women worked. See also **wool spinners and weavers.**

■ CARRIER

The **country carrier** was once the only link between market towns and the villages that made up its hinterland, few of which would have had direct access to a railway station. A number of these carriers were women, who had either taken over a deceased husband's business or operated it in tandem with another business, such as innkeeping. Ann Russell, for instance, ran the carrier's business in the little village of Denham in Suffolk in the 1870s, while husband James was a farmer and keeper of the Bell public house – her cart went from the village to Bury St Edmunds twice a week on market days, Wednesday and Saturday. In some cases, the women employed a man to drive the cart but female drivers were not unknown.

The carriers took passengers who wanted to get to market or to the railway station (for some country women a trip on the carrier's cart might be a once-a-year treat for 'special shopping'); their horse-drawn carts were covered but a single bench seat was usually the only other amenity offered. They operated at regular times, in all weathers and over all kinds of road conditions, which in the 19th century could often be extremely bad, with little more than rutted unmetalled lanes, dusty in summer and muddy in winter. They also offered a valuable service for those who could not travel themselves: taking orders for goods to be bought in the town shops or market, such as medicines, shoes, tools or items of clothing not to be found in the village; posting letters and parcels and bringing back those waiting for collection; transporting goods for small shopkeepers; even carrying livestock, suitably caged or tethered. The coming of motorised transport allowed carriers to travel farther and faster, and in the end the carrier's cart became the rural omnibus.

Trade directories list local carriers and their routes. The carriers themselves often became well-known local characters, mentioned in village histories and in local newspapers. Because of the link between carriers and early buses, some information can be found in histories of bus companies (such as those in Dorset, at www.countrybus.co.uk).

■ CARTOGRAPHER

Women's **historic involvement** in mapmaking usually extended only to tracing or colouring maps and plans (see **tracer**), until during the Second World War a small number of **Auxiliary Territorial Service (ATS)** girls were taken on in the Ordnance Office to be trained to draw maps. The ATS also worked with the RAF in revising maps and town plans by comparison with reconnaissance photographs.

However, there was one notable exception. In the 1930s Phyllis Pearsall CBE, (née Gross, 1906–1996), the daughter of a mapmaker, became so frustrated at not being able to find a good map of London that she began to explore on foot and draw up her own maps. She set up the Geographers Maps Co Ltd to publish her 'A-Z of London' in 1936, which still publishes that famous guide and A-Zs for other towns and cities. See *Mrs P's Journey: The Remarkable Story of the Woman Who Created the A-Z Map*, Sarah Hartley (Pocket Books, 2002); her story is also to be found at www.designmuseum. org/design/phyllis-pearsall.

■ CARTRIDGE MAKER

Gun **cartridge and** fuse making was almost wholly done by women, including at Woolwich Arsenal until the 1870s. Their work 'consists in cutting paper, plugging and gauging shot, forming the cartridge cases, making pulp insides, filling, twisting, lubricating, cutting, packing in bundles and finally in barrels. None of this work is injurious to the health . . . except perhaps the pressing, which is somewhat sickly work, and the sticking on the green bands, during which possibly some arsenite may be swallowed'. (*Industrial Classes*, 1876.)

Women were already working at this trade in workshops in Birmingham and Coventry before the First World War brought in thousands of female **munitions** employees. In 1886 H. Sutherland Edwards visited the Ardeer dynamite factory in Ayrshire for the *English Illustrated Magazine*. Women worked in small huts making cartridges by 'pushing the dynamite through copper tubes'; completed cartridges were taken from them by men stationed outside the huts. It was extremely dangerous work and an explosion had killed three of the women not long before. As Edwards rightly said: 'One little mistake, and the poor cartridge girl is blown from her wooden hut to the skies.'

■ Cashier

In larger shops from the mid-19th century one woman would act as cashier in a department, taking the money from customers (or preparing their bills) after they had been served by the counter assistants. Some shops had a system that carried money or receipts by pneumatic tube or overhead lines, with the cashier seated in isolated splendour at the centre of the web. A cashier also might be the woman who took money for tickets at a cinema or theatre box office; or she might work in an office handling money, keeping ledgers and so on.

■ Chainmaker

The chainmaking industry of the 1800s was centred on Cradley Heath, straddling the Worcestershire/Staffordshire border – in the 1890s over 1,000 tons of chains were being produced there every week, ranging from huge ships' mooring cables to handcuff links.

Although there were factories engaged in the making of the larger chains, it was still a cottage industry and the women who did much of the work were in effect **blacksmiths**. Robert H. Sherard visited the area for *Pearson's Magazine* in 1896 and described the scene: 'One may come across sheds with five or six women, each working at her anvil, that are all talking above the din of their hammers and the clanking of their chains, or they may be singing a discordant chorus; and, at first, the sight of this sociability makes one overlook the misery which, however, is only too visible, be it in the foul rags and preposterous boots that the women wear, or in their haggard faces and the faces of the frightened infants hanging to their mothers' breasts, as these ply the hammer, or sprawling in the mire on the floor, amidst the showers of fiery sparks.'

Iron rods were heated in the fire until red hot, then cut and twisted, the woman (or a child) working the bellows continuously. Each link was then inserted into the last link made and welded closed with a hand hammer or the Oliver – the heavy hammer worked by treadle also used by **nailmakers**. Girls ('blowing girls') could work two pairs of bellows at a time, for ten or twelve hours a day, 'the work being like that of a treadmill in a sulphurous atmosphere', and for that they could earn 3s to 4s a week. Women might also work in the smaller factories, operating the bellows to provide 'blast' to the furnace. As with the nailmakers, the 'fogger' acted as middleman, or, more usually here, middlewoman. Louisa Addleton, a chainmaker living at Cradley Heath, was also a 'fogger'.

Many of the women produced chain for the company run by Eliza Tinsley, who took over her husband's firm after his death in 1851 and moved to Cradley Heath in 1853. Eliza retired in 1872 but Eliza Tinsley & Co is still a leading chain supplier.

The terrible conditions and starvation wages eventually provoked the women into a strike in 1910, led by Mary Macarthur of the National Federation of Women Workers. After ten weeks, their right to a minimum wage was established (giving some of the women a 150% pay rise) and this is now seen as a milestone in labour history. In 2006 the first Women Chainmakers' Festival and rally was held at Dudley, in celebration of their achievement. The Black Country Living Museum is at Tipton Road, Dudley, DY1 4SQ (telephone: 0121 557 9643; www.bclm.co.uk). See *Chains and Chainmaking*, Charles Fogg (Shire Publications, 2008).

■ CHAINMAKER (GOLD OR SILVER)

A **completely different** occupation from that above was gold and silver chainmaking for the jewellery trade. The firm of G.E. Walton, situated in Birmingham's Jewellery Quarter, is said to have been the 'largest watch-key, and gold and silver chainmakers in the world' by the 1880s, and it was estimated that over 2,000 people were employed in the trade, including many women.

The smaller the links of the chains, the slower the work, and "it is said the difficulty of making the smaller chains is so great, that the women who make them cannot work above two hours at a time". To be a good gold chain maker, a girl must start young, commencing with "linking", and passing the chains on to the "finisher", who solders them. "Dipping", viz. placing the metal in aqua fortis, brightening or "charging", viz. putting small pieces of metal together to form supports inside a larger one, as in the case of ear-rings, are other branches of employment'. (*Industrial Classes*, 1876.) See also **jewellery worker**.

■ CHAMBERMAID

A woman employed usually in a hotel or boarding house to carry out housemaid duties, specifically cleaning rooms and bedmaking. (American usage sometimes equates chambermaids directly with domestic housemaids.) Before indoor plumbing was universal, she would also have to carry hot water upstairs for guests' baths and cold water for drinking and washing. Tips from guests formed a major element in her wage and she worked long hours, responsible to the housekeeper in a large hotel or the manager. There was effectively a 'servants' hall' in larger places, mirroring the set up in large country houses.

One girl started work at the Sawrey Hotel near Ambleside in 1935, aged 14, and was taught 'setting tables properly, waitressing and chambermaiding' for 8s a week and her board; she had to provide her own uniform of a blue dress and large white apron for the morning and a black dress and 'small fancy apron' for the afternoon, plus caps (*Cumbria Within Living Memory*, Cumbria Federation of WIs, Countryside Books, 1994).

■ CHARLADY, CHARWOMAN

A woman hired by the hour or day to do the heavy cleaning, inside and out, perhaps coming in once or twice a week. She never 'lived in' with other servants and would probably 'oblige' for several different households. By the 1920s the numbers of charladies (their preferred title by then, often shortened to 'char') had risen considerably as the difficulty in finding servants increased. By then, too, they were in demand by owners of flats or maisonettes who had no other cleaning help and nowhere for a servant to live if they could find or afford one. Often older women, their 'unimpeachable respectability' was described as 'somehow enhanced by their Victorian clothing'. See also **daily maid**.

■ Chauffeuse

In July 1915, when the loss of men to the Front in the First World War was beginning to open up new horizons of employment to women, *The Times* noticed an 'increasing tendency on the part of gentlewomen to take up various forms of domestic service . . . In one West End agency which deals only with gentlewomen there is an enormous demand for the feminine motor car driver who can do running repairs . . . An increasingly large number of women are qualifying as drivers, taking advantage of cheap tuition in various polytechnics and motoring schools, and they make up for their lack of experience of London traffic by their extreme carefulness. The usual wages in private service is from £1 resident to 35s or £2. . . .'.

It would have only been 'gentlewomen' who would have had the opportunity to learn to drive at this early stage of motoring, but those that did were as keen as their male counterparts on their motor cars. The Ladies' Automobile Club began meeting at Claridge's Hotel in 1904, proving that 'the woman motorist is in real earnest in the matter of horseless locomotion' (*Lady's Realm*). By the end of the war, a woman driver was no longer a curiosity.

■ Chevener

An embroiderer, in silk, of stockings or socks. Ann Birkin of Nottinghamshire was chevener to Queen Victoria and had a signed portrait of the Queen on her cottage wall until she died in 1909. In Lea Mills, Derbyshire in the early 1900s female cheveners added silk embroidery to men's socks; they worked at home, fetching the socks by the gross from the stocking factories. They had a different needle for each colour they were using, and the needles were stuck into cloth, much like a pincushion, until they needed them.

■ Chimney sweep

Marian Dye was a chimney sweep in Hertford in the mid-19th century, running the family business with her husband. She was a huge woman, said to have been over 6 ft tall and weighing over 18 stone. One morning in 1844 she arrived at Goldings, the house of the local MP, to sweep the kitchen chimney. Marian began work at 3 am because otherwise, once the servants got up at 6 am, the chimneys would be in use. She would have erected a screen around the kitchen fireplace, to catch the falling soot, before sending her son, James, up the chimney.

James's job was to scrape the soot from the walls of the chimney as he clambered up towards the roof – climbing boys had to be young and small. If all had gone well, Marian would have collected the soot (a valuable commodity, which could be sold on for fertilizer), cleaned up in the kitchen, hoisted James back on the cart and gone home with no one the wiser. But this time when he should have climbed to the top and signalled to his mother that he was through, he did not appear. Marian heard a noise behind the fireplace but could not get to him, so she ran off for help. It took hours for the brickwork to be chipped away, by which time the boy was found to have suffocated in deep soot.

James should not have been sent up the chimney at all, as in 1840 an act had prohibited the use of 'climbing boys', following a campaign from the late 18th century, that created a great deal of heat on both sides. Marian was by no means the only sweep to be caught using boys after 1840, but magistrates were often lenient in sentencing because, living in large houses themselves, they frequently agreed with the sweep that she could not otherwise clean properly – the machines that could do the job were fiercely resented for years. Only after a third prohibitive act in 1875 did the practice cease, but not before chimneys had claimed too many young lives.

In rural areas cottagers might clean their own chimneys, but in towns and for larger houses a professional chimney sweep would be called in, like Marian Dye – although men dominated the profession, women sweeps were, and are, by no means unknown. Hundreds are listed in the census returns, often widows – such as Ann Howard in Hitchin in 1851, who, aged 32, employed four men in her business. Although cleaner fuel and reduced dependence on coal for heating brought a decline in the profession by the mid 20th century, the necessity for sweeps has never gone away.

There is background information at www.chimneysweep.co.uk/history/history.html, or read *British Chimney Sweeps: Five Centuries of Chimney Sweeping* by Benita Cullingford (Book Guild, 2000), or *Chimneys and Chimney Sweeps*, Benita Cullingford (Shire Publications, 2003).

■ CHIROPODIST

The 'corn cutter' was a lowly form of life, as seen through the eyes of medical practitioners in the 19th century, but a necessary and (mostly) respectable one and it was a job that could prove remunerative if a good clientele could be built up.

Mrs Seymour Hill (d.1860) advertised herself as 'the celebrated corn cutter' (she was said to have been the original of 'Miss Moucher' in Dickens' *David Copperfield*) and following her death her London practice was scrapped over by the women who had worked for her. Miss Emily Bath, calling herself Miss Emley (because she had always been addressed as 'Miss Emily' or 'Emily'), had cards printed and distributed that emphasised she had been 'for many years with the late Mrs Seymour Hill' and set herself up in 'the profession of chiropodist' in 1861. The competition was not welcomed by Mrs Knight and Mrs Hayward, who had been left the bulk of Mrs Hill's property and were continuing her business.

There was little that could be done to stop 'Miss Emley' setting herself up as a chiropodist because there was no requirement to obtain professional qualifications or registration. At the turn of the 20th century, several court cases indicated that 'chiropody' was one of the personal services offered at 'disorderly houses' – including, in 1899, that of Florence Story, who advertised herself on her door in Great Portland Street as 'Nurse Florence, hospital certificated chiropodist'. It might also be included in a bona fide setting – but not always successfully, as Isobel Hawkridge of Barrow-in-Furness, Lancaster ('Madame Arthur, hairdresser and chiropodist') proved when she was made bankrupt in 1924.

All this was galling for the men and women who were serious about their occupation and determined to make it a respected adjunct of the medical profession. The National Society of Chiropodists was formed in 1912, the first such in Europe, with a founder member who was also one of the first female chiropodists (as opposed to corn cutters), Miss Catherine Norrie. Over the next 30 years four other societies were formed – the Northern Chiropodists Association in 1925, the Chelsea Chiropodists Association in 1926, the British Association of Chiropodists in 1931, and the Chiropodist Practitioners Group in 1942. All of these societies had their own journals. In 1945 they merged to form the Society of Chiropodists (today the Society for Chiropody and Podiatry; website: www.feetforlife.org) and with the coming of the National Health Service registration was made a requirement for employment. However, in the private sector it was still possible to be a 'Miss Emley' until 2002, when the title 'chiropodist' was protected by law. See *Past Imperfect: A Brief History of the Chiropody Profession*, Alan Ryecroft Whitby (2002). The records of the Society 1945–1996 are held at the University of Warwick (www2.warwick.ac.uk/services/library/mrc).

■ CHORUS GIRL

see ballet dancer.

■ CIRCUS PERFORMER, FAIRGROUND WORKER

The credit for creating the modern circus goes to Philip Astley in the late 18th century, who developed the idea from a riding school and performing with horses, to include acts by clowns, jugglers, trapeze artistes etc. Many circuses travelled around the country, performing for a few nights at a town before upping sticks and heading for the next engagement; others developed as static entertainments, such as the Tower Circus at Blackpool (see www.blackpoolcircusschool.co.uk/circus_history.html).

Women performers were an important part of the circus world – for example, Patsy Chinery, known as 'Pansy Zedora' in the ring and born plain Francis Murphy in Liverpool in 1879; in one act she was 'shot from a giant crossbow, flew through the air into a huge paper target, to be caught on the other side by her sister swinging from a trapeze'. The Theatre Museum website, which includes Pansy's story, has a wealth of photographs, postcards, cuttings and biographical information on people in the circus. John Turner's site (www.circusbiography.co.uk) relates to the project he is working on: 'an index of showmen, performers and other people connected with the circus in Britain' over the 19th and 20th centuries.

Some databases and indexes tend to lump circus and fairs together, which is why they have been put together here – but circus folk would have disliked that, as they considered themselves a cut above the fairground. As with the circus, some fairs travelled a circuit each year, while fairgrounds also developed as entertainment centres – such as the fairground at Bricket Wood in Hertfordshire, which attracted London crowds every weekend and bank holiday from the 1880s. Fairs have a very long history and many families have equally long associations with them – see *Fairfield Folk: A History of the British Fairground and its People*, and *Fairground Strollers and Showfolk*, both by Frances Brown (Ronda Books, 2nd ed. 1988, and 2001) for a fascinating background. The Fairground Heritage Trust, at Dingles Fairground Heritage Centre, Milford, Lifton, Devon PL16 0AT (www.fairground-heritage. org.uk) has preserved equipment, sideshows and memorabilia.

The National Fairground Archive at the University of Sheffield, Western Bank Library, Sheffield S10 2TN (www.nfa.dept.shef.ac.uk) includes material on both fairs and the circus and has a guide for family historians (under 'Using the NFA'). At http://users.nwon.com/pauline/Travellers.html there is a Showmen, Circus and Fairground Travellers Index, taken from census and other records. See also **actress**.

■ CIVIL SERVANT

In 1911, *Everywoman's Encyclopaedia* stated: 'The chief advantages which belong to the Civil Service as a sphere in which women may work include permanency of employment, regularity as regards hours, the prospect of a pension, and the comfort to be gained from working among those at least equal in the social scale.' Women were admitted into government employment in the Civil Service as typists from the mid-1890s, some 40 years after the Service had been opened to male entry by competitive examination rather than the system of patronage that had previously existed (see also **Post Office**).

By the 1930s there were about 70,000 female employees, mainly clerks, typists and shorthand-typists, but there were some specialists and a few women were being promoted through the ranks – Miss Isabel Anne Dickson, OBE, became the first and only woman assistant secretary in the Civil Service, in the Board of Education, having also been one of the first women appointed as an inspector of schools in 1905. Women were paid less than men on the same grades, a bone of contention still unresolved by the 1950s. They were also segregated from their male associates for work and for promotion prospects. In 1934, following a Royal Commission recommendation, it was agreed that all posts should be open to women, including administrative (except initially in the Colonial Office) and executive (except in the Defence Department). In 1923 the examinations for Assistant Inspectors of Taxes had been opened to women, which could lead to a career with the Inland Revenue.

Women were required to leave if they got married, though there was leeway in 'exceptional circumstances' for a head of department to keep individual women on if it was 'in the interests of the public service'. In 1932 the case of Miss A.C. Richmond, 'a first-class officer in the Ministry of Labour', hit the headlines when the male union objected to her being kept on after marriage – the government rebuff was that because of the marriage bar there were too few women in the higher ranks of the service, therefore keeping Miss Richmond on was in the public interest. It was a very arbitrary process, however. Miss M.L. Green, a botanist at the Royal Botanical Gardens at Kew and therefore a specialist officer, was another woman who managed to stay on in 1938, but the great majority of women who married simply left the service.

The National Archives has a Research Guide on Civil Service record holdings (Domestic Records Information 117), though it admits that the 'amount on female civil servants is limited'. The Federation of Women Civil Servants was formed in 1916 from existing female staff associations, and their records (1915–1942) are at the Women's Library (London Metropolitan University, 25 Old Castle Street, London E1 7NT; www.londonmet.ac.uk/thewomenslibrary). When an application was made to take the Civil Service examinations, applicants had to prove their age and these 'evidence of age' records (to 1948) are held at the Society of Genealogists; the name index can be searched online at www.findmypast.com.

■ CLAY WORKER

Women worked as surface labour at specialist clay works in Cornwall, Devon, and around Stourbridge in the 19th century. Cornwall provided the china clay and kaolin (the Chinese name for porcelain clay) essential for the production of fine china, and, today, the white mountains that are the waste product of the pits around St Austell are a reminder of the importance of this industry in the local economy for over two centuries.

China clay was first discovered in the area in 1745 and commercial use was under way by the 1820s. It proved to be the ingredient that would make it possible for Staffordshire pottery makers to produce wares that rivalled the best porcelain in the world and the process was a major employer of local labour, involving whole families. The women, 'balmaidens', worked at the surface of the pit. Once brought up by male workers, the clay had to be left to dry, after which it was cut into blocks. Women carried the blocks to dressing yards ('taking out clay'), where the clay was laid out again to dry further. Once completely dry, the blocks were cleaned by scraping them to get rid of any mould or sand, and then packed into wooden casks for transporting, all tasks done by women workers until the beginning of the 20th century.

On the Isle of Purbeck blue or ball clay was dug and formed the basis of the pottery industry in the area, notably Poole Pottery (although earlier it had been used for the manufacture of clay pipes). Once dug, the clay was taken to Furzebrook to be 'ripened' for about six months, by which time it was more elastic and workable.

Fireclay was dug in many places, usually in conjunction with coal mining, but in Stourbridge a special kind of heavy clay, completely different from the products above, was used to make pots for glasshouses and for gas retorts. Women formed the major part of the workforce on the surface of the quarries, breaking the clay into regular sized pieces and sorting it from discoloured and irregular lumps and stones.

Lynne Mayers, who specialises in the occupations of women in the West Country, wrote an article 'Was your great grandmother a balmaiden at the clay pits?' for the Cornwall Family History Society journal (no. 107, March 2003) which describes the women's work at the St Austell china clay pits; see **mine worker** for details of her website. See also *A History of the English China Clay Industry*, J.A. Buckley (Bradford Barton, 1997); and the Wheal Martyn China Clay Museum (Carthew, St Austell PL26 8XG; www.wheal-martyn.com) has access to the China Clay History Society and its archives.

■ CLERK

Usually an office worker (see **office staff**), although she may have worked in other environments such as hospital wards (see below), or the word may describe someone working in a telegraphy office. Before the widespread use of the typewriter, every piece of paper in an office had to be handwritten, and copies made by hand. In 1871 there were fewer than 1,500 female clerks, but by 1921 this number had rocketed to nearly 600,000.

Advice given to those wanting to apply as a 'commercial clerk' in 1911 was that they should be able to spell well, write with a clear 'commercial hand', have a basic knowledge of book-keeping, and be able to cope with shorthand and typing. That the adviser expected the applicants to be not only well educated but also middle class was plain: 'A very important point is punctuality. The better the clerk the fewer occasions will she plead "fog" as an excuse for being late on winter mornings, and in the summer she will very rarely leave the office five minutes before time to join a tennis party.'

■ CLINICAL CLERK

This was what we might now call a ward clerk, though the duties in the 19th century seem to have been a little more hands-on than would be expected today. When Augusta E. Mansford went into the Royal Free Hospital as a patient in 1895, she encountered a clinical clerk who completed the paperwork and even marked her up with blue pencil ready for the visit of the doctor an hour or so later: 'She was my idea of a strong-minded woman. Though her skirts were short, her hair was not, but lustrous brown plaits were coiled round and round a classic head, and her broad forehead, well-marked brows, clear grey eyes, and calm mouth, all inspired me with confidence'. (*Strand Magazine*, 1895.)

■ COFFEE STALL KEEPER

The coffee stall, open night and day, has long been a familiar feature of city streets. Henry Mayhew believed that the majority of those in London in the 1850s were kept by women. The stall might vary in size and amenities according to the district but it was often a two-wheeled barrow, with the water for the coffee carried in large tin cans over iron fire-pots heated by charcoal. The keeper would also provide sandwiches, bread and butter and cake to go with the coffee, tea and cocoa. See also **street seller**. Women also kept coffee houses, which by the mid-19th century had lost their earlier connection with merchants and intellectuals and were quite often simply working class meeting places.

■ COLOURMAKER

The making of ships' colours (flags) and pennants was restricted to female workers in naval dockyards such as Portsmouth and Chatham – the widows of naval men and, later in the 20th century, the widows of dockyard workers. The women at Portsmouth also made overalls, curtains and furnishings for ships and shore establishments. They were given special consideration by being allowed to leave work at 4 pm, half an hour before the male employees, so that they could avoid the rush at the dockyard gates (www.seayourhistory.org.uk).

■ COMPTOMETER OPERATOR

The comptometer was an American invention of the late 1880s that rapidly came into use in practically every office and was used by many women – a calculating machine with a numeric keyboard that was capable of adding and listing entries, operated by pulling a small lever at the side. It was still widely used after the Second World War.

■ CONDUCTRESS

Leader of an orchestra or choir. At the beginning of the 20th century this was not common, though by no means unknown, especially in amateur musical circles. In 1900 women musicians and a woman conductor were employed to play at the Women's Exhibition at Earl's Court. Male musicians who felt they had been ousted showed their feelings by 'raucous and derisive applause', cat-calling and rapping with sticks on the bandstand, but the unnamed conductor rose above it all with good humour and commonsense.

Also the name for a kind of stewardess on board ship, or a bus conductor.

■ CONFECTIONER

A maker or seller of sweets, chocolates, fudges, candies etc – women ran confectionery shops, or combined the trade with a baker's shop, general store or teashop. It was a trade thought suitable for middle class ladies. Some confectioners, however, were travellers, making their living with sweet stalls at fairgrounds and showgrounds, or in holiday resorts.

■ COOK

Although the upper classes and the restaurant trade perpetuated the myth that women could not produce the finest cuisine, female cooks of all types were more common than the male chef.

'Good plain cooks', or cook-generals, were a mainstay of middle class life up to the 1930s.

In large houses where the full panoply of servants were kept, the cook would be third in seniority in the female servants after the **housekeeper** and the **lady's maid**. She would be assisted by **kitchenmaids** and **scullery maids** (and would probably have come up through their ranks herself), and the kitchen would be her kingdom.

Cooks in general had a reputation for touchiness, perhaps brought on by the heat in the kitchen and the pressure of their work, so that employer and assistant alike might have to tread carefully. *Punch* cartoons of the 19th and early 20th centuries frequently portrayed the cook as a tyrant, rather fond of the bottle, over-familiar with the tradesmen, and protective of her right to her 'perquisites' – the dripping, bones, empty jars etc that she could sell on her own account. By 1910 mistresses were being told that this practice should be forbidden and to keep their own eye on the bills, but many a mistress with a good cook would overlook a little 'wastage' rather than lose her.

Her kind fared badly during the First World War: 'The only kind of servant who is without a post at the moment is the high class cook at £50 or £60 a year, for whom there is little demand, owing to the steady growth of thrift and the almost total cessation of private entertainment on any large scale. The highly-trained cook is not adaptable and stands out obstinately for the old elaborate kind of meal,' said *The Times* in July 1915.

The majority of households were, of course, small to middling-sized and then the cook might be one of only two or three servants, or she might be on her own altogether. She also might be a 'plain cook', preparing simple dishes and probably self taught, rather than an experienced and capable 'professed cook'. Other opportunities opened up for women cooks during the 19th and 20th centuries – in institutions such as workhouses, schools, hospitals and the armed services particularly. See also **domestic servant**.

■ COOK, ARMY

During the First World War, cooks were needed by the Army even before the women's services were formed. 'There is an ever increasing demand for women to act as Army cooks and waitresses in camps, hospitals, convalescent homes and officers' messes,' reported *The Times* in January 1917. 'The salary is £20 per annum, board and accommodation found, laundry allowance and free uniform, with the prospect also of the salary being raised in the near future. Women doing this work have also the satisfaction of knowing that they release men for military service. The military cooking section of the **Women's Legion**, Duke of York's Headquarters, Chelsea, have already enrolled 2,000 women for this service.'

■ COOK-GENERAL

Many families employed a cook-general, or 'general', who would have to combine cooking with domestic duties such as lighting fires, cleaning and sweeping, filling the coal scuttles and cleaning the boots, answering the door and washing up. In 1910 the advice on uniform was: 'Cooks should always wear washing dresses and white aprons, with coarse ones for cleaning purposes. Black dresses and fine aprons are usually worn in the afternoon. Frequently cooks do not wear caps, except in houses where they are expected to answer the front door'.

The cook-general was increasingly in demand as it became more difficult to find servants in the 1920s and 1930s: 'Where only one other servant is kept it is wisest to advertise for a cook-general rather than a cook, as, when so styled, the latter at times goes on strike and refuses to assist in the housework.'

The careers of some cooks highlighted the fears of employers. Ada Brennan confessed in August 1922 that she had carried out robberies at houses in London where she had been employed as cook-general. After only one day in service at a house at Beaufort Gardens she ransacked the place and absconded with jewellery, plate and linen to the value of £150, plus £20 in notes. At her next job, in Finsbury Park, she absconded after two days' service with goods valued at £50. However, there was another side to the story of the living-in servant, as a court case in 1928 demonstrated. Laura Easy, a cook-general, described as a frail little woman, had gone to bed at 9.35 pm instead of 10 pm and refused to get dressed again to post a letter, for which she was told she could not have her day off on Sunday. She slipped out anyway, but when she returned she was locked out of her room and struck on the legs with a stick by her employer: Murray Fletcher Rogers was ordered to pay a fine of £2 and costs for assault, but the decision was overturned on appeal because there was no independent corroboration of Laura's story.

It was no wonder that servants were becoming scarce. In 1925 an advertisement appeared in *The Times* offering a £3 reward to anyone who could help find 'a really reliable and industrious cook-general'.

■ COOK, VISITING

A few women hired themselves out as visiting cooks. In the 1880s it was said that 'for really clever visiting cooks there is ample employment. We know two excellent middle-aged women who earn more than a livelihood by cooking dinners and suppers for people.' It was the ideal solution for a mistress who gave only the occasional dinner party.

■ COOKERY INSTRUCTOR/TEACHER

In 1874 the National School of Cookery was founded in Exhibition Road, South Kensington, by Sir Henry Cole (1808–1882), who was an active public figure and patron of the arts. The first Lady Superintendent was Lady Broome, who had written a 'little book' on *First Principles of Cookery*, but she soon left to follow her husband abroad and Mrs Edith Clarke (d.1919) took on the post, staying for the next 44 years. She had a tremendous influence on the teaching of cookery teachers and instructors, so much so that at her death the teaching of domestic science in schools was put down to her 'inspiration and foresight'. The School closed finally in 1962 as the National Training College of Domestic Subjects.

There was much concern in the last quarter of the 19th century that working class girls were not being taught the basics of cookery and good housewifery to fit them for their role as wife and mother, and the School held classes for local children and 'female pupil-teachers' in 'artisan cookery'. At the same

A class at a board school in London in the early 1900s, 'making tarts, and a few looking after a joint of beef – which a group of the teachers will buy for their own dinner'. (Living London, 1902)

time, cookery instruction was seen as a suitable and useful job for 'ladies' to undertake, after a period of training. Instructors might find work in colleges or schools, or take private pupils – young middle class women were also being urged to take a course in cookery to 'finish' their education. In 1881 the School was estimated to have awarded 148 diplomas in teaching, and trained over 12,000 people in classes throughout the country; by 1913 over 2,000 teachers had been trained for posts in public elementary schools, secondary and private schools, high schools and training colleges.

Other training schools could be found at Edinburgh, Glasgow, Leeds, Nottingham, Liverpool, Manchester, Wakefield, and Birmingham. The National Training School itself employed 'a considerable number' of teachers, loaning them out for demonstrations and lectures throughout the country.

■ COPYWRITER

Advertising agencies emerged during the late 19th century in response to an increasingly crowded marketplace, first in the USA, where it was quickly realised that the great majority of purchases were made by women. However, the copywriters who created the slogans and advertisements were almost all male. The League of Advertising Women of New York was formed in 1912, but a similar movement does not seem to have existed in Britain. During the 1920s and 1930s copywriting was seen as an attractive job for an educated and literate woman – the writer Dorothy L. Sayers worked from 1922 to 1931 as a copywriter at the London advertising agency, Benson's. She was good at her job but later condemned it for creating need where none existed.

■ CORK CUTTER

In 1806 the *Book of Trades or Library of the Useful Arts* said that both men and women worked at cork cutting and called it the 'blackest and dirtiest of all the trades'. This was probably because of the method used to prepare the cork – the bark of a species of oak tree, grown around the Mediterranean and imported into England – for cutting and shaping into the familiar bottle stoppers and also larger items such as shoe soles and heels. It was a trade dating back to the 17th century. The pieces of cork were heated over open flames so that they softened and tightened before being worked on, the blackened areas being scraped off like burnt toast. Corkcutters worked in small workshops and the trade became increasingly mechanised through the 1800s. Mrs Rose Ann Stokes was a 'cork cutter (dealer)' at Thetford in the 1870s, and in 1881 Jane Beach, a 55-year-old widow, was a cork cutter employing four men and one boy in Shadwell, East London.

■ CORSETMAKER, CORSETIÈRE

The fashions of the 19th and early 20th centuries demanded well-made undergarments, and particularly corsets. Corsetmaking needed much the same skills as tailoring, and garments made to measure were the ideal for most fashionable women, who would buy them from specialist corsetmakers, either working from home or in shops. Many staymakers worked for the corsetières at home to order, making the intricate and substantial garments.

Mass production made good quality corsets available to a wider range of customers by the 1900s. One of the specialist companies, the Spirella Corset Company of Great Britain, formed in 1910, had a factory at Letchworth, the First Garden City; Mrs F. Wright was the first corsetière at the factory and large numbers of local women worked there, carrying out many of the processes by hand, such as putting the laces in the corsets.

See the website www.corsetiere.net for a great deal of information about the 20th century corsetmakers and their corsets, including many photographs. To gain an idea of the work involved in making a corset, see *Waisted Efforts: An illustrated Guide to Corset Making* by R. Doyle (Sartorial Press Publications, 1997); or for history, *Corsets and Crinolines*, Norah Waugh (Routledge, 1954).

■ COSTER GIRL/WOMAN

A **costermonger was** a street seller of fruit, vegetables, fish and provisions and it was common for their daughters to be sent out onto the streets to sell from the age of about seven, beginning probably with oranges, apples, violets or watercress. By the time they were 15 or so, they would be walking barefoot eight or ten miles a day, carrying a basket of produce – anything from sprats to apples – weighing near 200 cwt on their head, so that when they put their burden down at the end of the day their necks were cricked and their heads felt 'as light as a feather'. Otherwise they might exhibit their wares on a heavy tray, a strap around the neck holding it in front. From the centre of the city the younger women would walk out to the nearby towns. Older women were more likely to have a regular fruit or vegetable street stall. Most of these coster girls married or lived with costermongers in their turn. See **street seller.**

■ COTTON SPINNER AND WEAVER

By 1851 the cotton industry was the third largest employer in Britain (after agriculture and domestic service), providing work for over 250,000 women. Fifty years later the workforce was dominated by women. Despite the long hours and often poor working conditions, many women found greater freedom and better pay in the mills than they could expect elsewhere. Female weavers were amongst the highest paid women workers in industry. For years the industry led the world, despite the hardships caused by the cotton famine during the American Civil War in the 1860s, until its gradual decline began during the 1920s and 1930s.

While Lancashire was the acknowledged 'Cotton County', spinning and weaving took place at mills around the country. In 1893 Hamish Hendry

The Lancashire mill girl's familiar and distinctive clothing, with a shawl to cover her head.

visited the Paisley works of J. & P. Coats, manufacturers of cotton thread, and wrote about it for *Good Words*. The process by which cotton was prepared had been roughly the same for decades, although in earlier times much of the preparation and cleaning was done by hand.

Raw cotton arrived at the factory in bales and had first to be cleaned of dirt. This was done by machine in 1893, the cotton being revolved on cylinders that teased the fibres out into a layer of uniform thickness. This layer of cotton went through a carding-engine, where 'several millions of small sharp wire teeth' combed it into 'a soft light fleece', rounded into a coil called a 'sliver'. A drawing-frame stretched the sliver out into long and even strands of cotton. Next came a slubbing-frame and a roving-frame, each of which drew the thread out again and twisted it, to be wound onto a bobbin – now the spinning process could begin. On the spinning mule, its 'pure white bobbins stretching away, row upon row, in this vast building', the cotton was spun into yarn. At Paisley, this would be used to make sewing cotton thread, but where the spun cotton was intended for weaving it would now go to the powerlooms in the weaving sheds. Here the basic method involved the use of a shuttle to throw the weft between the divided threads of the warp to produce woven cloth, or cotton tape.

Women were involved at every stage of this process, including the spinning, which in the earlier 19th century tended to be dominated by male workers. This is a large subject and it is not possible here to more than touch on the many processes that it involved and the technological advances that affected day to day working life, both in spinning and weaving. There is a huge range of general material available for the cotton industry and its workers. There may even be surviving employee or trade union records for individual firms but to find them luck will play a part in being able to identify the mill where a woman worked.

Information from archives, museums and libraries in the North West, including a bibliography, extracts from books, and photographs, is gathered at www.spinningtheweb.org.uk; while an introduction to the ways in which the Industrial Revolution affected Lancashire is given at www.cottontimes.co.uk. At the Helmshore Textile Museum, Holcombe Road, Helmshore, Rossendale BB4 4NP, demonstrations and exhibitions are held in the original textile mills – this is only one of many local museums that over recent years have concentrated on recreating life in the cotton mills and towns. See www.paisleythread.org for more about the mills of Coats and others; Coats' archives are held by Glasgow University Archives Service. There is a dictionary of cotton fibres and weaves at www.ntgi.net/ICCF&D/cotton.htm. The 18th century New Lanark mills in southern Scotland are now a World Heritage Site (www.newlanark.org).

A helpful start for reading about the industry (which is online at Spinning the Web, above) is *Cotton: A Select Bibliography on Cotton in North West England*, Nigel Alan Rudyard and Terry Wyke (Manchester University Press, 1997); see also *The Cotton Industry*, Chris Alpin (Shire Publications, 2003) for a brief introduction. *The Hungry Mills*, Norman Longmate (Hamish Hamilton, 1978) tells the story of the hardships of the 1860s. To bring the story up to date, see *Memories of the Lancashire Cotton Mills*, Ron Freethy (Countryside Books, 2008).

See also **fustian cutter; lacemaker (bobbin net); weaver.**

▒ COWKEEPER

A woman who kept one or more cows in a town location to provide fresh milk for customers. In 1851 Jane Clarke, a 40-year-old single woman, was a 'Cowkeeper, grocer etc' in Gloucester Street in the Mile End area of London.

▒ CRACKER MAKER

Thomas Smith marketed the first crackers in the late 1840s, originally with a wrapped sweet in the cardboard tube. It was the crack of the snap that made them completely original, though, which he created

Even in city back streets, up to the turn of the 20th century a cow or two might be kept for fresh milk.

with a small strip of saltpetre pasted onto thin card – he launched 'Bangs of Expectation' in 1860. It was also the noise that gave early crackers the name 'cosaques', because it sounded like the crack of a cossack's whip. Other firms began to make crackers too – Caleys, and Hovells, for example – but Tom Smith's remained the market leader.

By end of the 19th century Smith's was producing about 13 million crackers a year and exporting all over the world. The manufacturing process was very labour intensive – machines made the boxes and assembled the papers but women rolled, glued and tied the crackers by hand, as well as putting in the essential novelties, hats and jokes. Alice Adelaide Morgan, born in 1910, worked at the Smith's factory in Finsbury Square, London from the age of 14 until she married in her mid-twenties. She remembered that the crackers for the Royal Family were made there, and that every year a member of the Royal Household came to the factory with small packages to be put inside them – but the women working there were never told what they were.

The website www.christmasarchives.com/crackers.html has useful background information on the history of crackers. Unfortunately, the Tom Smith's factory and archive was destroyed by bombing during the Second World War.

A 'cracker maker' may also sometimes be a female worker in a **firework** factory.

■ CURDS AND WHEY SELLER

A **street trade** of the 19th century mostly carried out by women, in the summer months. They bought skim milk from a dairy, scalded, cooled and sweetened it and added rennet to make it set. In an hour it was ready – the curd was the solid and the whey the liquid that ran out when it was cut into. It was served in mugs or glasses, from a stall 'covered with a white cloth, or in some cases an oil-cloth, and on this the curds, in a bright kettle or pan, are deposited'. See **street seller.**

■ CUTLERY WORKER

The **cutlery industry,** based in Sheffield, employed women on the finishing processes for knives, forks, spoons, tools, razors, files, saws, scissors and surgical instruments: in 1871 there were nearly 2,000 female workers.

The industry was a dirty and unhealthy one, but women did mostly the lighter work – making up and finishing the products, particularly by adding bone, ivory or wood handles and if necessary lacquering them, and 'dressing and scouring', i.e. scouring the metal with sandpaper and polishing it to a good finish (earning 7s to 12s a week in the 1870s). For examples of the trade see the website of the Sheffield Industrial Museums Trust (www.simt. co.uk/collections/collections-1-2-1.html). *A History of Sheffield*, David Hey (Carnegie Publications, 2005) has details of the cutlery industry.

■ DAILY MAID, DAILY

By the 1920s, with living space at a premium for many people in smaller houses and flats, employing a daily **house-parlourmaid** or **cook** for a set number of hours each day was often the only way they could manage to have a servant. (If all they wanted was cleaning, see **charlady, charwoman**.) 'Frequently she is a woman of a competent and superior type, the wife, perhaps, of a disabled soldier, obliged to return to service in this form, highly recommended by the better-class registry which supplies her.' (*Good Housekeeping* magazine, 1923.)

■ DAIRYMAID

A good dairymaid could be worth her weight in gold to a dairy farmer producing butter and cheese for sale. While a hill farm, or any small farm, might make butter or cheese for family consumption only in the summer when the milk was at its best, a dairy farm would be in production all year round for market.

On many farms the dairying was done by the farmer's wife, who would in any case probably oversee the work in the dairy, but often on larger farms a woman with specific responsibilities was employed. By the mid-19th century, the dairymaid was also making an appearance in middle-class suburban villa establishments, where the mistress of the house might have a fancy to keep a cow or two and some poultry, in which case the maid would combine her duties in the dairy with other household service.

In the 20th century, when it was feared that the old skills were being lost, dairy schools (recognised by the Board of Education) were set up to bolster the industry and teach a new generation how to make good butter and cheese – the one in Gloucester in the 1930s was run by a Miss Collet. The dairy teachers were employed by the local county council.

On some farms the dairymaid would also help with the milking of the cows (see **milkmaid**), but usually any connection between the cowshed and the dairy was kept to a minimum. Cleanliness was absolutely vital and much of a dairymaid's time was spent in washing and scouring clean her equipment and utensils. It was in the churning and kneading, for butter, that a dairymaid's skill was tested, and likewise in the cutting up of the milk curds and the pressing and storing of cheeses.

For an idea of the kind of equipment used in the dairy, see *Dairying Bygones*, Arthur Ingram (Shire Publications, 2002), or pictures on the website www.fellpony.f9.co.uk (Dales farming). Many county or agricultural shows had competitions for dairying, and reports may appear in local newspapers.

■ DEACONESS

To become a deaconess (an 'accredited lay worker') was the only way in which a woman could train theologically and minister to a community in the Anglican church in the 19th century – she was a single woman, 'set apart' but, unlike a male deacon, not ordained. The role was formally recognised in 1891 but it would be 1987 before women were admitted to the order of deacon (and 1994 before they were admited to the priesthood).

The deaconess movement was a significant factor in the second half of the 19th century, coming at a time when women were creating a new image of themselves as an independent sisterhood in nursing, education and what we now call social work. In 1862 Elizabeth Catherine Ferard received her licence from Bishop Tait of London, the first woman to do so. She founded a community of deaconesses, which was also a religious sisterhood – the (Deaconess) Community of St Andrew, working originally in a poor parish in the King's Cross area of London and at the Great Northern Hospital; St Andrew's House is now the world headquarters of the Anglican Communion. Isabella Gilmore was another influential figure, licensed in 1887; see *Isabella Gilmore, Sister to William Morris*, Janet Grierson (SPCK, 1962). There is more information on women and the Anglican Church at www.watchwomen.com. See also **minister of religion**.

■ DENTIST

In the mid-19th century the dentistry profession was completely unregulated and there was no way of knowing if a person was competent or not – surgeons might carry out dentistry as a speciality, but others who practised included chemists and even watch-repairers (because they were craftsmen who could produce false teeth and dental aids), and training was by apprenticeship rather than approved courses of study and examination.

From 1860 the Licentiate in Dental Surgery (LDS) was granted by the Royal College of Surgeons (and names of dentists appear on the Medical Directory after 1866). In 1878 the British Dentists Act laid down that only those who had gained recognised training could call themselves a 'dentist' or 'dental surgeon' and be included on a new Dentists' Register – but, as there was no actual legal requirement to register, control of the profession remained elusive.

Dental schools existed from the 1850s, for instance at Birmingham Dental Hospital and under the Royal College of Surgeons at Edinburgh. They were slow to accept female students and the first woman to qualify as a dentist in Britain was Lilian Lindsay (1871–1960) in 1895; she graduated in dentistry at the Edinburgh Dental School and had a distinguished career, becoming president of the British Dental Association in 1946. There were, however, women practising as dentists before that – Dr Harriet Boswell, for instance, at 25 Queen Anne Street, London, in the early 1890s.

There were also women who had a less professional approach. In *A Wanderer in London*, E.V. Lucas wrote in 1911 of being 'fascinated by the despatch, the cleverness, and the want of principle of a woman who sold patent medicines from a wagonette, and pulled out teeth for nothing by way of an advertisement. Tooth after tooth she snatched from the bleeding jaws of the Commercial Road, beneath a naphtha lamp, talking the while with that high-pitched assurance which belongs to women who have a genius for business, and selling pain-killers and pills by the score between the extractions.'

The Dentists' Register has been maintained since 1879, with name, address and qualification. It was not until 1921 that all practising dentists had to be on the register, and to have a qualification from a recognised dental school.

The British Dental Association was founded in 1880 and the museum has information on how to trace dentist ancestors; photographs and archives: the museum is at 64 Wimpole Street, London W1G 8YS (www.bda.org/museum). There is an online history of professional dentistry at the website of the Faculty of Dental Surgery, Royal College of Surgeons of Edinburgh (www.rcsed.ac.uk/site/682/default.aspx). Not particularly about women dentists but great fun is *The Strange Story of False Teeth*, John Woodforde

(Routledge and Kegan Paul, 1983) – although it does mention Helen Mayo, whose evidence about a victim's teeth in 1949 helped to convict John Haigh of the Acid Bath Murder.

■ DINNER LADY

A much maligned woman, blamed for memories of soggy cabbage, gristly meat pies and lumpy custard, the 'dinner lady' arrived with the first school meal; she prepared, cooked and served the food in the school dining room.

From the 1860s voluntary groups in cities such as Manchester, Newcastle upon Tyne, Birmingham and London began to provide hot dinners for poor children, but it was once compulsory education was begun in the 1870s, when it became all too clear that thousands of children were so ill-fed as to be on the edge of starvation, that some school boards also became involved. The poor diet of the working class was a particular cause for concern when Army recruitment for the South African War in 1899 revealed an underclass of ill-nourished workers, stunted in growth.

In 1906 the Education (Provision of Meals) Act gave local authorities the powers to provide hot meals in elementary schools, paid for by parents or the imposition of a local rate. Uptake was patchy throughout the inter-war years, with some authorities more generous than others; in Bradford 'children could have porridge, bread and treacle and milk for breakfast and a variety of cooked dishes for dinner, including onion soup, hashed beef, shepherd's pie, fish and potato pie, baked jam roll and rice pudding,' according to John Burnett ('Eat your greens', *History Today*, March 2006). However, school meals for all became a statutory provision under the 1944 Education Act.

Dinner ladies and school cooks were the employees of the School Meals Service of the local education authority and any staff records that may survive will be found usually in county archives.

■ DISPENSER, DISPENSING ASSISTANT

Training as a hospital dispenser took a three-year apprenticeship under a qualified chemist, but when, in the days before the National Health Service, GPs often had their own dispensaries on site in their practices and made up medicines and pills on the spot, they might accept someone with the less advanced Apothecaries' Assistant qualification.

The dispensing assistant, frequently a woman, was also part receptionist, part first-aider, part book-keeper and general all-round assistant. There is a description of one woman's experiences in the 1940s in *Hampshire Within Living Memory*, Hampshire Federation of WIs (Countryside Books, 1994): 'One was expected to test urine and blood samples for a diversity of medical conditions; deal with accidents and emergencies when the doctors were out of the surgery; sterilise instruments and assist at minor operations. Book-keeping, filing, wages and general clerical work, not to mention typing, were all part of the job. Additionally it helped if one could unblock drains, smooth ruffled feathers and make a good cup of tea.' See **pharmacist**.

■ DOCTOR, SURGEON

The **arguments against** accepting women as medical students and then as qualified medical practitioners seem now fairly illogical – they were too emotional; their brains were smaller than a man's; they could not take the rowdy atmosphere of the dissecting room or the operating room (and

The effect of a female doctor on a young man's heart rate was a cause for concern to Punch *in 1865.*

the male medical students were indeed rowdy); they could not be alone with a male patient etc. In 1878 Sir William Jenner went so far as to say that he would rather see his daughter dead than as a medical student. Yet the history of women in medicine is one of stubborn, dedicated individuals who refused to allow considerable obstacles to put them off their chosen course.

Elizabeth Blackwell of Bristol (1821–1910) was the first woman to have her name included on the Medical Register, in 1859, but her training and career were in America and it was Elizabeth Garrett (1836–1917) who became the first registered English female doctor, in 1865 (see **apothecary**). The Medical Register had only made its appearance in 1859, following the Medical Act 1858 that required all those practising as physicians, surgeons, doctors or apothecaries to have followed a recognised course of study and be registered by the Medical Council.

Many early women doctors gained their degrees from universities in Zurich or Paris. In 1869 Sophia Jex-Blake (1840–1912) managed to be accepted into the School of Medicine at Edinburgh Infirmary, although the authorities would not allow her to qualify. The situation only eased a little with the founding of the School of Medicine for Women in Brunswick Square, London in 1874, and the establishment of the Hospital for Women in the Marylebone Road by Dr Garrett, and the Edinburgh School of Medicine for Women by Dr Jex-Blake, allowing women to get the practical experience they needed.

In 1876 an act allowed qualifying bodies to grant medical registration 'without distinction of sex', but added the rider that nothing in the act made it compulsory to open their examinations to women. Some schools of medicine followed the spirit of this permissive act and admitted women students, including the Kings and Queens College of Physicians in Dublin and the schools of the Royal Free Hospital and London University, but many did not. The Birmingham University Medical School's first female medical student matriculated in 1900 (even though the Women's Hospital had 'unlawfully but enthusiastically' appointed a female Resident Physician in 1877 – Dr Louisa Atkins, MD Zurich); the School did, though, have the honour of training Hilda Shufflebotham, later Dame Hilda Lloyd (and then Dame Hilda Rose), who became the first female president of the university in 1949, and the first female professor of a medical royal college, in obstetrics and gynaecology (see www.medicine.bham.ac.uk). Manchester University's first female graduate from its School of Medicine was Dr Catherine Chisholm in 1904.

Women were admitted as members of the British Medical Association in 1892, when there were about 200 female doctors in the country. Mary Emily Dowson was the first female surgeon to be registered (approved by the Royal College of Surgeons in Dublin in 1886) and Dr Eleanor Davies-Colley became the first female Fellow of the Royal College of Surgeons in 1911. Female doctors could be found in hospitals, workhouses, private practice, general practice and the operating theatre.

Women doctors were from the beginning sought after in certain countries abroad, particularly India. In the late 19th and early 20th centuries there were frequent appeals by the Medical Women for India Movement for qualified women to take up teaching and clinical posts in hospitals and clinics on the sub-continent, where millions of women either could not be treated by a male doctor for religious reasons, or lacked the money to pay for care, and where female students needed tuition and role models. In 1874, for instance, the Madras Medical College opened its doors to female students. This was a secular movement, separate from that of the missionary, societies (see **missionary**).

The names of female doctors will appear in the Medical Register. The Wellcome Library has a list of sources for 'Women in Medicine' (http://library.wellcome.ac.uk/doc_WTL039962.html), and the Guildhall Library's advice on sources for finding surgeons, physicians and other medical practitioners is a good background guide to the profession (www.history.ac.uk/gh/apoths.htm).

The Royal College of General Practitioners (www.rcgp.org.uk/default.aspx?page=93) has advice for family historians, as does the Royal College of Surgeons of England (www.rcseng.ac.uk/library/services/familyresearch). The Royal College of Physicians (www.rcplondon.ac.uk/heritage/munksroll) has an index to obituaries, and the BMA (www.bma.org.uk/ap.nsf/Content/LIBBiographicalinformation) has biographical information. Outside England there is the Royal College of Surgeons of Edinburgh (www.rcsed.ac.uk); the Royal College of Physicians and Surgeons of Glasgow (www.rcpsg.ac.uk); and the College of Medicine at the University of Edingburgh (www.mvm.ed.ac.uk/history/history4.htm).

■ DOMESTIC SERVANT

Domestic service was a major employer of female labour until after the First World War, although unfortunately unless they were living in, finding out where a servant worked will be almost impossible. See under the job title, eg **cook, housekeeper, lady's maid, parlourmaid** etc. There are many books about servant life, all of which have bibliographies for further reading. Try *The Rise and Fall of the Victorian Servant*, Pamela Horn (Sutton Publishing, 1995); *Life Below Stairs in the 20th Century*, Pamela Horn (Sutton Publishing, 2001); *Below Stairs in the Great Country Houses*, Adeline Hartcup (Sidgwick and Jackson, 1980); *The Complete Servant*, by Samuel and Sarah Adams, ed. Ann Daly (1825 edition reprinted, Southover Press, 1989); *The Victorian Domestic Servant*, Trevor May (Shire Publications, 2006).

■ DRESSMAKER

Dressmaking was another important employer of women and girls by the late 19th century – in the 1880s a third of the clothing labour force in London was in the trade, in one of its several guises. It could be a seasonal trade (busiest times were said to be March to July and October to November), with irregular hours according to the orders that had to be completed. The strict code of dress in Victorian times for mourning was one of the greatest supports of dressmakers large and small, as whole families might have to replace or adapt clothing at short notice; the death of public figures also ensured them a busy time. (Shroud-making was a sideline

A sleevehand in 1893 – garment-making was often broken down into its separate parts and each woman worked only on her section.

too – Ann Lee of Coventry was recorded as 'dressmaker and shroudmaker' in 1871.) The popularity and increasing supply of ready-made clothing changed the market over the turn of the century, with more hands being employed in factories or as outworkers, or in the large department or drapers' stores.

At the peak of the profession were the high-class Court dressmakers, creating fashionable clothes for society women and for debutantes who were to be presented at Court. The Royal Archives website (www.royal.gov.uk) states categorically that: 'Court dressmakers were the people who made clothes for members of the general public who attended functions at Court, rather than specifically for the Queen or other members of the Royal Family'; unless of course they also held a Royal Warrant. This was what you might call 'the Madame dressmaker'. One famous Court dressmaker was Madame Clapham (1856–1952) of Hull, who forged an enviable reputation in the 1890s and 1900s (see www.hullcc.gov.uk/museumcollections, and some of her beautiful creations can be seen online at www.mylearning.org). After the First World War the demand for such elaborate dresses began to decline. A Court dressmaker's business could be very profitable, but behind the luxurious façade a small army of poorly paid workroom seamstresses and apprentices might have to work night and day to complete orders on time.

Dressmakers were employed in quantity by department stores such as Peter Robinson's or Selfridges, where the rates of pay were better than working for a Court dressmaker in a smaller establishment. In some cases the girls lived in at the shop: 'The "young ladies" resident in the houses of the higher firms, such as Messrs Howell & James, Regent Street, Messrs Lewes & Allenby, etc, are thoroughly well cared for, the salaries varying, according to capability, from £20 to £200 a year' (*Girl's Own Paper*, 1883). Most made-to-measure work was done by hand, 'machinists' normally just stitching linings. A large part of their work was altering clothing for customers.

A dressmaker might work on her own account, taking in orders from private clients and working at home – particularly a married woman who had had to give up work. She might also be a 'visiting dressmaker', going to the homes of clients and working there for a few hours a week: 'A visiting dressmaker receives from 2s to 2s 6d a day, and her principal meals are provided for her' (*Girl's Own Paper*, 1883).

Girls leaving school were usually taken on as apprentices. The period of training with a Court dressmaker might be two years, or anything up to five years for a big store. The conditions of the apprenticeship could vary – sometimes the girls were paid nothing for a year, their parents having to find a premium for them to be taken on. In the 1930s an apprentice in Cumbria was paid 4s 6d for a 40 hour week, in comparison to a fully qualified dressmaker at 29s.

One girl who was apprenticed to the dressmaking department of Richmans, an exclusive store in Walsall, in the 1920s, found her first job was picking pins up off the floor and taking out tacking thread. The room the girls worked in had treadle sewing machines, a coke stove for heating the flat irons used to press clothing, and a gas ring for the very heavy iron that was used to press bigger items such as coats. The discipline was strict and all work took place at large tables covered with brown paper. Each girl was trained either as a 'skirt hand' or a 'bodice hand'. This division of labour was common (caused partly by the increasing complexity of women's dresses in the later 19th century and partly by the sewing machine, which instead of freeing women simply gave them ever more complicated work to do) and being a dressmaker did not necessarily mean that she worked on whole garments.

The women at the bottom of the trade were those who were employed in the background – the 'sweated labour' that periodically throughout the 19th century was highlighted as a shameful affront to those who bought fashionable clothes (see also **tailoress**). Anyone called simply a 'seamstress' is likely to have been in this category, employed at starvation wages in dreadful conditions, sometimes at home, sometimes in sweat shops, working 14 to 18 hour days.

The website www.fashion-era.com/the_seamstress.htm has a lot of background information, about the profession as well as every aspect of clothing. A study of any fashion book covering the period will provide a good idea of the clothing over which dressmakers laboured; e.g. *A Visual History of Costume: The Nineteenth Century*, Vanda Foster (Batsford, 1992), or *Everyday Fashions of the Twentieth Century*, Avril Lansdell (Shire Publications).

■ DYEWORKS

Before 1856 all dyes came from natural sources, but in that year William Perkin discovered a method of factory mass-production that gave rise to the synthetic dye industry. His first colour – mauveine, a deep, intense purple – was so successful that Queen Victoria appeared in a gown of that shade in 1862, and the industry went from strength to strength until it hit a slump in the 1920s and 1930s. Women and children were employed in the industry, as unskilled labour and particularly in the bleaching process (see **bleacher**).

The Colour Museum of the Society of Dyers and Colourists (Perkin House, 82 Grattan Road, Bradford BD1 2JB; website: www.colour-experience.org) has some material on those involved in the industry and photographs, and the University of Bradford has a 'Dyeing Collection' (www.bradford.ac.uk/library/special/dyeing.php). More detail on modern dyes is available at www.makingthemodernworld.org.uk.

The bleaching ground at Monteith's dyeworks, Glasgow in 1844. After cotton cloth had been bleached ready for dyeing it was brought out by women to the bleach-fields in 28 ft lengths and laid flat on the grass for a few hours to oxidise. If it rained, all had to be quickly gathered up. There were sometimes as many as 5,000 pieces lying on the field at one time.

■ Electroplate worker

The 19th-century electroplate industry was based mainly around Birmingham and Sheffield, Elkington's of Birmingham having possessed the patent since 1840 for coating a base metal (nickel or copper) with silver by electrolysis. The items produced, which could closely imitate silver, including jewellery, were of such good quality that from 1896 it became necessary to mark them with the initials 'EPNS' (for 'electroplated nickel silver'). By the 1880s Elkington's alone was employing some 2,000 workers, many of them female. The nickel used in manufacture was a danger to women, more than to men, as it was not only an allergen but could cause miscarriages and birth defects. Wages were higher in Birmingham: a burnisher there could earn up to 20s a week, while one in Sheffield might only get 12s. There is information on Elkington's at www.jquarter. members.beeb.net/walk5.htm, where you also learn that the most famous piece they produced was the Wimbledon Ladies Singles Trophy. See also **burnisher; jewellery worker.**

■ Emery (glass) papermaker

Emery was a very hard mineral, used for polishing, for which it first had to be pulverised and the powder sorted into grades of fineness: 'The glass and emery are pounded in a mill, and were formerly sifted by hand by girls and women in hand sieves, though this is now done by machinery; and during this process an immense deal of the most irritating dust is set free, and necessarily inhaled, and particularly during the sieving out the first set or "flow", when the powder is finest. This is probably one of the most unhealthy employments that there is.' (*Industrial Classes*, 1876.)

■ Enameller

An enameller might work in a number of industries – with glass or china, for instance, or enamelling tin advertising signs. As the process involved lead, it could be a dangerous environment (see also **white lead worker**). The Departmental Committee on White Lead in 1897 interviewed 20-year-old Annie Harrison, who worked at Messrs Ralph & Jordan's in

Bilston 'brushing' tin signs after painting and before enamelling: the dust thrown off got into the girls' clothing and was also swallowed, so that they coughed up coloured balls of phlegm. Harriet Walters, just 17 years old, had died four years earlier while working at the same factory – the only 'respirators' the girls had were tattered handkerchiefs to put over their mouths.

■ ENGINEER

Engineering was predominantly a male environment, but there are examples of women working in various aspects of the profession in the 19th and early 20th centuries. Civil engineering covers building structures such as bridges, railways or roads. Mechanical engineers worked on everything 'from the minutest component parts of a railway engine, to the full-grown locomotive in all its beauty of paint and brass work; from the smallest detail of a spindle, to the enormous plant of a cotton mill, with its hundreds and thousands of intricate details'. They might also be called 'machine makers' in Victorian times, and included agricultural implement makers – Mrs Anna Taylor of Mickfield in Suffolk, for instance, is recorded as an agricultural implement maker, corn drill manufacturer, gunmaker and engineer in the 1870s. There were also a small number of women employed in engineering and machine works.

There were a few female students of engineering in the 1910s (including Jessie Young and Christina Foster, studying sanitary engineering at the Royal Technical College in 1911) but it was the upheaval of the First World War that opened more opportunities. The Women's Engineering Society, formed in 1919 by Lady Margaret Eliza Parsons, emerged from the Engineering Committee of the National Council of Women that had been set up during the war to consider the interests of the women employed by their thousands in munitions work. Many had been dismissed by their employers to allow returning servicemen to get back into work, but there were still enough women who wanted to remain in engineering to make forming their own society worthwhile, giving them support and encouragement in an often hostile working environment. From the initial branch in London, others quickly followed in Newcastle, Manchester and the Midlands. Their ranks were swelled in the Second World War, when again women took on skilled engineering work in factories and the services, and post-1945 women were accepted onto all university engineering courses. Apprenticeships, however, which provided the essential on-the-job training, were few and far between – notable exceptions were the firms of Rolls-Royce and Metropolitan Vickers.

The Women's Engineering Society is based at Michael Faraday House, Six Hills Way, Stevenage, Hertfordshire SG1 2AY (www.wes.org.uk), but the best place to start looking at the history of women in engineering is the Institute of Engineering and Technology's website (www.theiet. org), which has an online exhibition on 'Women in Engineering' and an Archives Research Guide on the same subject. Their library and archives are at Savoy Place, London WC2R 0BL and are open to the public but see the website first for details of how to make an appointment for research. The *Woman Engineer* journal has been published since 1919 and copies are held at the IET.

A website run by Nina Baker has a list of women engineers in Scotland from the 19th century (http://uk.geocities.com/scottishengineers), including those who studied at Glasgow University in the 1920s. The Institution of Civil Engineers, 1 Great George Street, Westminster, London SW1P 3AA, was founded in 1818, and it has an archive of membership records (www. ice.org.uk). The Institution of Mechanical Engineers, 1 Birdcage Walk, Westminster, London SW1H 9JJ (www.imeche.org.uk) was founded in 1847 and has a membership archive.

■ ENGINEER, MARINE

This was seagoing engineering, with the chief engineer the master of the engine room and answerable to no one but the captain. Under him (or her) were second, third etc engineers, and below them the 'greasers', who oiled and attended to the machinery, the stokers, who shovelled coal into the furnaces, and the 'trimmers', who moved the coal from the bunkers where it was stored. Below the waterline, in artificial light at all times, surrounded by heavy machinery with moving parts, steam and heat, with the ship rolling and pitching – this was not a workplace that would have attracted many women.

In the 1930s careers advice regarding becoming a marine engineer in the mercantile service was aimed solely at boys – 'The boy who wishes to enter this service first of all becomes apprenticed to a firm of shipbuilders or specialists in the manufacture of marine engines.' Yet at the time a woman was in her second decade as a sea-going engineer – the first female member of the Institute of Marine Engineers, Victoria Drummond (1894–1978), in whose name an award is still given today by NUMAST (the marine officers' union).

Her full story is told in *The Remarkable Life of Victoria Drummond, Marine Engineer* by Jean Cherry Drummond (Institute of Marine Engineers, 1994). She came from a privileged background, being a god-daughter of Queen Victoria, but had to start at the bottom in her chosen career. In 1916 she was taken on as an apprentice by the Northern Garage, Perth, and then at the Caledon shipworks, Dundee, and six years later she went to sea as Tenth Engineer on the SS *Anchises* for the Blue Funnel Line, earning £12 a month. She retired in 1962 as a chief engineer. During the Second World War she worked on convoys – dangerous and draining work, particularly for those in the engine room, who would be the last to be saved if the ship went down – and was awarded the MBE for devotion to duty, and the Lloyds war medal for bravery at sea after she took sole control of an engine room and kept it running while under attack. See www.plimsoll.org, or the website of the Institute of Marine Engineers (www.imarest.org).

■ ENGRAVER

Wood engraving was said in the 1880s to be 'a most remunerative occupation for women. The tools are few, and the wooden blocks clean and easily carried about, so as to be ready to be taken up at any time.' At least three years' experience was thought essential for making a good wage. Engraving on glass or metal, such as the backs of watches, also attracted female artists.

In 1860 *Once a Week* carried a report which highlighted the antagonism often displayed by male workers when women were employed: 'Three young ladies, after a preliminary training at the Marlborough House School of Design, applied to him [Mr Bennett] for occupation in engraving the backs of gold watches. Although perfect strangers to this kind of work, in six months, he tells us, they became as practised artists as a mere apprentice would have been in six years. At the end of this time, when they were making each three pounds a week by their labour, the men in the shop struck. These "foreigners", as they were termed, must go, or they would;

and Mr Bennett was obliged, sadly against his will, to comply with their wishes. These brave girls, however, were not to be beaten; they immediately turned their attention to engraving on glass, and are now employed at this delicate employment, and earn as much thereat as they did before as watch engravers.'

■ ENVELOPE MAKER

A trade carried out by stationers that employed women, either creasing and bending the paper, or gumming, folding and banding. Much of the work was done by machine from the 1870s but hand-folding and gumming was still done by outworkers. See also **papermaker**.

■ ESCORT AGENCY PROPRIETOR

Running an escort agency has sadly insalubrious connotations these days, but when 'Mrs Horace Farquharson' opened what is believed to have been the first escort agency in 1937 she had far better things in mind. If you were being presented at Court and had no 'connections' of your own, you could pay £5,000 to have a duchess take you under her wing, or £3,000 for a marchioness. The company of the younger son of a peer for the evening would set you back just £3 a time.

■ Factory inspector

The first two women factory inspectors, May Abraham and Mary Muirhead Paterson, were appointed in 1893 in response to growing agitation for female participation in the national regulation and investigation of factories and workplaces where women and girls were employed (as opposed to local regulation, where their duties overlapped to a certain extent with those of a **sanitary inspector**). It was believed that the workwomen would say things to a female inspector which they would not to a man and this proved true to a certain extent, though the inspectors still had to press their investigations into dangerous practices and sweated trades with some courage. The story is told in *Lady Inspectors: The Campaign for a Better Workplace 1893–1921*, Mary Drake McFeely (Basil Blackwell, 1988).

These women were also pioneers in government service: Hilda Martindale (1875–1952), for instance, one of the first women factory inspectors, in 1903 wrote an influential report on lead poisoning in brickworks and by 1914 was Senior Lady Inspector. In 1933 she joined the Treasury, one of the first women to reach the higher levels of the Civil Service (see **civil servant**).

■ Fairground worker

see **circus performer**.

■ Farm servant

The **farm servant** not only worked in the farmhouse, on indoor duties common to the **general servant**, but also in the dairy and the poultry yard, and at busy times might be expected to be outdoors in the fields, perhaps hoeing, picking or assisting at the harvest and haymaking.

Farm servants were often taken on at the local hiring fairs ('mop' or 'statute' fairs) for a set term. Although this system was gradually disappearing in the South and Midlands by the mid to late 19th century, in the North the hiring fairs were still going strong up to the 1920s and 1930s. The *Newcastle Daily Journal* reported on 25 May 1920: 'The oldest farmers do not recollect more animated or dearer hirings than those for women at Cockermouth yesterday. Servants were snapped up before they reached the hall set apart for the conduct of negotiations. Experienced women commanded £30 for the term, second class hands up to £25 and even inexperienced girls got £18.'

■ FARMER

Farmers were quite frequently female, usually (but not always) women who had inherited the land from a father, brother or husband – in 1851, for instance, 69-year-old Miss Jane Clarke was farming 40 acres at Nether Alderley in Cheshire, and employing two male farm labourers and a female farm servant. As such they had the same responsibilities as male farmers with regard to poor rates or service as parish officers such as constables or churchwardens, and may well appear in parish records. See *Farming: Sources for Local Historians*, Peter Edwards (Batsford, 1991). They will be listed in local directories, usually with the name of the farm. Maps can also be a useful source for tracing farms.

■ FILM, TELEVISION AND RADIO

By the start of the First World War there were at least 600 cinemas in Greater London – and taking the country as a whole the number must have run into the thousands – and the foundations for what became the 'British Hollywood' had been laid at Elstree.

Women can be found at every stage of the industry, from the film set to the cinema, though discovering which of many hundreds of small companies they may have worked for will be difficult. Books about the British studios, such as *Elstree: The British Hollywood*, Patricia Warren (Columbus Books Ltd, 1988), are useful for background and bibliographies, and see the website of the British Film Institute for information about their resources of catalogues and trade magazines (www.bfi.org.uk/filmtvinfo/library/).

There is also an interesting website of the AHRB Centre for British Film and Television Studies that lists the names of people found to be connected with the film business in London 1894–1914 (http://londonfilm.bbk.ac.uk) – here, for instance, are Eveleen B.A. Arton, a film renter and dealer who ran the Artograph Company in the early 1900s; Miss Carlton, proprietor of the Picture Theatre at Kingston in 1914; and Hannah Abrahams, of the Electric Palladium in Camden Town in the 1920s – giving an idea of the wide range of possibilities for employment.

Caryl Doncaster was a producer of documentaries for the BBC in the 1950s; she is talking here to the Governor of Wandsworth Prison.

Until the 1950s, when commercial television arrived in the UK, anyone working in radio or television would have been an employee of the British Broadcasting Corporation (BBC). Radio broadcasts began in 1922 (Radio Scotland was formed in 1923), and the first edition of *Woman's Hour* was heard in May 1923; the first female radio announcer and newsreader, Sheila Borrett, did not follow until ten years later. The first woman to appear in a BBC television broadcast was Adele Dixon on 2 November 1936: she sang *Here's looking at you* in a show of the same name, which was beamed out to 400 TV sets within 25 miles of Alexandra Palace. As television announcers, Elizabeth Cowell and Jasmine Bligh take the first honours; requirements, of course, were not only a good voice but also an attractive face – and in those days the pay was better on radio than on television.

Women broadcasters were few and far between, though there were other noteworthy individuals – such as Audrey Russell, who was the BBC's first woman news reporter and their only accredited woman war correspondent in the Second World War (post-war she was the first woman appointed to the newly formed Home Service reporting unit), or Una Marson, the first black programme maker at the BBC, in the 1940s (see *The Life of Una Marson 1905–1965*, Delia Jarrett-Macauley, Manchester University Press, 1998).

The BBC website (www.bbc.co.uk) has many interesting pages on radio and television history. The British Film Institute website, above, will also be useful for the history of television. The National Media Museum at Bradford has collections relating to film, television and radio (www. nationalmediamuseum.org.uk).

■ FIREWOMAN

While a small number of women worked in some way with local volunteer fire crews in the 19th and early 20th centuries, it was the creation of the Auxiliary Fire Service (AFS) in 1938, in preparation for war, that opened opportunities for female staff. All recruitment was done at this time by local authorities, but in August 1941 the National Fire Service (NFS) was formed in response to the devastation of the Blitz, and the service taken out of local hands. The difficulties of forming a coherent whole from a mass of individual town services with different organisations and equipment cannot be underestimated.

The pay for women in 1941 ranged from £3 a week to £400 per annum for the top grade. The first course for women officers opened in February 1942 at Brighton and 50 women took part, receiving training in 'welfare work, communications, and messenger service'. They were never expected to actually fight fires (some undoubtedly did, but a professional female firefighter would not arrive until 1982) but were taught drill and how to operate a light pump – their purpose was to release men from indoor duties onto the pumps. At its peak in March 1943, there were 29,000 women working full time in the NFS, and 41,000 part time. In 1948 the NFS was disbanded and the service returned to local authorities.

'Firewatchers' were not part of the NFS, but were volunteers who watched for fires caused by bombing, often stationing themselves on rooftops of factories, churches etc. Many women did this after their day's work.

A History of the British Fire Service, G.V. Blackstone (Fire Protection Association, 2nd edn, 1996) gives a broad picture of the service. Individual records may be difficult to find, depending on the area. For the London area, for instance, see the London Fire Brigade website (www.london-fire. gov.uk/about_us/our_history/your_history.asp).

■ FIREWORK MAKER

One of the most famous firework manufacturers, Messrs C.T. Brock & Co, were established as firework makers in the 18th century and female workers were prominent in their factories through the 19th and 20th centuries, moving out of London to Hertfordshire and then in the 1970s to Norfolk and Scotland.

In 1891 an article about their 50-acre factory in South Norwood appeared in the *Strand Magazine*. Women were engaged particularly in making 'coloured lights' in the dry rolling shed: 'They sit at slate tables, with paste-pot and brush handy, and piles of paper in front of them cut to a square about the size sufficient to hold half-an-ounce of tobacco.

Making crackers in a fireworks factory in 1891, running the paper cylinders filled with gunpowder through a press.

The thin rolls of paper are shaped with a steel rod, and are used for the great set pieces. A girl can roll twenty gross of cases for coloured lights in a day.' Elsewhere they made crackers, filling small paper cylinders with fine-grain gunpowder, and Catherine wheels.

At the website www.photolondon.org.uk there is a 1930s photograph of women workers in black overalls – the 'filler girls', who handled the powder – when 'Brocks fireworks factory consisted of many small bunkers, widely dispersed over the Gander Green Lane area of Cheam'.

There were many smaller fireworks manufacturers all over the country. An interesting site for anyone with firework-making ancestors is that of the UK Pyrotechnics Society (www.pyrosociety.org.uk), which has a forum page for questions and comments, many of them historically based.

FIRST AID NURSING YEOMANRY (FANY)

The **FANY was** formed in 1907, the brainchild of a veteran of the South African War who felt there was a role on the battlefield for a small mobile force of mounted, trained nurses who could save lives by filling the gap between the fighting men and the Army's medical corps. The women who responded to Capt Edward Baker's recruitment advertising were trained in first aid, cavalry drill (though the 'mounted' aspect fell before the advent of motorised transport) and army discipline, and they were a very independent bunch.

That feistiness came to the fore when the First World War broke out. FANY was a voluntary service, supported by public contributions, and the two women at its head – Grace Ashley-Smith and Lilian Franklin – were determined it would serve wherever the nurses could save lives. The War Office was not interested in using them, but the Belgian government was, so that Ashley-Smith was working in Antwerp within a few weeks, joined by the first FANY volunteers. The fall of Belgium cut that short, but the experience gained had been invaluable, and, when the FANYs returned to France shortly afterwards, they had their own ambulance. In Calais they took over the Hospital Lamarck for the Belgian Army, and were soon accepted as invaluable help on the British side as well. For the rest of the war they earned respect and admiration for their courage in the most dangerous and stressful conditions. They went wherever they were needed, whether nursing the dying and wounded behind the lines or driving ambulances to the trenches to bring back stretcher cases.

*The FANYs were among the first women to go to the front line during the
First World War, and they worked closely with the French and Belgian forces
as well as the British.*

Still a voluntary organisation (as they have remained), FANY stayed
together after the war and offered its services to the government – an offer
taken up during the General Strike of 1926, when the women drove for
the War Office and Great Scotland Yard. Recruitment continued through
the 1930s and in 1936 the name was changed to the Women's Transport
Service (FANY). In 1938 they were asked to recruit for and form the Motor
Driver Companies of the new **Auxiliary Territorial Service** (ATS), which
they continued to do until the spring of 1940 when that part of FANY
was incorporated into the ATS. Many members transferred (though they
kept their FANY arm flashes on the ATS uniform).

The FANYs went on, though, with separate units, serving with the Polish
Army in England as canteen workers and drivers, the British Red Cross
as ambulance drivers, and the 'Alnwick Unit' as hospital drivers. Many of
the women served in addition as clerks, wireless operators, drivers etc with

government departments. Abroad, they drove ambulances for the Finnish government, and the Kenya Section worked with the military in East Africa. Some of the FANYs transferred to the **Special Operations Executive** (SOE) and famously played their part behind enemy lines.

In 1907 the FANY uniform was a dark blue riding skirt topped by a scarlet tunic and scarlet service cap, but by 1910 this dashing outfit had toned down to the khaki it would remain. Their badge was a Maltese Cross enclosed within a circle. In 1999 they were renamed yet again, and are currently known as FANY (Princess Royal's Volunteer Corps).

Their official website (www.fany.org.uk) has background information. There is a centenary project to record the memories of surviving FANYs and SOE agents (www.our-secret-war.org/The_FANYs.html). There is also a list of those who died during the two wars, commemorated at St Paul's church, Knightsbridge (www.stephen-stratford.co.uk/wts.htm).

Amongst useful books are *The FANY in Peace and War*, Hugh Popham (Pen and Sword, 2003), *In Obedience to Instructions: FANY and the SOE in the Mediterranean*, Margaret Pawly (Leo Cooper, 1999), and *War Girls: The First Aid Nursing Yeomanry in the Great War*, Janet Lee (Manchester University Press, 2005). Remember to search for records under Women's Transport Service (WTS) as well as under FANY.

■ FISH CURER

Smoking fish to preserve it is usually thought of as a coastal trade, but strangely there was a haddock curing industry in London, in Camberwell, in the 19th century and at least up to the First World War – and if it was there, it was probably to be found in other inland settings where there was a thriving fish market. George R. Sims went 'Off the beaten track' for the *Strand Magazine* in 1904 and found women working at a trade that could prepare and smoke four tons of haddock a day, working in two shifts – the day shift did the preparation and the night shift the smoking: 'In the centre is a big table or bench, at which two women and a number of men are "sounding" the fresh haddocks, splitting them open and decapitating them with marvellous rapidity.'

■ FISHER WOMAN, FISHER LASS

The fishing industry could not have existed without the labour of women. Practice varied around the coast, but in many places they made nets and dried them after the catch had been brought in, gathered limpets and mussels for bait and then baited the lines, helped to launch the boats and to bring them in – and in some areas they carried the fishermen out to their boats through the shallow water, so that they did not start their long and arduous work soaking wet.

It was in the preparation and packing of the catch that women were dominant – only if the fish could be quickly preserved or despatched to the inland markets or for export would anyone make a living. In Cornwall some of the pilchard catch was going into tins by the 1890s: the local women washed the fish before drying them off and then boiling them for a very short time and packing them carefully into the familiar flat sardine tins and covering them with olive oil.

Otherwise, large quantities of the fish were salted, as described in the *Strand Magazine* in 1891: 'salt being plentifully used and the heads placed outwards. The row of carefully arranged pilchards is then thatched over and left to pickle for about a month. The pay is pretty good for this work, the children even getting 3d per hour. The pile is then undone, the fish packed with great care into barrels, and by means of a long lever with a heavy stone hooked on at the end, pressed down tightly. It is then ready for the market.' Much of this salted fish was exported to Italy.

However, it was in the East Coast herring industry, from Scotland down to Suffolk, that women were most important. Every year, until the 1940s, Scottish women followed the herring harvest south from the Shetlands in early summer to Yarmouth in the autumn, working in the herring yards along the way gutting and cleaning the fish and packing them into barrels for transport (again, there was a big export trade, this time with Germany and Russia).

In some places they lived in specially built sheds, much as the hop pickers did for their harvest work, while in others they found lodgings with local people. This was the case in Lowestoft, where cottage rooms were cleared for their arrival. They brought their belongings with them in wooden chests and lived four or five to a room; at the end of the season they spent some of their money on presents and clothes and then disappeared back to Scotland until the next time, usually travelling by sea along the coast. When they were not working they were noted for their knitting, which they did even as they walked around.

Packing Cornish pilchards in salt, the heads outwards,
to 'pickle' for a month, 1891.

At work they got some protection from their clothing, especially the 'thick, black, oily skirt and apron, which at the end of the day would stand alone when they stepped out of it' and black rubber boots, with their fingers wound round with cloth against the sharp knives, but gutting 50 to 60 herrings a minute all day, every day would still have left them stinking of fish and covered with slime, blood and fish scales. By all accounts, they were tough, independent and in general loud and cheerful.

Local histories of fishing ports like Lowestoft often include chapters on the work of women; and see books like *Yorkshire Fisherfolk*, Peter Frank (Phillimore, 2002). For the East Coast fisher lasses the place to start is with the website www.geocities.com/transport_and_society/routine.html, which has pages on the women's work, as well as a bibliography and many links to other sites, including a very early short film of the girls gutting fish. *Walking Through Scotland's History*, Ian Mitchell (National Museums of Scotland, 2001) has a chapter on the women's annual migration (which is also online at the website above). See also 'Herring women', Karen Foy, *Ancestors* magazine, April 2007.

■ FLAX WORKER

Linen was manufactured from the stalk fibres of the flax plant. Flax mills in the North and Scotland employed female workers in the preparation processes, including 'retting', i.e. rotting or steeping in water to break down the fibres and produce the typically silky flax, which was then sorted and baled for the linen manufacturers. Attempts were made to grow flax commercially in England in the 1930s and 1940s to lessen our dependence on imports and by 1944 over 60,000 acres were under cultivation and flax mills in operation in Norfolk, Suffolk and elsewhere, largely employing women. See also **linen spinner and weaver; weaver.**

■ FLORIST

A woman selling flowers from a shop, rather than the **flower girls** working on the streets, and relatively rarely found until the 20th century. A girl wanting to work in floristry would take up an apprenticeship in a shop or nursery.

■ FLOWER GIRL

Henry Mayhew in the 1860s divided flower girls into two classes. There were the young women who, as prostitutes, used flowers as a way to approach and proposition a man, and the genuine article who made their living selling flowers on the streets. An article by P.F. William Ryan in *Living London* in 1902 sub-divided them even further. Some concentrated on button-holes and targeted businessmen, perhaps at the Royal Exchange or by waiting outside the main railway stations; some made up small bouquets or sold loose flowers, mainly aimed at women purchasers. A few made public houses their selling ground, or toured residential streets. The working class neighbourhoods of the East End were as well covered by the flower girls as the more prosperous areas, and Sunday was usually a working day too – selling outside hospitals being popular.

■ FLOWERER

An embroiderer of muslin. See **tambourer.**

*Less a flower girl than a flower lady, at her pitch in
Piccadilly Circus in the 1940s.*

■ FUR PULLER

Pulling the fur off rabbit skins – getting the loose down off with a blunt knife so that the fur could be used to line cloaks and jackets, the down in stuffing beds and pillows – provided a living for some women in the 19th and early 20th centuries, both in town and country. It was a particularly busy time during the Crimean War when the fur was in demand for soldiers' coat linings.

'The fur puller sits in a small barn, or out-house, on a low stool. She has a trough in front of her, into which she drops the down as she pulls it off the rabbit-skins with her knife. . . . The down gets into her nose and mouth. Her hair and clothes are white with it, She generally suffers from what she calls "breathlessness", for her lungs are filled with the fine down, and she is always more or less choked.' (*Toilers in London, or Inquiries concerning Female Labour in the Metropolis*, 1889; www.victorianlondon. org.) The women also cut out the bones from the rabbit tails, which were used for manure, and prepared old pieces of rabbit skin for use as cheap blankets and fur hats. In the late 1920s a Mrs Eagle of Brandon in Suffolk was getting rabbits delivered to her home and would sit all day skinning them for local furriers' factories.

■ FUSTIAN CUTTER

Fustian was a coarse, thick cotton cloth from which corduroy, velveteen and other varieties of finished cloth were prepared. The cloth (in rolls sometimes 150 yards long) was laid out flat on special tables called frames and held steady at each end by rollers, for women fustian cutters using a special sharp knife to walk the length skimming the top and cutting through the weft just enough to form a pile on one surface. The cutters would walk miles, up one side of the frame and back down the other, their hands having to be steady enough to cut evenly even at the end of a long day, otherwise they would be penalised in their pay.

Right to the end of the 19th century velvet dealers set up special mills to cut fustian, or the job was carried out in fustian shops, or in attic spaces over cottages – anywhere where there was enough space to set up the extremely long tables. By the 1940s machines had taken over in the industry and all the 'walking shops' had closed by the 1950s. The work was carried out in many places around the country – one major centre of the trade was around Warrington, Lymm and the surrounding villages in Cheshire. A woman apprenticed for two years to a shop in Lymm in the 1910s recalled being paid about 35s for a 77 hour week. Mow Cop in Staffordshire had three mills – see the website http://mowcop.info/htm/fustian.htm for a useful background to the trade.

■ GAMEKEEPER

A female gamekeeper was a rarity but not unknown. On Thomas Coke's Holkham estate in Norfolk in the first half of the 19th century one of the gamekeepers was 'black-eyed Polly Fishburn', who eventually went to Yorkshire to work on the estate of Coke's son-in-law. Adeline Hartcup in *Below Stairs in the Great Country Houses* (Sidgwick and Jackson, 1980) tells her story and adds that in later life Polly 'grew strange side-whiskers to match her butch style of dress'.

The First World War, as with other 'male' jobs, found women willing and able to take on gamekeeping, and the *Sunday Chronicle* in May 1916 reported: 'Miss Hilary Dent, engaged as a gamekeeper by Lord Montagu of Beaulieu, is the pioneer in this particular form of feminine activity. As soon as the idea was suggested to Lord Montagu he was sufficiently broadminded to recognise its possibility, and Miss Dent was forthwith engaged, the only reservation being that she was not allowed to go on night duty unaccompanied.' (Noted in Clifford Morsley's *News from the English Countryside 1851–1950*, Harrap, 1983.)

Her duties would have included not only the care of Lord Montagu's game on the estate and the control of vermin but also involvement in and organisation of shooting parties, and the protection of game from poachers, who often came armed, hence the embargo on solo night-time patrols.

■ GANGWORKER, GANGMASTER

In areas where there was not sufficient farm labour locally available, or where there was a strong seasonal demand, e.g. for weeding, hoeing etc, the gang system was sometimes used by farmers, earliest reports dating from the 1820s. Groups of men, women and children were hired by the day to work in the fields, often coming from other villages or outside the neighbourhood, usually through a gangmaster who handled all the negotiations with the farmers and paid the workers.

The system was subject to a great deal of criticism, not only because the workers were poorly paid but also because the women working in mixed-sex gangs were thought to be at risk of moral corruption. Evidence was examined by a Royal Commission in 1862 and in 1867 the Agricultural Gangs Act was passed, ensuring the compulsory six-month licensing of gangmasters by local magistrates, and that women could not be employed in the same gang as men 'unless a female licensed to act as Gangmaster is also present with that Gang'. Gang labour continues to be used to the present day (usually today with migrant workers).

■ GARDENER

Gardening has always had an appeal for women but their involvement was usually on an amateur basis until the later 19th century, when women gardeners can be found in census records. Outside the great houses, the mecca of professional gardening must be the Botanical Gardens at Kew and the first women gardeners to be taken on there were Annie Gulvin and Alice Hutchins, who had studied at Swanley Horticultural College, in 1896: the staff registers had no suitable columns for women and they had to be recorded as 'boys'. Annie had to leave in 1900 when she married and Alice was gone by 1902, and despite good, and slightly surprised, reports on their work, no more women crossed the threshold until during the First World War. The first women students were not taken onto the three-year postgraduate course until the 1950s.

Earlier than this, Fanny Rollo Wilkinson can lay claim to being the first professional female landscape gardener, amongst her designs being Myatt's Fields Park in Brixton and the gardens at the New Hospital for Women in Euston Road in the 1880s, although her case is exceptional in that she was within the talented and influential circle that included the Garretts and later the Pankhursts.

Most 19th century male gardeners served long apprenticeships on one of the landed estates or at Kew, but the establishment of horticultural colleges meant that women could take up the profession without necessarily having to break untrained into the rigid hierarchy under the traditional head gardener. Apart from local authority horticultural colleges, a college for lady gardeners was established at Glynde in 1901 by Frances Wolseley (1872–1936), under the patronage of Gertrude Jekyll and Mrs C.W. Earle, which gave women the opportunity to train as professional gardeners and horticulturalists. In 1896 a magazine mentioned that 'many noblemen and gentlemen now employ female gardeners. The late Duchess of Montrose used to employ a lady, at a large salary, to advise about and superintend her orchid collection, and both the Duchess of Devonshire and the Duchess of Newcastle have lady gardeners in their employ.'

The Museum of Garden History, Lambeth Palace Road, London SE1 7LB (www.museumgardenhistory.org) is a great place to start – not long ago they had an exhibition on professional women gardeners. The archives of the Royal Botanical Gardens are at Kew and their website (www.kew.org/library/archfaqs.html) has advice for family historians. *The Dictionary of British and Irish Botanists and Horticulturalists*, Ray Desmond (Taylor & Francis and Natural History Museum, 1994) includes plant collectors, flower painters and garden designers.

■ GENERAL SERVANT, GENERAL, MAID-OF-ALL-WORK

The servant with possibly the hardest job of all, the 'general', was a lone servant employed by households who could not afford or did not have room for more (see also **cook-general**). Although she could be an older woman, Mrs Beeton sympathised especially with young girls: 'She starts in life, probably a girl of thirteen, with some small tradesman's wife as her mistress, just a step above her in the social scale.' She did all the domestic work throughout the house: she cleaned, cooked, served at table, washed, ran messages and undertook any other duties imposed by the mistress. If she was lucky, her lonely life was eased by a kind family; if not, it could be a depressing and exhausting existence.

'Print dresses, with neat white aprons and caps, should be worn for mornings, and large coarse aprons should be used when stoves have to be cleaned or scullery work done. A black dress, pretty muslin apron and cap, should be worn in the afternoon,' was advised in 1911. The general's hours were then likely to include one evening a week off (from 6 pm to 10 pm), alternate Sunday afternoons and evenings, and perhaps an extra afternoon and evening once a month, with a week to a fortnight's holiday a year. Apart from that, all her time was spent in the house. At that time, her wages were anything from £12 to £24 a year.

General servants were not only employed in private houses – the sheer drudgery endured by some women in this job can be gauged from this description of 'Domestic Slavery in the West End' that appeared in *The*

Dinnertime at a boarding house in the early 1900s. The servants in such places were often overworked for very little pay.

Times in 1878, concerning 'a young servant girl, of 17 years, in a fashionable lodging house near Piccadilly':

'The cooking was done by the landlady, assisted by a young girl of 14 who also undertook a certain amount of cleaning below stairs. The remaining work rested entirely upon the shoulders of the servant of 17. Every morning she began by filling seven baths, for each of which she carried two cans of water from the basement to the bedroom floors of a four-storied house. She then supplied every room with coal, and swept and dusted three sitting rooms. Three breakfast tables were next laid, and cleared after use. Every bedroom having been put in order, the work of lunch began, and dinner, of course, followed in the evening. When at last the meals were over, and china and plate had been cleaned and replaced, fresh duties succeeded. There were cabs to be called, and the maid-of-all-work must remain up until all the lodgers had returned home from the theatre or parties. She was never once in bed before 12, seldom before 1, and sometimes as late as half-past 2. She was expected to be at her post by 6 in the morning . . . Her food consisted of scraps from the dishes, and even from the plates, of the lodgers and their maids. She seldom tasted a potato, and never any other vegetable or pudding.'

See also **domestic servant.**

■ GINGER BEER SELLER

Ginger **beer, lemonade** and other fruit sherbets could be bought on the streets in summer in Victorian times, the sellers male in the majority but with a number of women in their number. Some made their own ginger beer (water, ginger, 'lemon-acid', essence of cloves, yeast and sugar) while others bought from the manufacturers. The apex of the profession was to run a ginger beer fountain; in 1861 Henry Mayhew describes one, drawn by two ponies: 'It is made of mahogany and presents somewhat the form of an upright piano on wheels. It has two pumps, and the brass of the pump-handles and the glass receivers is always kept bright and clean, so that the whole glitters handsomely to the light.'

For a full description of the brewing and trade, see Mayhew, *London Labour and the London Poor,* vol 1.

■ GLASSMAKER

Some **2,000 women** were employed in the manufacture of glass in the 1870s. Four types of glass were made in factories at the time: plate glass for mirrors and windows, crown and sheet glass for ordinary windows, flint glass for ornamental work such as lamps etc, and bottle glass. Prior to that time women had worked in the manufacture of black bottle glass, taking the bottles from the kilns, but by the last quarter of the 19th century they were employed usually only on polishing ('smoothing') plate glass, or on 'cutting, roughing, or obscuring' flint glass for lamp globes etc, or in painting or enamelling (see **enameller**) – from 1867 it was against the law for women to be employed in any part of a factory where melting (or 'annealing') glass was carried out. Rates of pay for roughing, cleaning and smoothing were from 6s to 10s a week in the 1870s.

For a background to the techniques involved in glassmaking, see *Glass*

G

and Glassmaking, Roger Dodsworth (Shire Publications, 1998). The Red House Glass Cone (High Street, Wordsley, Stourbridge, West Midlands DY8 4AZ; www.dudley.gov.uk/redhousecone) is one of only four glass cones (something like a bottle kiln in pottery making) in Britain and is now a heritage site; in the same area is the Broadfields House Glass Museum, Compton Drive, Kingswinford DY6 9NS (www.dudley.gov.uk/glassmuseum).

There were of course also several famous glassmaking firms in Scotland, including Edinburgh Crystal, Caithness Glass and Selkirk Glass, all of which have their own websites; www.futuremuseum.co.uk has a great deal about Scottish industries in the south-west.

■ GLOVEMAKER

Glovemaking was an important home industry for women in several areas of the country. In some places it was a part of the leather industry (Worcestershire, Wiltshire and Oxfordshire, for instance), while elsewhere (Hampshire, Dorset, Somerset, for example) the gloves were knitted or of fine fabrics.

Worcester was a significant centre of the leather glove industry and the firm of Dent, Allcroft & Co, for instance, employed men to go around the local villages with stocks of unsewn gloves and to pick up the finished product – at the village of Redmarley D'Abitot an agent called at the Rose and Crown twice a week until in the 20th century machines took over much of the trade in hand-made gloves. The process in the 1880s was described as follows: 'Glove-sewing is mostly done by the aid of a "clam" stand, something like a vice, which is held between the feet and knees. The glove is slipped into the "clam", the cut edges being almost level with the top surface, which is of brass, and is really a series of fine teeth. The needle – a very short one – is passed between these teeth, the worker being thus guided to regular stitches. . . . the women of the villages are mostly kept to the thumbs and fingers, while the backs and "topping" are, for the most part, done by persons in the city itself.'

Woodstock in Oxfordshire had also long been a glovemaking area, including specialist sporting gloves. In the factories, 'the men cut the skins, pressed them, and then cut them into the pattern of the gloves. The pointing on the backs was done and the ends of the stitching tied. Then workers fitted thumbs and fourchettes in place. The gloves were taken in dozens round to the outworkers to stitch and complete in their own homes.' (*Oxfordshire Within Living Memory*, Oxfordshire Federation of WIs, Countryside Books, 1994.)

Knitted gloves were still being made by Dorset women in the 1940s for firms over the county border in Yeovil, with agents collecting from the villages. They used a yarn called 'silkette', which was soft and hardwearing, and were paid one shilling a pair. The women were so proficient that they could walk while they knitted: 'They never seemed to look at what they were doing, and I should think they could even manage it in their sleep!' recalled one knitter's daughter (*Dorset Within Living Memory*, Dorset Federation of WIs, Countryside Books, 1996).

See **leather worker** for background to the leather industry; also **hosiery worker** and **knitter**.

Stitching a glove by hand at the cottage door in the 1940s, using a clamp to hold the piece in position.

■ GOLDSMITH, SILVERSMITH

Women working in gold and silver were by no means uncommon and records at the Goldsmith's Company show that female goldsmiths and silversmiths were treated seriously by their male counterparts. Confusingly, the term 'goldsmith' also covered women working in silver and silver plate. For both men and women it had for centuries described a wide range of activities relating to precious metals, including unofficial banking and pawnbroking. It also encompassed those who were in the retail side of the business if they were members of the Goldsmith's Company, while by the late 1700s being termed a 'silversmith' usually implied someone who actually created the pieces, either as a manufacturer or a worker. In fact, the names of over 300 women appear in the Goldsmith's Company's records from 1685 to 1845 and their occupations include spoonmaker, bucklemaker, watchmaker, (watch) casemaker, hiltmaker, jeweller, cutler, chainmaker, chaser, engraver, and finisher. Many women worked as smallworkers or largeworkers, i.e. outworkers who made small pieces such as thimbles or larger items to order, or who chased, engraved or burnished the finished goods.

Women seem to have in general learned by experience, working initially with other members of their family or their husbands, before being recognised in their own right. Some registered their own maker's mark, and created work valued today for its beauty and variety, but many more women worked in the trade than the recorded marks suggest. In the early 19th century, Rebecca Emes, for instance, ran 'the largest manufacturing business' of the time with her partner Edward Barnard in London and registered her mark; while Mary Godley worked in silver flatting (producing sheet silver from ingots); Ann and Elizabeth French were silvercasters in Birmingham; Elizabeth Packer was a watchmaker in Reading; and Rebecca Jacobs a silversmith in Portsmouth – but no records exist of their registration.

Women Silversmiths 1685–1845, Philippa Glanville and Jennifer Faulds Goldsborough (Thames & Hudson, 1990) is the essential introduction to the subject, with references to sources and a name list of more than 300 women workers. The website of the Goldsmiths' Company is at www. thegoldsmiths.co.uk. See also **burnisher; jewellery worker.**

■ GOVERNESS

Governessing was almost the only profession open to women from an educated middle class (or impoverished upper class) background before the last quarter of the 19th century, and it was often a path taken by those who had no alternative but to make their own living, due to bereavement or bankruptcy in the family. The resident governess is the one most familiar to us from literature – in 1850 two very different governesses had just been presented to the world: Becky Sharp in *Vanity Fair,* and *Jane Eyre.* Until the 1880s there were consistently more women seeking posts than posts for them to fill. Some took the option of emigration, though in practice they often discovered that a background in domestic service was of more use and value in the new colonies.

The governess occupied an often uncomfortable middle ground between servant and employer, providing a paid service yet maintaining a claim to be a lady rather than a menial. Living in, her world was the schoolroom. However, there were several other types of governess.

The visiting or daily governess came to the house to teach the children, but lived at home; 'She is not hired as a caretaker and trainer of youth, nor as an example of manners and morals, and her responsibilities cease with the lesson she gives' (*Girl's Own Paper*, 1883). Nursery governesses taught children (including boys) from four to eight years of age, concentrating on reading and writing, although their poorly paid duties might include generally looking after the children. Preparatory governesses taught girls aged about eight to twelve (left at home when the boys had gone off to preparatory – 'prep' – school), giving them a grounding in essentials such as English grammar, history, geography (or 'the globe'), drawing etc. Holiday governesses would accompany a family away from home; and governesses were also employed in private schools. Finishing governesses took on the education and polishing of young ladies in their mid-teens; this advertisement appeared in 'Situations Wanted' in 1870:

'A FINISHING GOVERNESS (married) has three days disengaged. Converses with her pupils only in pure French, German, or Italian (long residence abroad). Teaches successfully literature, advanced arithmetic, music and drawing. High testimonials. – Alpha, 10 St Mark's-crescent, Notting-hill, W.'

By the end of the 19th century the growing opportunities for more satisfying and independent female employment, combined with the increasing number of schools for girls, smaller families, a greater desire for privacy in the family, and the rise of the professional nursery nurse, meant a sharp decline in the number of resident governesses, though the upper classes continued to rely on them well into the 20th century.

When a governess became ill or old, she had little to fall back on and the Governesses Benevolent Institution was founded in 1843 to offer support for a small number each year; records are at the London Metropolitan Archives. See *The Victorian Governess*, Kathryn Hughes (Hambledon

Press, 1993) and *The Governess: An Anthology*, eds. Trev Broughton and Ruth Symes (Sutton, 1997) for background.

■ GUNMAKING

Women were employed in the 19th century in the gunmaking factories of Staffordshire, Warwickshire and Worcestershire – and particularly at the centre of the industry in Birmingham – in some of the finishing processes: 'making-off', sandpapering and polishing, and barrel smoothing. It was dirty and laborious work.

■ HAIRDRESSER

Although wealthier women relied on a lady's maid to dress their hair, in the outside world hairdressing was a man's profession until the end of the 19th century. In 1883 the *Girl's Own Paper* noted that hairdressing was admirably suited to women, but for 'the almost unaccountable fact that women actually like to submit their heads to the manipulation of men.' Some still do, of course, but at least they have a choice.

However, there were increasing openings for girls to enter the profession, as the *Paper* noted: 'For some years the great Bond-street hairdressers, Messrs Trufitt & Douglas, have been in the habit of taking apprentices, and in their rooms ladies can always be attended by women. A moderately clever girl is ready to give help in the hairdressing salon in six or nine months, and the wages are from 32 shillings to 35 shillings a week. . . . A few girls earn a respectable living as visiting hairdressers, but it must be much less fatiguing and more profitable to work in a shop, and especially if the girl understands the preparation of supplementary hair, and the making of hair chains, brooches and other ornaments, which would employ her leisure time.'

It was dressing long hair into different styles, rather than cutting it, that was usually required. Not until short hair became fashionable in the 1920s did the scissors truly come into play. Girls increasingly chose hairdressing as a career from that time too, with salons opening up in towns and villages all over the country. They were taken on as apprentices for two years, and worked as an 'improver' for another year before being considered qualified. At the same time, technological advances brought electrical appliances into the salon, such as the 'permanent wave' machines and hairdryers, and an array of shampoos, conditioners and colours.

Recalling her apprenticeship to a Folkestone hairdresser in the 1930s, one woman 'learned to make shampoo from soft soap, sewed little muslin bags into which we put dried camomile flowers to use as a rinse for fair hair, learned to shampoo, cut and set hair and also to Marcel wave with tongs. We also singed hair if requested, and a permanent wave was a mammoth task with the customer strung up to a machine and the whole business, to

me, fraught with danger!' (*East Kent Within Living Memory*, East Kent Federation of WIs, Countryside Books, 1993.)

The National Hairdressers Federation was formed in 1942 but its antecedents go back to the 19th century when local hairdressers formed their own associations (www.nhf.biz). The *Hairdressers Journal* began appearing in 1882. See *Good hair days: A history of British hairdressing* by Caroline Cox (Quartet Books, 1999).

■ HANDYWOMAN

An unregistered midwife. See also **nurse, monthly.**

■ HAT MAKER, FELT

Felt was the foundation of the majority of men's hats and although the hat makers were predominantly male, women outworkers were employed to trim and finish hats of all kinds, from the sober bowler through to the exotic fez.

The manufacturing industry was concentrated in Stockport, Denton (Manchester) and London, though hatters can be found in many other places and in the 20th century the Luton hat industry compensated for the decline in straw hat manufacture by expanding into felt hats. The use of felt dated from the 16th century – it was made from a mixture of fur (beaver, hare, rabbit, coypu), goat or camel hair, and wool, which was matted together, cut, shrunk, blocked to shape, dyed, and finally trimmed and finished. The making of the hats was originally done by hatters in their own workshops but by the end of the 19th century factory production had taken over most of the market.

The women who worked on the hats did a variety of tasks, including sewing in linings and adding trimming to the outside. Most worked in their own homes, but in some cases small workshops were set up, as in the village of Poynton, near Stockport. The Female Branch of the Felt Hat Trimmers Association was formed in 1890. In the 1920s and 1930s felt hats gained greatly in popularity with women, particularly in styles such as the cloche and the beret.

See **milliner;** the Stockport Hatworks museum, in particular, has a great deal on felt hat making.

■ HAT MAKER, STRAW

The straw hat making industry was centred on the Bedfordshire towns of Luton and Dunstable, and St Albans in Hertfordshire, which employed hundreds of workers, many of them women, in the factories and as outworkers. It was a prosperous industry through the second half of the 19th century but declined after 1920 with the increased popularity of felt hats.

Straw plait (see **straw plaiter**) was hand-sewn into bonnets and hats until sewing machines became available from the 1870s (at first, just ordinary domestic sewing machines, which still made the process much quicker and easier, but then increasingly sophisticated industrial machines – hand-sewing continued to a certain extent for the finest, most ornate styles of hats). The sewers and pressers worked to a pattern according to current fashions, some at home and others in small factories as makers-up, who then sold on to the larger factories.

The hats were stiffened by being immersed in gelatine, then steamed to soften so that they could be shaped on wooden blocks. The blockmakers were the original hat designers, and it was not till the 1900s that factories began employing women millinery designers. Trimming provided the finishing touches – trimming weavers, makers and manufacturers are found in the same areas as the hat industry. Sometimes braids of horsehair or straw plaited with another material, such as silk, were used as a trimming, but more usually the women used artificial flowers, ribbons and other fabrics.

'Chip bonnet' makers worked with shavings of willow or poplar, plaited like straw, while 'Brazilian' hat makers used strips of palm leaves and the hat was woven entire, working from the crown out, and not sewn.

'Straw hat manufacturers' are also found in many other towns and cities round the country, and these were probably workshops producing for a local market, perhaps even buying in the plain shells from the factories and making up hats as required. See also **milliner**.

For background see, for instance, *Luton: Hat Industry 1750-2000*, Luton Museum Education Service (2003); *Luton and the Hat Industry*, Charles Freeman (Luton Museum, 1964); *Vyse Sons & Co Ltd: 200 Years of Millinery* (1965); or see www.galaxy.bedfordshire.gov.uk/webingres/luton. Examples of the hats made in the factories are on display at Wardown Park Museum, Old Bedford Road, Luton LU2 7HA (telephone: 01582 546722).

■ HEALTH VISITOR

As a municipal employee in the late 1890s and early 1900s, a woman called a health visitor was in some areas one and the same as the lady sanitary inspector, or else she worked for a charitable foundation dedicated to providing nursing care in slum homes (and probably at the same time spreading the Christian message) and was a forerunner of the district nurse (see nurse, district). In 1898 the *Lancet* was of the opinion that 'an intelligent, well-educated and kindly woman' could do the job.

However, the Notification of Births Act 1907 stated that a 'trained health visitor' was to 'call on the mother at home to teach her how to protect her baby's health'. The health visitor was initially very specifically targeted at the working class mother, whose ignorance was blamed for many infant deaths.

'She enters each home with the consent of the occupants, and teaches the housewife the importance of cleanliness and proper ventilation and explains the dangers of dirt and overcrowding. She instructs her in the choice of suitable food and clothing, shows her how to cook, and especially points out the dangers of using impure water, at the same time explaining how best to prevent its contamination and that of food generally. She helps to nurse the sick, and promotes a knowledge of home nursing and all that relates to the care of young children. One of the health visitor's most important duties also is to attend on women during or shortly after childbirth.' (*Everywoman's Encyclopaedia*, 1911.)

The salary varied from place to place, from about £50 to £100 per annum. In Hertfordshire, Miss Burnside, the County Inspector of Midwives, was named also County Health Visitor in 1911 and appointed 70 health visitors, most of whom were midwives or district nurses.

The high rate of infant mortality in poor areas was brought down to an all-time low by the 1920s with the advent of this new profession, and midwifery remained an essential element of health visiting until 1938. After the war, new duties were assigned the visitor, including school health. With the coming of the NHS in 1948, the emphasis was to turn to the family as a whole, long-term illness, and hospital after-care.

In 1896 the Women's Sanitary Inspectors Association was formed by seven female Sanitary Inspectors in London and within ten years had over 60 members around the country. In 1915 the name changed to the Women's Sanitary Inspectors and Health Visitors Association, which in 1918 registered as a trade union, now with over 3,000 members including health visitors, school nurses, TB visitors etc. Then in 1929 it became the Women's Public Health Visitors Association, in 1962 the Health Visitors Association, and is now the Community Practitioners and Health Visitors Association. The archives are held by the Wellcome Institute under 'Public Health' (http://library.wellcome.ac.uk/doc_WTL039941.html); see also Sanitary Inspectors Association of Scotland. Records of employees of town, borough and county councils will be held by county record offices. For background see, for example, *Nursing, Midwifery and Health Visiting since 1900*, Peta Allan & Moya Jolley (Faber & Faber, 1982).

■ HOP PICKER

The harvest, usually in September, was the 'grand jubilee' of hop-growing areas and an important source of extra income for the families of not only the local labourers, but also the tens of thousands of (mostly) women and children who left the cities each year for probably their only breath of fresh air. About 60,000 acres of hops were being harvested in England in 1880, predominantly in Kent, Sussex and Herefordshire. The annual exodus of London's East Enders for the fields of Kent and Sussex has passed into folklore, while for Herefordshire it was the Black Country and the mining villages of Wales that provided the labour. Some regular pickers wrote beforehand to farmers to 'book' their place, others went on the off-chance and took what they could find. All lived in tents or semi-permanent huts erected by the farmers close to the fields.

In the spring local village women were employed in the hopfields to tie in the early main shoots of the bines so that they would grow upwards on the poles. Come harvest, the poles, with the bines still attached, were lifted and taken to the waiting pickers at their bins (large bags suspended from a wooden framework), where the hop flowers were picked off by hand, as free of leaves and stalks as possible. When full the bins were emptied and a tally kept of the amount, as the pickers were paid by the volume, not weight. While the hops disappeared off to the oast houses to be dried, the pickers tackled more poles. At the end of the day the cry of 'Pull no more bines' went up, and work ceased. The wage paid to the pickers varied from year to year, depending on the quality and extent of the crop, but it was enough to keep whole families, often under the supervision of the mother while the husband remained at his own work, coming back year after year.

There are many books and articles recalling the hop pickers: see for instance *Old Days in the Kent Hop Gardens* (West Kent Federation of WIs, 1962); *Pull No More Bines*, Gilda O'Neill (The Women's Press, 1990); *Herefordshire Within Living Memory*, Herefordshire Federation of WIs (Countryside Books, 1993); *Hops and Hop Picking*, Richard Filmer (Shire Publications). The Museum of Kent Life holds a Hop Picking Festival each year (Lock Lane, Sandling, Maidstone, Kent ME14 3AU; www.museum-kentlife.co.uk or www.hoppingdowninkent.org.uk).

■ HOSIERY WORKER

The hosiery industry had its origins with the framework knitters of the Midlands, based mainly in Leicestershire, Nottinghamshire and Derbyshire. Although it was one of the most extensive and prosperous of domestic industries in the 18th century, by the mid-19th century it was in a long, terminal decline; for background to the industry see *Framework Knitting*, Marilyn Palmer (Shire Publications). One of the causes of that decline was competition from factory production, and by the late 19th century the hosiery industry had reinvented itself very successfully, with production now heavily dependent on female labour in factories and as outworkers.

One of the centres of manufacture of socks and stockings was Hinckley in Leicestershire, where the first factory was in production in 1855 (www.hinckley-online.co.uk/hosiery.shtml). Women doing outwork for the manufacturers were provided with knitting machines until the 1920s, although by the 1950s their work was mainly mending. In the factories the knitters were responsible for perhaps a dozen machines – in contrast to many other industries the finishing and packing was done by men. 'There was much variety in stockings, from pure silk down through rayon, wool and lisle; fully fashioned or the cheaper circular knits, which were sold in Woolworths in the early 1930s for sixpence a stocking,' recalled one knitter (*Leicestershire and Rutland Within Living Memory*, Leicestershire and Rutland Federation of WIs, Countryside Books, 1994).

Leicester had many hosiery factories in the 20th century, including well-known underwear manufacturers such as Chilprufe and Corah, and for local girls being 'in the hosiery' meant working as machinists, pressers, cutters and graders on anything from heavy-duty pure wool men's combinations, to 'passion killer' directoire knickers or delicate silk stockings.

The East Midlands Oral History Archive (www.le.ac.uk/emoha/community/resources/hosiery/index2.html) has a great deal on 'Leicestershire Hosiery' in the 20th century, with details and photographs of all the processes and products. *Knitting Together: Memories of Leicestershire's Hosiery Industry*, Geoffrey Bowles and Siobhan Kirrane (Leicester Museum Service, 1990) follows the same lines. There is information on hosiery manufacture in Dumfriesshire and Galloway, which had a thriving industry until the late 20th century, at www.futuremuseum.co.uk. *The British Hosiery and Knitwear Industry: Its History and Organisation*, F.A. Wells (David and Charles, 1972) looks at the industry as a whole.

■ HOSPITAL STAFF

Hospitals were like small communities, employing not only medical and nursing staff but also housekeeping and laundry staff, therapists, office staff, catering staff and so on. To find the records that survive for a particular hospital, look at the Hospital Record Database, created by the Wellcome Library and online at The National Archives (www.nationalarchives.gov.uk/hospitalrecords/). Many of the older hospitals have had histories published, and a local county library or archive will be able to identify relevant books.

■ HOTEL KEEPER

The hotel, as opposed to the inn, was a Victorian creation that grew out of the new opportunities for road and rail travel and the expansion of seaside and spa resorts. Female hotel keepers are common. Some even became famous, like the larger than life cockney Rosa Lewis (1867–1952), who provided 'not an 'otel but an 'ome from 'ome for my friends' (including Edward VII) at the Cavendish in Jermyn Street, London.

They would either be a manageress, appointed by a board or an individual owner, or, like Rosa, owned the hotel themselves. Advertisements in tourist guidebooks or directories usually specify either 'manageress' or 'proprietress' – Miss Boulding, for instance, was manageress of the Zetland Hotel at Saltburn-by-the-Sea in Yorkshire in 1874, a 150-bed 'Hotel of the North' with 'splendid Coffee-Rooms, large Drawing and Music Rooms, Bed-Rooms, Rooms *en suite*, Smoke and Billiard Rooms, etc.' Some ran small family hotels, perhaps little bigger or better than a boarding house (see **boarding house keeper**), while others like Miss Boulding were in charge of large and prosperous concerns, and it was a job that required a good commercial sense as well as an aptitude for housekeeping.

The Golden Age of British Hotels, Derek Taylor and David Bush (Northwood Publications, 1974) is a good general introduction to the period. Hotels still in business often have a reference to their history on their website.

■ HOUSEKEEPER

The **most senior** of the female staff employed in the servants' hall, second in command only to the mistress of the big house. It was a prestigious and responsible position, that called for quite varied talents – which some were able to fulfil and in the process become prized members of staff. Elizabeth Payne, for instance, was housekeeper for the Dukes of Bedford at Woburn Abbey for almost 30 years from 1865. As a matter of courtesy, housekeepers were awarded the title of 'Mrs' whether married or not.

The housekeeper had the power to hire and fire the maidservants (though not usually the **cook**, the **lady's maid** or the **nanny**). The store rooms, stillroom, china and linen closets were under her control and she doled out supplies and kept accounts. She had her own private rooms below stairs, where she took meals with the other senior staff, and she did not wear a uniform as such, though would usually be dressed in black. The household keys would jingle at her waist, a badge of office in themselves.

Apart from her management and financial responsibilities, the housekeeper apparently had to know how to make wines, preserves and pickles, pot pourri and scented flower waters, candied fruit and sweets, which she produced in the stillroom, perhaps with the assistance of a **stillroom maid**. She, not the cook, baked the finest pastries and cakes, and afternoon tea was her special forte; she also made the elaborate desserts for upstairs dinner. Her skills extended to simple first aid and, again in the stillroom, to the mixing of herbal potions, medicines and cosmetics. When the family travelled, the housekeeper was often left behind in charge of the house – in the great houses she might earn a tip or two by showing visitors round the public rooms like a modern tourist guide. See also **domestic servant**.

Women may also be recorded as 'housekeepers' who never set foot in a servants' hall. It is not unusual to find entries in the census returns for a housekeeper in quite humble homes; usually this is because there is no wife or matriarch and she is looking after the cottage and the family, perhaps for a wage but more probably for her food and a roof over her head.

Housekeepers may also be found in large institutions such as hospitals, possibly having trained in domestic economy, or in responsible positions in such places as judges' lodgings, schools and colleges.

■ HOUSEMAID

In the very big houses or stately homes, such as Belvoir in Leicestershire, there would have been a head or upper housemaid to superintend the work of the under housemaids, having usually been one of those under housemaids herself. She herself would have done the lighter housework, such as dusting, especially of valuable items, and seeing to the best bedrooms. The housemaids might have had their own sitting room, and one or two of them may have travelled with the family. In the great majority of households, however, a single housemaid was employed, perhaps having to overlap her duties with those of **parlourmaid**, **waiting maid**, **cook** etc, where these were also employed, or to help with the children.

'It is most important that a housemaid should be methodical and punctual, be an early riser, clean and neat in work and person' – a good housemaid was essential for a comfortable, well-kept home for she, after all, did the housework, aired the beds and the rooms, and catered to her

A family snapshot of two young women in service in Lancashire in the early 1900s, Sarah Jane Whittaker, housemaid, and Violet Matilda Derry, the cook. (Jean Owen)

family's little whims. In rooms crowded with Victorian clutter, with no modern appliances such as vacuum cleaners before the 1920s, she worked from about 6 am to late in the evening.

Her duties would have varied from place to place, but followed a similar pattern – attending to fires, cleaning grates and stoves, dusting, cleaning carpets, floors and furniture, brushing the stairs, carrying water upstairs, making beds and cleaning bedrooms, emptying basins and chamberpots, laying and clearing tables, getting beds ready for the night. If there was no 'boy' to do it, she would clean the boots and shoes, and carry coals. In quiet moments, she would help with mending and renovating the household linen, and skill with a needle was highly prized. Whatever she was doing, she had to be ready at all times to answer the bell rung by a member of the family. In 1911 wages were quoted as head housemaid £23 to £30 a year, under-housemaid £16 to £20; single housemaid £18 to £22. See also **domestic servant**.

■ HOUSE-PARLOURMAID

A combination of **housemaid** and **parlourmaid**, with all the duties to carry out. See also **daily maid**.

◼ ILLUSTRATOR

During the last quarter of the 19th century there was a huge increase in the number of national and local newspapers and magazines, many of them aimed at women readers. Photography could not yet provide all the illustrations required and drawings filled the gap, giving artists employment as illustrators – other openings could be found in, for example, book illustration, advertising or greetings cards, and artists may have worked in all and more of these fields.

On newspapers and in some journals they filled the role of a present-day press photographer, accompanying the reporter to an interview or investigation. Some female illustrators disguised their sex by using only initials when signing drawings, but others can be found listed in acknowledgement pages, e.g. Dorothy Hardy in the *Strand Magazine* in 1896. Unfortunately it will prove to be difficult to trace many of the women who worked on a freelance basis. Some help may be provided by the *Dictionary of 19th Century British Book Illustrators and Caricaturists*, Simon Houfe (Antiques Collectors Club, 2nd edn, 1999) and *Dictionary of 20th Century British Book Illustrators*, Alan Horne (Antiques Collectors Club, 1994). There is also an online list of 19th and 20th century Scottish illustrators at www.nls.uk/collections/rarebooks/collections/illustrators.html. See also **artist**.

◼ INTERIOR DESIGNER/DECORATOR

In the last quarter of the 19th century books began to be written appealing directly to women wanting to decorate or design their own homes, as well as articles in popular magazines aimed at women living on their own, perhaps in one or two rooms. The element of gaining control over their environment was important, chiming with the increasing independence of working women. The first professional interior designers in England are believed to have been Agnes Garrett (sister of Dr Elizabeth Garrett) and her cousin Rhoda Garrett. They wrote a book, *Suggestions for House Decoration*, in 1876 and were employed by the new women's colleges at both Oxford and Cambridge universities and on private commissions. They even designed a bedroom layout for the Paris Exhibition of 1878. For their story see *Architecture in*

Mrs Staples was a prolific illustrator of stories and articles in Victorian and Edwardian magazines, under the name M. Ellen Edwards, or simply M.E.E..

the Family Way: Doctors, Houses and Women 1870–1900, Annmarie Adams (McGill-Queen's Press, 2001).

■ IRONER

see **laundress**.

■ IRONWORKER (MINES, IRON FOUNDRIES)

By the last quarter of the 19th century female labour in ironworks and foundries was to be found mainly in South Wales, probably because alternative employment was scarce in the remote valleys. The women unloaded the ore coming out of the mines, broke large pieces down, and filled boxes for the furnaces – heavy work in a dusty environment. In the ironworks and foundries women swept the floors and made up piles or stacks of puddled iron ready for reheating in the mill furnace. 'Tip girls' tipped molten slag and rubbish, cleaned out the carriages and returned them to the furnaces – they wore a scarf or handkerchief across their mouths to keep out the dust and a thick apron to protect their bodies from the heat.

Apart from Wales, reference to women in iron foundries is rare at this time – in south Staffordshire some were employed in wheeling cinders from the furnaces, and in some foundries women were occasionally employed as core makers. These are pieces of well-baked sand used for filling up the holes or hollows in castings, while there are occasional finds of women recorded as 'iron foundry workers' in Cornwall and the West. See also **mine worker**.

The ironworking processes can be seen at the Black Country Museum, Tipton Road, Dudley DY1 4SQ (www.bclm.co.uk).

■ JAPANNER

Japanning was an important industry around Wolverhampton, Bilston and Birmingham in the 19th century and employed many women, though it had died out by the 1920s. Japanned ware was very fashionable in the 18th and 19th centuries, involving a process whereby a dark varnish was applied to tin or metalware to make it black and shiny. It was carried out in workshops, as well as in a handful of large factories. There was also a thriving industry at Pontypool in Montgomeryshire from the early 18th century; the history is at www.pontypoolmuseum.org.uk. Background to the Wolverhampton factories is given at www.wolverhamptonhistory.org.uk. The site www.japanware.org has a great deal of information on the workmanship and the products.

■ JEWELLERY WORKER

Major centres for gold and silver work and for jewellery making in the later 19th and early 20th centuries were Clerkenwell in London and Birmingham's Jewellery Quarter, where there were not only larger manufacturers making use of modern machinery, but also small workshops employing any number from 5 to 50 people, many of them women working as stampers and polishers.

Birmingham was known in particular for mass-producing cheaper jewellery as well as quality pieces. In the late 19th century gold ornaments, such as earrings or lockets, were created from blanks or discs that were stamped in a screw-press and cut to shape: it was a task that needed a good eye and good reflexes as it was easy to leave a finger under the heavy press – it was said to be the 'badge of a good [?] stamper to be minus the usual allowance of fingers'. There is a Museum of the Jewellery Quarter at 75 Vyse Street, Hockley, Birmingham B18 6HA (telephone: 0121 554 3598; www.birminghamuk.com/go/index). See also **chainmaker (gold or silver); electroplate worker; goldsmith.**

■ JOURNALIST

By 1896 there were over 200 members of the Society of Women Journalists, and there was keen competition for every advertised post. They were barred from the Gallery of the House of Commons but every other type of reporting was open to those with the ability. Some women occupied prominent positions by that time – Mrs Rachel Beer (1858–1927) was already editor of the *Observer* when she bought the *Sunday Times* in 1893 and became not only the first female editor of a national newspaper, but the only editor ever to have worked on two national newspapers at the same time, which she continued to do until 1904. Flora Shaw (later Lady Flora Lugard, 1852–1929) began her journalistic career in 1886, writing for the *Pall Mall Gazette* and the *Manchester Guardian*, but from 1892 to 1900 was the Colonial Editor on *The Times* and the highest paid woman journalist of her day.

There were many more lowly women who worked as freelances. Susan Carpenter, for instance, worked for the Press Association, and her work was syndicated around the country – in the 1891 census she is rather coyly referred to as a 'literary worker'.

For most female writers, however, the opportunities came in 'women's columns', writing about fashion, food, gossip, beauty, relationships etc for national or local newspapers, or magazines, and many articles are anonymous or the writer's identity is hidden behind a pseudonym. It will be difficult to trace them without some indication of who they wrote for. If it can be identified, most newspapers have had histories published and all have their own websites. There is a biographical dictionary of British and Irish journalists of all kinds at www.scoop-database.com (fee for use).

■ KINDERGARTEN TEACHER

Today, we might use the word 'kindergarten' for any school or class for very young children, but in the late 19th century it had a very specific meaning and a woman recorded as a kindergarten teacher was not just a schoolmistress. Then, it related to a school or group organised on the principles of Friedrich Froebel, who had opened the first kindergarten ('garden of children') in Germany in 1837. A woman trained in Froebelian theory would, put simply, allow the children to learn through their play, letting them take in ideas and express them through drawing, modelling etc, as well as develop their natural love of Nature. The practical teaching continued to evolve from Froebel's initially rather vague philosophy and influenced the teaching of all young children by the mid-20th century.

The Froebel Educational Institute was founded in 1892, and is now part of Roehampton University; see www.froebel.org.uk.

■ KITCHENMAID

In effect, the assistant cook. She cleaned the kitchen and the work surfaces, tended the fires, heated water and washed up dishes. How much cleaning and washing she did would depend on whether a **scullery maid** was also employed – she might also have to clean the front door, the hall and passages, the area steps, the larder and the butler's pantry.

She was involved in the preparation of all meals throughout the day, from breakfast to supper, for everyone in the household, including the servants. She assisted the **cook** by making sauces, preparing vegetables, gathering ingredients together ready for a meal, baking bread, tending the plain roasting or boiling of joints of meat, and preparing meat and fish. If she wanted to better herself, the next stage up would be to apply for a cook's position herself. See also **domestic servant**.

Kitchenmaids would be employed not only in private households but also in institutions, schools, colleges etc. Sometimes one took advantage of the ready availability of quite expensive foodstuffs to make a little more income on the side, as did Jane Jenkins in 1876, who stole two legs and loins of mutton, 3 lb of butter, 2 lb of sugar, a bottle of beef tea and 'other articles' from the kitchens of St Bartholomew's Hospital.

■ KNITTER

Knitting was a female cottage industry in many places around Britain and included the making of gloves, socks, stockings, hats, and jumpers or pullovers. It usually supplemented the family income, the women being outworkers for a particular industry, or for a tourist trade. The Victoria and Albert Museum has background on the various types of regional knitting – Shetlands, Fair Isle, Yorkshire Dales, Aran Islands, Channel Islands – at www.vam.ac.uk/collections/fashion/features/knitting/regional/index.htm. See also **glovemaker; hosiery worker.**

■ LACEMAKER

Lacemaking as a home industry had a long and prosperous history in England, from the time lace became a fashionable accessory in the 16th century. In the East Midlands (Bedfordshire, Buckinghamshire, Northamptonshire and Huntingdonshire) and in Devon (especially around Honiton, but stretching over a wide area and into Wiltshire and Dorset), lacemaking was a major employer of women and children, with skilled craftswomen able to earn the equivalent of an agricultural labourer's wage.

The British pillow lace industry was at its height in the early years of the 19th century, when war with Napoleon prevented lace being imported from across the Channel (though it provided a good opportunity for the smugglers along the south coast). Pillow lace – also called thread, bone or bobbin lace – was created upon a straw-filled pillow-like base, the design pricked out with pins from a printed pattern. Thread, latterly cotton, was twisted and interlaced around the pins, the ends weighted in place by bobbins made of bone or wood. If possible, women worked at their cottage doors or outside in good weather to get the light, singly or in groups. Children learnt the art in lace schools, where working at their pillows was favoured over education.

Lace dealers supplied the women with thread and patterns, and bought the finished pieces. Some of them were women, such as Abigail Chick (b.1782) who collected lace from Honiton and sold it in the fashionable resorts of Bath, Cheltenham and Brighton.

Honiton lace was especially sought after, being popular with the Royal Family (lace for Queen Victoria's wedding dress in 1840, including the veil that was buried with her 60 years later, was ordered from Miss Jane Bidney of Beer, and a succession of Devon women were thereafter appointed Royal lacemaker). However, the long and slow decline in the hand-made industry had already begun and although it never disappeared entirely it was only a shadow of its former self by the end of the 19th century (the 1851 census recorded over 26,000 lacemakers in Bedfordshire, Buckinghamshire and Northamptonshire; by 1891 the number was down to just over 3,000). Attempts were made at reviving it, for instance by the formation of the Midlands Lace Association in 1891 and by Devon County Council in 1902, but it would never make a full commercial recovery.

There are illustrated examples of all the different types of lace, plus patterns, on the website of Jo Edkins' Lace School (http://gwydir.demon. co.uk/jo/lace/index.htm), or see *Pillow Lace and Bobbins*, Jeffrey Hopewell (Shire Publications). Books also abound, such as *History of the Honiton Lace Industry*, H.J. Yallop (University of Exeter, 1992). There is a 'Lace reading list' at www.vam.ac.uk/collections/textiles/resources/reading/lace/index.html.

Museums are also excellent places to learn more about the craft, such as the Allhallows Lace and Pottery Museum, High Street, Honiton, Devon EX14 1PG (www.honitonmuseum.co.uk), the Cowper and Newton Museum, Olney, Buckinghamshire (www.mkheritage.co.uk/cnm/lace/index/html), or the Luton Museum, Wardown Park, Luton LU2 7HA (www.luton.gov.uk).

▪ LACEMAKER (BOBBIN-NET)

It was not only the trade in European lace, revived after the end of the Napoleonic Wars, that took pillow lace into a decline but also competition from a machine-made lace substitute – bobbin-net. This was not actually traditional lace but bore a strong resemblance to it and it became the basis for the ubiquitous Victorian lace curtain.

It had been clear since the late 18th century that there was no reason why the patterns of lace could not be replicated by machine. Originating with a lace-loom invented by John Heathcote (who moved to Tiverton), the new industry became rooted predominantly in and around Nottingham and soon employed thousands of workers, many of them women. Smaller factories were also in operation in Devon, Somerset, Norfolk, Glasgow, London and parts of Ireland.

In 1884 Bernard H. Becker visited the works of Mr Birkin at Kimberley (Nottingham) for the *English Illustrated Magazine* and described the machine lace industry, which, he said, 'bears about the same relation to simple weaving that a watch does to a wheelbarrow'. Mr Birkin was manufacturing lace curtains and the process had by now become extremely sophisticated, producing patterns of great intricacy.

The crowded room at Birkin's Kimberley factory in 1884 where the lengths of manufactured lace were examined and finished by hand.

Cotton yarn came to the factory from Lancashire and in the lower rooms of the building was wound from the spools onto bobbins – sometimes as many as 3,000 of them on one machine-work done by women. The loom was set up by using a Jacquard card perforated to guide the thread in the desired pattern – 'an infinite, and, to the unpractised eye, almost maddening variety of movements is brought about, and the most intricate patterns produced by a machine which appears to possess intelligence of its own.' The lace that was produced, however, was rarely without faults, so it had to be examined and repaired by hand; it might also need trimming, and to be cut to lengths. The material was then finished by gassing (singeing it in a gas flame to remove fluff), bleaching and starching. As Mr Becker described the advances made in the imitation of quality lace by machinery, he could only conclude that 'everything that can be done with bobbin and cushion, crotchet-needle, or tambour-hook were in a fair way of being composed by machinery. Only the very finest hand-work remains unapproachable.'

The Nottingham Museum of Costumes and Textiles is at 51 Castle Gate, Nottingham NG1 6AF (telephone: 0115 915 3500); it has published books such as *Nottingham Lace*, Zillah Halls (1973). There is some background to the industry at www.bbc.co.uk/legacies/work/england/nottingham/article_ 1.shtml.

There was also a thriving lace industry in Ayrshire, where Alexander Morton promoted machine lace to boost the failing hand weaving business. See www.futuremuseum.co.uk, under its Textiles collection, for a full history and photographs.

■ LADY'S MAID

In the servant hierarchy in wealthier homes, the lady's maid ranked second, just below the housekeeper. Entitled to be known as 'Miss So-and-so' rather than plain 'So-and-so', the lady's maid was not always a popular member of the staff below stairs, as some had a tendency to identify themselves too closely with their 'betters' and to put on airs. It involved the maid in a very intimate relationship with her mistress and honesty and reliability were highly prized, as were a good education and a neat, attractive appearance. The route to employment usually lay through experience, gained as a personal maid to younger members of a family (as a 'young lady's maid' or waiting maid), and most lady's maids rose to the position in their late twenties or thirties.

The duties of the lady's maid altered little over the 19th and 20th centuries. 'It will be her business to dress, re-dress and undress her lady', summed up her *raison d'être* but described only part of her responsibilities. Every morning she laid out her lady's clothes and made sure her rooms were warm and comfortable, which might mean supervising the housemaid or doing the dusting and light cleaning herself, as well as lighting the fire and getting up hot water for washing (pre-indoor plumbing) or running a bath. When summoned to her lady by bell, she prepared her for the morning – doing her hair and helping her to dress. She would expect to re-dress her lady after lunch, in preparation for the afternoon activity of visiting or being visited, and again before dinner – or going out – in the evening, and then to wait up for her to return and help her to prepare for bed.

In between these flurries of activity, she had plenty to occupy her. Clothing and accessories had to be cared for, no easy task and requiring great expertise to do properly; cleaning, stain removal and repair all had to be attended to, as well as minor adjustments to dresses and major overhauls to react to fashion. 'In summer, particularly, an iron will be constantly required,' wrote Mrs Beeton in 1860, and no wonder – those light muslin dresses were extremely pretty but needed 'smoothing out' every time they were worn. Delicate fabrics, furs, feathers, jewels and all the other ingredients of my lady's wardrobe were the responsibility of her maid. As Mrs Beeton wrote, she had to be a 'tolerably expert milliner and dressmaker, a good hairdresser, and possess some chemical knowledge of the cosmetics with which the toilet-table is supplied, in order to use them with safety and effect' (particularly important when cosmetics had to be made up by hand).

Hairdressing was a very important part of the maid's duties, and a deft hand and understanding of the often extremely intricate hair fashions were essential for a girl with ambitions. The maid would normally travel with her lady, and packing the quantities of clothes and personal accessories necessary for the journey or visit was her responsibility. She could also be called upon to read aloud, or to act as a companion and sit with her mistress, particularly by older women or invalids. See also **domestic servant.**

■ LANDLADY

Might refer to a **boarding house keeper**, taking in paying guests, or to a woman running a public house or inn, perhaps with her husband: see **publican.**

■ LAUNDRESS, LAUNDERER

Wealthy families might employ a **laundrymaid**, or some might have a **washerwoman** come in on a regular but casual basis to work on the premises, but from the later 19th century the rising middle and professional classes more often sent their washing outside the home to a professional laundress (the home washing machine was available from the 1930s, but would not be in general use until the 1950s).

The time-honoured system was for washing to be delivered to the laundress at the start of the week for return by Saturday. This meant pressure to wash, dry and iron to schedule, no matter what the weather was like, and many laundresses worked a minimum of a 12-hour day and quite often at least 15 hours. They had a reputation in the 19th century for being tough, strong and hard-drinking, and many commercial laundries provided beer for the women as part of the contract of employment.

The first task was to fetch enough water to fill the huge coppers in which the washing would be boiled and to rinse it all afterwards. Clothes and linen had to be sorted and delicate items left to one side to be washed carefully by hand; otherwise the load was soaked, boiled, rinsed, wrung and scrubbed until clean. There were no detergents until the early 20th century, and soap, such as Lever's Sunlight Soap, was used as the cleaning agent. To get as much water out as possible, items would be put through the rollers of the mangle – in some cases women specialised in this stage of the procedure and a manglewoman might charge for the use of her mangle or simply do the work herself. Mangling also pressed out some of the creases, making ironing a little easier. New 'wringers', available from ironmongers from the 1890s, took away much of the manglewoman's work.

Drying was always a problem. In towns and cities, where smoke from coal fires and factory chimneys and general air-borne dirt would have soiled clean linen as soon as it went into the open air, much of the washing had to be hung inside to dry, above the heads of the laundresses. In the country, or in suburban areas where the air was cleaner, drying grounds were

National Telephone **272.**

THE . . .

Gloucester "Model" Laundry, Ltd.

❧ ❧

SISSON ROAD, GLOUCESTER

PERFECTION IN WASHING.

Flannels washed in Distilled Water, imparting a soft feeling and preventing all shrinking.

Gentlemen's Shirts, Collars and Cuffs, Ladies' Fine Linen and Dresses laundered in perfect style.

Curtains Cleaned equal to new.
Household work a speciality.

Our vans collect in all parts of the Town and District on receipt of a message or a post-card

An advertisement for the Gloucester 'Model' Laundry in 1912.

used, perhaps shared by several laundresses. This was still common into the 20th century: in 1907 in the first Garden City, at Letchworth, Miss Miller's Home Laundry advertised 'Hand work only. No chemicals. Large open-air drying ground. Shirts and collars a speciality.' In a wet season, getting the washing dry was a major headache for any laundry business. Once dry, it had to be ironed, using solid, cast-iron flat irons; delicate things such as lace or frills would still have to be done separately, using special goffering irons.

A hand laundry was, as its name suggests, a laundry where the work was done by hand and the term came to differentiate smaller concerns from the power or steam laundries that evolved from the turn of the century. While the hand or cottage laundry might be in someone's home, or in adapted premises, the steam laundries used large and up to date machinery, employing more staff and able to offer a cheaper and quicker service.

Rotary washers could cope with larger loads and cut out the laborious wash-wring-soak-wring cycle, while the heated rollers of calendering machines could replace the mangle and press large as well as small items. Even then, not everything could be coped with by a machine and most delicate work still had to be done by hand. Dry cleaning (*nettoyage à sec*) was introduced in the 1870s by Achille Serre from France and was used by wealthier clients for silks, velvets, cashmere and other expensive fabrics but it would not come within an ordinary family's budget until after the 1940s.

This was an almost entirely female industry, and the women suffered poor working conditions. They had to stand for long periods and handle heavily soiled garments and linen, in rooms that were badly ventilated, hot and humid, sometimes reaching a temperature of 90° F. The wet fabrics were heavy to lift and the machinery, particularly the moving rollers of the calendars, dangerous. The gas-heated irons that came into general use by the 1890s gave off fumes that caused headaches for the ironers. Rose Squire, a factory inspector in the 1890s, described meeting 'middle-aged and draggled, down-trodden creatures, ill-paid, and constant sufferers from rheumatism and from ulcerated legs due to long standing'. However, they did have the confidence of steady employment; in the *Strand Magazine* in 1904 George R. Sims noted that in Notting Dale (an area off Notting Hill in London and a thriving 'laundry-land') 'the women are the principal wage-earners . . . It is a common thing in the Dale for a man to boast that he is going to marry a laundry girl and do nothing for the rest of his life.'

English Laundresses: A Social History 1850–1930, Patricia Malcolmson (University of Illinois Press, 1986) describes the working conditions of the laundresses. Every growing town and city spawned a thriving laundry industry; for instance, there is information on the laundresses of Headington, who washed for the colleges, churches, hotels and private families of Oxford in the late 19th century, at www.headington.org.uk/history/misc/laundresses.htm.

■ LAUNDRYMAID

Only in wealthy households would a laundrymaid be employed, and certainly by the end of the 19th century, especially in towns, the professional steam laundries had made sending washing out to be done the modern way for middle and upper class families (see **laundress**).

A laundrymaid was responsible for washing all the family and household linen and clothing, and it would take her a week to do so. Every Monday, she received all the items for that week's wash and noted them all in her laundry book – clothing and linen was expensive and had a ready secondhand market; any losses in the wash would be a question mark against the laundrymaid's honesty. For the next three days she soaked, washed and rinsed in the separate wash house, all the hot water having to be brought in and heated in the copper. She needed to know how to get out stains and grease, and how to treat fabrics as diverse and delicate as satin, silk, muslin and wool. Thursday and Friday were taken up with mangling (squeezing the excess water out), starching, and ironing – an art in itself in the days of heavy flat irons heated by the fire. Drying must have been a nightmare at times in the British climate; linen especially was often spread or hung outside to bleach and dry at the same time.

Women working in hospital laundries were also sometimes called laundrymaids – Guy's Hospital in the 1920s was employing about 40 laundrymaids in the steam laundry, under a laundry superintendent. Later they would be known as laundry assistants.

■ LAW COPYING

Copying documents by hand was essential in the days before typewriters and from the 1860s there was an office for women clerks specialising in law copying, based in Lincolns Inn Fields. It was created by Maria Rye, who also founded the Female Middle Class Emigration Society in 1862. In 1860 the Society for Promoting the Employment of Women had begun holding courses in law copying. By the 1890s, the fee for a course in 'law copying and engrossing' was £8 8s.

■ LAWYER

Women were not admitted as either barristers (advocates in Scotland) – the lawyers who appear in court to argue a case – or solicitors, who do the day to day legal work such as conveyancing, wills etc, until after the Sex Disqualification Removal Act of 1919, despite continued attempts to gain access to lectures and training.

A solicitor had to serve an apprenticeship of two years as an articled clerk, and pass the examination of the Law Society, before being admitted to a court. In 1913 the Law Society refused to allow four women to sit the examinations but in 1922 Carrie Morrison (d.1950) became the first woman to qualify as a solicitor (see www.ambrose.appelbe.co.uk/ CarrieMorrison.htm), closely followed by Maud Crofts, Mary Pickup and Mary Sykes. It was expensive to get articles and by 1931 there were still only about 100 women acting as solicitors; the Association of Women Solicitors was founded in 1923 (www.womensolicitors.org.uk). The Law Association (110–113 Chancery Lane, London), which regulates the system for solicitors, has information on its website on 'How to trace a past solicitor' (www.lawsociety.org.uk/productsandservices/libraryservices/nonmembers/ historicalresearchers.law) and you can also request a search in their records. The papers of solicitors are sometimes deposited at local record offices.

Barristers in England went through their training at one of the four Inns of Court in London, culminating in the Bar Examination (compulsory since 1872), when if successful they were 'called to the Bar'. Then began practical experience as a pupil in chambers, until finally they were allowed to begin taking briefs of their own. Helena Normanton (1882–1957) was admitted to the Middle Temple in 1919 (having been refused entry the previous year) and in 1922 became the first woman to be called to the Bar and to practise law – Ivy Williams (1877–1966) was actually the first woman to qualify as a barrister but she went back to lecturing in law at Oxford and did not appear in court. Helena Normanton was also one of the first two women (the other was Rose Heilbron of Gray's Inn) to become a King's Counsel, in 1949.

Much of the information available for researching lawyers predates 1919 and so is not useful when tracing women; see *My Ancestor Was a Lawyer*, Brian Brooks and Mark Herber (Society of Genealogists, 2005) for a general background. The annual Law List of barristers, solicitors etc would be the best place to start: it is available at the Law Society, The National Archives and other large repositories. Each of the Inns of Court has its own website (www.graysinn.org.uk; www.lincolnsinn.org. uk; www.middletemple.org.uk; www.innertemple.org.uk) with histories and other information. The Law Society of Scotland (www.lawscot.org. uk), the governing body for Scottish solicitors, has information on the Scottish court system; the Faculty of Advocates is the governing body for advocates (www.advocates.org.uk).

■ LEAD SHOT MAKING

Lead shot for pistols and muskets was made by dropping molten lead (mixed with antimony and arsenic) through a large colander, from a height, into a tub of water, creating 'a stream of silvery rain'. The lead separated into perfectly spherical balls, solid by the time they hit the water. They were dried and passed through a sieve to grade out the different sizes.

In the mid-19th century the next stage in the process was done by women, seated at a table at which they separated out any misshapen shot – the board was at an incline and perfect shot rolled quickly down into the furthest box, while any slightly imperfect spheres went more slowly and fell into a box immediately under the lip of the table. The shot was weighed into 28lb bags and women sewed the bags up ready for sale. By the end of the century, the processes were much the same, but the separation process was more usually done by machine – women still sewed the bags of shot by hand.

■ LEAD SMELTING

In 1871 one fifth of those recorded in the census as working in lead manufacture were women. Lead was mined principally in the vicinity of coal mines (e.g. at Alston in Cumberland, on the Tyne west of Newcastle, at Bagillt in Flintshire, and at Wanlock Head in Lanarkshire, to name a few). When the lead had been mined and brought up, women and children worked on the surface (the 'knockers, chippers and washers'), sorting, separating and washing the ore free from impurities. This was year-round work, in all weathers. One of the dangers of the lead smelting process to those who worked anywhere nearby was the sulphurous lead smoke that belched continually from the smelters, though the introduction of the long chimney from the 1860s did something to disperse the poisonous fumes.

The Peak District Mining Museum, The Pavilion, Matlock Bath, Derbyshire DE4 3NR (www.peakmines.co.uk) has more information.

■ LEAD WORKER

see **lead shot making; lead smelting; white lead worker.**

■ LEATHER WORKER

In country areas the work of the saddler, harnessmaker or whipmaker was commonly in male hands, but in the factories of the Midlands it was a different story. In Walsall by 1851 there were 75 firms engaged in the leather industry, and the factories continued to employ female labourers throughout the 19th century and into the 20th. By the early 1890s two Royal Commissions had investigated the 'sweated trade' of the leather industry and concluded that these women were working long hours in poor conditions, their wages only a half or third of those of their male counterparts; they were paid on a piecework rate, while the men were paid by the hour. Union pressure also meant that women were the first to be laid off when trade was slow, and there was considerable opposition from male saddlers to the employment of women as stitchers.

Apart from a wide range of saddles and harness, the factories were turning out 'bridles, head collars, martingales, cruppers, horse breaking tackle, horse boots, muzzles, dog collars and leads, belts, purses, straps, saddle bags, horse collars, gig saddles, padlocks, leather rosettes and fronts, girths, whip sockets, rein holders, leggings, cigar cases, pocket books and many other lines' (*Walsall Past and Present*, Howard Clark, 1905). In 1871 Catherine Darby, an 81-year-old widow, was employed as a 'whip braider' in Daventry.

Some of the work was done by machine but hand stitching was thought to be stronger and better quality. One witness to the Royal Commission of 1893/4, a partner in a firm of saddlery and harness makers in Walsall, described the work done by the women stitchers: 'The better class work was all done by hand. The leather is fixed in a "clamp" so as to leave both hands free, the hole is made with a very sharp awl, and the threads put through and drawn tightly together. The women wear a leather pad fastened on to the palm of the hand by a leather ring on their middle finger. In one room women were seaming saddle seats instead of stitching them; the two parts put together were of much thinner leather and the needle was used instead of the awl; the women used thimbles and had guards on the third and fourth fingers. These seamers were considerably older than the other women in the factory. The black harness stitching having to be done with black thread was said to be trying to the eyes.'

Female labour was called upon particularly at times when orders were high, as during the South Africa War at the end of the 19th century, when military orders for saddlery etc came from the War Office

When, during the 20th century, the motor car began to take over from the horse as the principal means of transport the industry had to diversify into new products to stay alive. New lighter leather goods became popular through the 1920s and 1930s, such as travelling bags, wallets, blotters and other 'fancy goods'.

Walsall Leather Museum (in a restored leather factory at Littleton Street West, Walsall WS2 8EQ) has an excellent website (www.walsall.gov.uk/index/leisure_and_culture/leathermuseum.htm) which has much about the industry and publications for sale, including *Stitching and Skiving: Walsall's Women Leatherworkers*. See also **glovemaker**.

■ LIBRARIAN

The prospects of a woman employed in a library may not be dazzling, nor may the rate of pay be such as to encourage recruits to the profession', but at least the work was interesting and less routine than that in an office: advice that reflected the mixed feelings about librarianship in the 1880s.

In 1871 the first female librarians had begun working in public libraries in Manchester and opportunities for employment gradually spread throughout the country. In 1877 the Library Association was formed (www.la-hq.org.uk; now part of the Chartered Institute of Library and Information Professionals). By 1910 there were over 2,700 librarians and assistants employed by local authorities or academic bodies in Britain, 41% of them women, and within fifteen years women were outnumbering men in the profession. It was still, however, poorly paid, a woman teacher receiving something like £104 per annum against a librarian's £90 (or even less in small county libraries).

In 1911 it was reckoned to be a job for an 'educated middle class girl': 'The duties which fall to the lot of the junior assistants comprise the ordinary counter work of issuing and exchanging books, keeping the borrowers' register, getting the magazines ready for the tables and preparing them for binding. The seniors supervise all this work, and have to do the classification for the catalogue and take charge of the reference department.' To be considered for a senior post, taking the professional examinations of the Library Association was necessary. Records of librarians may be found where they were employed, i.e. in local authority records or those of universities or other organisations.

■ LIGHTHOUSE KEEPER

Female lighthouse keepers were fairly common in the USA by the end of the 19th century but in this country it is generally believed that the first female was appointed in the 1970s. However, there were women keepers in the 1800s, who had been allowed to take over in their own right after a husband, brother or father died.

This seems to have been particularly common in the north of England on the Mersey and the list of 'Liverpool's Lighthouse Keepers' (online at www.fhsc.org.uk/fhsc/keepers.doc) includes several women, including Ann Urmston at Bidston lighthouse 1835–1869 and Ann Jones at Leasowe 1854–1867. That there may have been others around the country is shown by the inclusion as lighthouse keepers in the census from 1841 to 1871 of Mary and Sarah Field at Cromer lighthouse with their brother Ellis. Information on records and the Mersey Docks and Harbour Board can be found at www.liverpoolmuseums.org.uk/maritime/archive/mdhc.asp.

One of the most famous was Elizabeth Williams, who was lighthouse keeper at Leasowe (between New Brighton and Hoylake, on the Cheshire side of the Mersey) from 1894 to 1908. When her husband died in 1894, she so impressed the Mersey Docks and Harbour Board that they appointed her permanently to the post; she employed one of her 13 children, a daughter, as an assistant. In 1896 she was interviewed for *Woman's Life* and pointed out that she was getting the same pay as her late husband, 'In fact, I'm in the same position as a man, only I don't wear the uniform. They chaff me about that, you know.' Her duties were 'Keeping the light going – that's all. The first thing in the morning I do my official work, as I call it, and after that I turn to household work; but I am generally dressed by about one o'clock. At sunset I have the light to look after, and from then to sunrise – sixteen hours in winter – it must be kept burning brightly.' After the Leasowe lighthouse ceased to be lit in 1908, Elizabeth kept it open as a successful teahouse for visitors. She died in 1935.

■ LINEN SPINNER AND WEAVER

Barnsley was one centre of the linen weaving industry in England in the 18th and 19th centuries, the first factory opening there in the 1840s, following a long tradition of handloom weaving. Barnsley produced a heavy, good quality linen cloth, with a significant export market, but the industry was failing by the 20th century. In Scotland there was also a thriving industry, for instance at Laurencekirk, Aberdeenshire, and Brechin. All the factories employed a large number of women workers.

The industry was particularly important in Ireland, and around Belfast in the 19th and 20th centuries – the website of the Copeland company in Belfast has a background history (www.copelandlinens.co.uk/history. htm). See *Barnsley's Linen Industry*, John Goodchild (1983); and www. futuremuseum.co.uk for details of 'linen manufacture in Nithsdale'. The Victoria and Albert Museum has a 'Linen reading list' at www.vam.ac.uk/ collections/textiles/resources/reading/linen/index.html. See also **cotton spinner and weaver; weaver.**

■ LODGING HOUSE KEEPER

A lodging house is not the same as rooms or apartments let as lodgings. Charles Booth in the 1880s defined a common lodging house (also called a low lodging house, or doss-house) as 'a house in which beds are let out for the night or by the week, in rooms where three or more persons not belonging to the same family may sleep at the same time'; they had to provide and cook their own food.

It was a wretched place for the poor, many of them one step away from the night shelter or the park bench, run by a landlord or landlady (who might own more than one house) and a paid 'deputy', who did the day to day (and all-night) supervision. T.W. Wilkinson described a visit to a doss-house in 1902 (*Living London*):

'In the corner beyond the fireplace a buxom female figure is eying the depleted collection of cracked crockery ranged on the shelves, her sleeves upturned over massive biceps. She is the "deputy", the domestic ruler of about 200 men. Her office is, even in hotels of this class, open to both sexes, each of which has qualifications for it denied to the other. Woman's strong point is the celerity and dispatch she displays in carrying out certain very necessary operations connected with bed-making. Hence the comfort of a house where females are entrusted with that work . . . Man's superiority lies in quelling disturbances and "chucking".'

In Ipswich in 1875, 42 out of 59 lodging houses were run by women. The character of a house depended greatly on the person in charge. Henry Mayhew relates that in the 1850s on the road from London to Birmingham, Mrs Bull's house at Northampton (twelve beds) and Mrs Leach's at Birmingham (30 beds) were 'comfortable and decent', while at Barnwell, near Cambridge, 'Yorkshire Betty' (30 beds) was 'a motherly body, but she's no ways particular in her management. Higgledy-piggledy; men and women, altogether.' Conditions in the houses improved a little once a police licence was required and county councils were given powers of inspection in the 1880s.

■ MAID-OF-ALL-WORK

see general servant.

■ MANGLEWOMAN

see laundress.

■ MANNEQUIN

see model, fashion.

■ MANTLE MAKER

A mantle was an outdoor garment that developed from a type of cape in the 1800s to a mixture of coat and cloak by the 1830s and remained popular. It usually had wide sleeves or else armhole slits, making it easy to wear with the sometimes expansive Victorian fashions. See dressmaker; tailoress.

■ MANTUA MAKER

By the second half of the 19th century the term was rather arcane and interchangeable with dressmaker. A mantua was originally a specific type of woman's gown, popular from the 17th century, made in one piece and requiring skill to make and fit properly – and therefore made by a professional rather than at home. It was loose, worn without boning, and open at the front showing the long petticoat beneath, but still caught in at the waist and flattering; fabrics were usually expensive and dressy. By the late 19th century the term was no longer in common use, though some examples can still be found – a Mrs Simmons, for instance, applied for a judicial separation from her husband in 1881, having supported him and their children for the past eight years 'from the profits of her business as a mantua maker'.

■ MARKET GARDENER

As the populations of towns and cities grew in the second half of the 19th century, so did the number of market gardens in the countryside around them to provide fresh vegetables, fruit, flowers and herbs – acres of peas, cabbages, carrots, beans, onions, broccoli, sprouts, cauliflowers, artichokes, lettuces, potatoes, fruits, lavender, camomile, parsley, mint etc were being grown within six miles of central London in the 1880s.

Women ran market gardens on their own account as well as working on them (see **picker**). In 1881, for instance, Fanny Allard, a 45-year-old widow with six children, was a market gardener at Evesham. One (unnamed) lady in Kent, the 'daughter of a naval officer', was described in a magazine in 1896: 'Six years ago, with a capital of less than £300, this lady went into the vegetable growing and mushroom culture business, and now she has extended her operations twenty-fold, and is known to everybody in the wholesale trade for the high-class products she sends to market.'

■ MASSAGE CORPS

see **physiotherapist**.

■ MASSEUSE

A woman who performs massage as part of a health or beauty treatment, or for therapeutic or remedial purposes. Unfortunately, the masseuse has frequently been liable to misunderstanding, 'massage' being such a common euphemism for other services. See **physiotherapist**.

■ MATCH GIRL

Although the 'poor little match girl' wrung Victorian hearts as she died in the snow, the young women who worked in the match factories in the

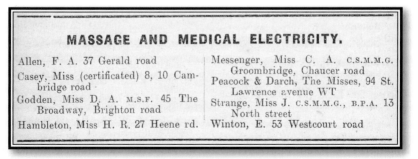

MASSAGE AND MEDICAL ELECTRICITY.

Allen, F. A. 37 Gerald road	Messenger, Miss C. A. c.s.m.m.g. Groombridge, Chaucer road
Casey, Miss (certificated) 8, 10 Cambridge road	Peacock & Darch, The Misses, 94 St. Lawrence avenue WT
Godden, Miss D. A. m.s.f. 45 The Broadway, Brighton road	Strange, Miss J. c.s.m.m.g., b.p.a. 13 North street
Hambleton, Miss H. R. 27 Heene rd.	Winton, E. 53 Westcourt road

The title 'physiotherapist' would soon replace 'masseuse', when these entries appeared in the Worthing and District Blue Book directory in 1934.

late 19th century were a different kettle of fish altogether – 'Most of them have an exuberancy of spirits truly astonishing,' wrote Montagu Williams in 1894. 'It must be admitted, however, that to have half-a-dozen of these girls marching down the Bow Road singing at the top of their voices the chorus of "Ta-ra-ra Boom-de-ay" or "Knocked 'em in the Old Kent Road" – these are at the present moment their favourites – is a little irritating to quiet-loving citizens. . . . Dress is a very important consideration with these young women. They have fashions of their own; they delight in a quantity of colour; and they can no more live without their large hats and huge feathers than 'Arry can live without his bell-bottom trousers.'

Charles Booth in 1897 heard that they were 'a rough set of girls . . . they fight like men and are not interfered with by the police.' The London match girls have passed into history for their successful strike against repressive management and poor wages at the Bryant and May factory in 1880.

There were matchmakers in all major cities and originally the work was mostly carried out in small home workshops, when it was described as 'one of the lowest, dirtiest, and worst paid of employments', before it moved into factories. For 'lucifer' matches, blocks of wood were first cut into splints, each the length of two matches, and the wood then dried out before being dipped into a mixture of white phosphorus. Women prepared the matches by cutting the splints in half and packing the matches into boxes. Careless handling (speed was essential as they were paid by results) meant that the phosphorus got onto their hands and was easily transferred to their faces and mouths.

It was known to be an unhealthy trade from the 1840s – what became known as 'phossy jaw', or necrosis, was a disfiguring and potentially fatal disease. It began with toothache, at which point the girls might have their teeth pulled out to try to stop the progression of the disease; otherwise 'the jaw and gums swelled, the teeth dropped out, abscesses formed, and the jaw-bone eventually came away in pieces'. Not only that, but in the early days the phosphorus impregnated their clothing, and workers 'shone with a pale, lambent light, so that they became offensive both to the sight and smell, and were almost pariahs to their fellows'. Replacing the white phosphorus with red phosphorus, and better ventilation and cleanliness in the factories, gradually improved matters but in the 1890s inspectors were still coming across odd cases of phossy jaw.

Read Montagu Williams' full article from *Round London: Down East and Up West* online at www.victorianlondon.org. *A Match to Fire the Thames,* Ann Stafford (Hodder & Stoughton, 1961) relates the story of the match girls' historic strike; the TUC website (www.unionhistory.info/matchworkers) has page images of the strike register, containing hundreds of women's names. For the history of Bryant & May see *The Match Makers,* Patrick Beaver, 1985.

■ MATRON, HOSPITAL

In the early 19th century a hospital matron was not usually a nurse but a housekeeper, frequently with experience in domestic service. The matron as a formidable, all-powerful head nurse, an object of fear and awe even to medical staff, was a role that developed in the late 19th and 20th centuries and was enshrined in the National Health Service in 1948, when together with the Medical Superintendent and the Clerk of Works she formed part of the triumvirate that ruled each hospital. The connection with housekeeping continued, however, as she had responsibility for domestic staff as well as nurses – when Emily McManus took up the post of Matron at Guy's Hospital in 1927 her staff included a Matron's Housekeeping Sister, and this continued after 1948. See **nurse; superintendent, lady.**

■ MATRON, POLICE

A woman employed by police forces in the 19th and early 20th centuries to be responsible for female prisoners, including searching them on arrest (see **searcher**). She might be called in on an ad hoc basis for anything concerning women or children, before the advent of the **policewoman.**

■ MATRON, PRISON

see **prison staff.**

■ MATRON, SCHOOL

The post of matron in a large boarding or public school might be either that of a housekeeper, overseeing the cooking, laundry and all domestic management, or that of infirmary or sickroom matron, in a nursing role and with nursing qualifications. In either case, she would probably live in at the school and, just as the workhouse matron was often the wife of the master, so the school matron might be the wife of the house or head master.

■ MATRON, WORKHOUSE

The workhouse, that potent symbol of fear and repression, was a creation of the Poor Law Amendment Act 1834. Boards of Guardians were charged with providing workhouse accommodation that would be a deterrent to anyone thinking of claiming poor relief, and in most cases the houses were new buildings, prison-like and chill, that served a group of parishes, or union. The conditions inside were meant to be tough and they certainly were, but staff were also appointed under rigorous controls – though whether they imposed a fair or a foul regime rather depended on the people themselves and the interest the Guardians took in the paupers.

The matron was appointed by the Board and was often the wife of the workhouse master, it being convenient for the Board if the two came as a combined package, but this was not universal – in 1891 Elizabeth Burlton, a widow aged 53, was matron of the union workhouse at Shaftesbury St James, while the master was George O. Genge, a 32-year-old unmarried man. In this case, Elizabeth had as assistant matron her 18-year-old daughter, Ellen. Regulations also made provision for the appointment of a 'matron of a workhouse having no master', in which case a minimum requirement was that she be able to keep accounts and provide a 'bond of two sureties . . . as security for the faithful performance of her duty'. The assistant matron was often the wife of the porter, and may have been known as a porteress.

The staff lived a life as regimented as their charges. The matron's duties were laid down by the Poor Law Commission. She was to assist the master in the general management and be in overall charge of the housekeeping duties of the workhouse – the washing, cooking and so on – though the female paupers did the actual work; in smaller workhouses where no cook was employed she might also take charge in the kitchens.

Her day was full: she was to oversee the female paupers at their employment; superintend the making and mending of clothes and linen – every pauper was supposed to have clean linen and stockings once a week and clean sheets on the bed once a month; take overall charge of the care of the sick and of the children, usually with the aid of a nurse and a schoolmistress; and take responsibility for the 'moral conduct and orderly behaviour' of the women and children. When women came into the house, either as inmates or 'casuals' (tramps) she admitted them – relieved them of any money or valuables, bathed, deloused and clothed them in the workhouse uniform, marked with the name of the union. At night she made the rounds of the female wards, to see that everyone was in bed and the lights and fires were out. Her salary was substantially less than that of the master, but if she served for more than 20 years she might be eligible for a pension.

See *Workhouse*, Simon Fowler (The National Archives, 2007), or *The Victorian Workhouse*, Trevor May (Shire Publications, 2003) for background. The website www.workhouses.org.uk is excellent on all aspects of workhouse life, including the staff. Because they were government employees some records of appointments, salaries etc may be found at The National Archives; matrons also kept a report book, which may survive with other workhouse records, perhaps in local record offices.

■ MECHANIZED TRANSPORT CORPS (MTC)

Founded in 1939 (as the Mechanized Transport Training Corps) by Mrs G.M. Cook and intended as a part-time voluntary service for women who could not join the services, it remained a civilian organisation during the Second World War, providing women for driving and motorcycle courier work with foreign governments, several ministries and the American Ambulance of Great Britain. The women were recruited in two groups, for home service and abroad. The Home Service Group worked closely with the Women's Voluntary Service and performed essential courier and transport work during the Blitz, including the evacuation of hospitals and driving ambulances. Abroad they worked, for example, in France, Belgium, Greece and Kenya. Members were in France in 1939, notably with the Hadfield-Spears Unit (ambulance and surgical); all returned safely after the British retreat in 1940, though two MTC drivers – Bessie Myers and Mary Darby – spent some time in captivity. (Bessie Myers wrote about her experiences in *Captured*, published in 1941.)

The khaki uniform was similar to that of the ATS but had to be purchased for £14, and initially the Corps was supported by subscriptions and the 10s 6d annual membership fees paid by its members, which led to some accusations of its being an organisation to which only the better-off could belong – why didn't they just join the ATS? However, after conscription was brought in, in November 1941, MTC members were officially recognised and paid, working under the Ministry of Transport. The Corps was disbanded at the end of 1945.

Equivalent ranks (ATS ranks in brackets): other ranks – Driver (Private); Cadet Officer (L/Corporal); Section Cadet Officer (Corporal); Company Cadet Officer (Sergeant); officers – Ensign (2nd Subaltern), Lieutenant (Subaltern), Captain (Junior Commander), Commander (Senior Commander), Commandant (Chief Commander, Senior Commandant (Deputy Controller), Corps Commander (Chief Controller).

■ MIDWIFE

Midwifery must have a claim to be the second oldest profession, if not the oldest. It was an important and trusted position within a community from ancient times. From the 16th century midwives had to have a licence from the Church to practise – not because the Church was concerned with the safety of the mother or the birth, but because midwives were sanctioned to baptise a baby that was not expected to live long enough for the local clergyman to perform the sacrament, thus receiving it into the Church and allowing it to have Christian burial. In some areas this system of 'nominations' continued into the 19th century and records can be found in Diocesan Record Offices (normally now the County Record Office).

During the 18th century there was a greater involvement of doctors, male of course, and the 'man-midwife' or accoucher made his appearance, a development that was greatly resented by female midwives. It was during the 18th century, too, that the first calls came for midwives to be registered, and the conviction that some form of training and control was necessary deepened as the 19th century progressed. In 1881 the Trained Midwives Registration Society was formed (later the Midwives' Institute) and their initial report concluded that over a million births each year were attended only by women – 'These women are under no control or regulation whatever in England.'

These were overwhelmingly home births (even by 1927 only 15% of live births were in hospital), and it was not surprising that women feared childbirth – the odds of surviving it were not encouraging and every family must have known horror stories of the mothers and babies that did not. Jennifer Worth wrote about her life as a midwife in the 1950s (*Call the*

Midwife, Merton Books, 2002) and her experiences would have been familiar to any Victorian or early 20th-century mother in a working class district – the terrible conditions of the housing, the bugs and the dirt, the overcrowding, the lack of water and sanitary facilities. The husband was sent off to the pub, the older children were taken off to a neighbour, and in the dim light (still gaslight in some places) the midwife did her work as best she could. There were no telephones and no way of contacting a doctor other than by sending someone off with a message. At least medical knowledge and drugs had advanced somewhat – one midwife who trained in the early 1900s recalled that 'there were no drugs. Some midwives gave them gin.'

From the 1880s the lobbying for registration gained ground. It was claimed that deaths of both mothers and babies were due to inefficiency or lack of skill of the midwife – some were said not to use antiseptics or even to wash, or refused to send for a doctor if complications set in. They were blamed too for trailing infection from house to house.

In 1902 the Midwives Act set up the Central Midwives Board. The 'name or title of midwife' was only to be used by women certified to practice and registration with the Board was compulsory; a woman who did not comply would be taken to court and liable to 'penal servitude'. It was also laid down that 'no woman shall, habitually or for gain, attend women in childbirth otherwise than under the direction of a qualified medical practitioner, unless she be certified under this act'. Doctors had resisted registration because they believed it might affect the number of cases they would attend (and thus their fees), and without a doctor present midwives were restricted to attending only 'normal' births, and could not use instruments in deliveries. Only in 1936 were they enabled to administer anaesthetic or painkillers.

There were, of course, many women who had been midwives for years, did their work well, and wanted to continue. The act allowed any woman who could prove that 'she had been for at least one year in *bona fide* practice as a midwife and that she bears a good character' to be admitted to the register and a period of grace was allowed for them to apply. Over 22,000 midwives were on the register by 1905, some 12,000 of them '*bona fide* midwives'.

Until 1936 midwives charged their patients a fee, which was cheaper than calling the doctor but still expensive for poorer families unless they qualified for free treatment. The Midwives Act of that year established a salaried midwifery service under local authority control, so that midwives could either stay as they were or join the scheme. In 1941 the Midwives' Institute became the College of Midwives, and received the Royal Charter in 1947.

See **nurse** for more information on sources (and also see **nurse, monthly**). The website of the Royal College of Midwives (www.rcm.org.uk) has historical background information; the college's records, including the Midwives' Roll 1872–1983 are at The National Archives. The website of the UK Centre for the History of Nursing and Midwifery at the University of Manchester (www.ukchnm.org/education/bibliographies/midwives-and-midwifery) has a bibliography of books on all aspects of the profession. See also *The Midwife's Tale: An Oral History from Handywoman to Professional Midwife*, Nicky Leap and Billie Hunter (Scarlet Press, 1993).

■ MILITARY CLOTHING MAKER

In 1860 the Royal Army Clothing Department in Pimlico was newly built as the Military Clothing Establishment. Until then the government had 'bought in' clothing from contractors, but after the scandal of shortages during the Crimean War soldiers' uniforms were now to be made on site. 'In one apartment we see women sewing soldiers' jackets with the new sewing-machines, and doing the work ten times quicker, stronger, and better than it was done of old by manual labour,' said *Once a Week*.

Nearly 40 years later, Frank Lamburn, writing in *Pearson's Magazine* in 1896, found that many of the garments were going out to contract, but that still 'those turned out on the premises necessitate the employment of about fourteen hundred women, all of them piece-workers, and all at work within the four walls of the factory'. Covering seven acres, this was a huge enterprise and it handled everything needed by a soldier, from his razor to his boots and his bearskin.

In the clothing department, male 'viewers' were responsible for the progress, from the piece of cloth to the finished garment. The cloth for trousers, tunic etc was first cut into pieces and taken to the viewers' room, where girls put with each piece all the buttons, braid and thread that was necessary, rolled it up into a bundle and took it to the factory women – each woman was responsible for a garment all the way through, including doing their own ironing, though some women only did button-holes; it was estimated that over 10 million buttons were sewn on each year. The maker took the finished item back to the viewer and the whole process started again. 'It is a curious fact,' noted Lamburn, 'that in the making of khaki uniforms the presence of a certain chemical in the dye results in heating the needle of the sewing machine to a degree that would render it useless unless it were soaped after each passage through the cloth.' Presumably it didn't do the women much good either.

Shirts were cut out on the premises and sent out to be made up by soldiers' wives and widows in their own homes – 'an inferior class of work', according to Lamburn. (Sailors' wives and widows were employed in naval ports.) See also **shirtmaker**.

■ MILKMAID

A woman who milked cows, sometimes but not necessarily the same as the dairymaid. The name might also apply to women who sold milk direct from the cow in public parks in the earlier 19th century, although it was a dying trade by the 1850s. Henry Mayhew talked to one old woman in St James's Park, London: 'It's not at all a lively sort of life, selling milk from the cows, though some think it's a gay time in the Park! I've often been dull enough, and could see nothing to interest one, sitting alongside a cow.'

■ MILLER

Female millers were not uncommon, having taken over the business from a husband or father. They would normally, like female blacksmiths, have been the proprietors of the mill and employed labour for the heavy work – one example was Edith Munt of Cromer mill in Hertfordshire, who had been left the milling business by her husband in 1837 and was still recorded in the census as a 'milleress' in 1851, then aged 68; Edith employed her son and two men.

The miller was an important figure in the local community well into the 19th century, though with increasing imports of foreign grain from the 1870s much of the milling began to be concentrated in the hands of major manufacturers, with the result that local mills gradually declined. Women were also employed by millers for the final stage in manufacture, when the flour was packed into cotton bags for sale, as they were at Edlesborough in Buckinghamshire in the 1920s and 1930s.

There is much about mills and millers at the Mills Archive Trust (www. millarchive.com); the Trust is based at Watlington House, 44 Watlington Street, Reading RG1 4RJ but an appointment is necessary to visit, see the website. For an introduction, see *Corn Milling*, Martin Watts (Shire Publications).

▪ MILLINER

A maker, designer and trimmer of ladies' hats, the basic shapes usually bought ready made from wholesalers and then being trimmed to order or to the milliner's designs. Opening a milliner's shop was considered a suitable occupation for a lady – 'It costs far more to start a milliner's shop than a tea-room,' warned the *Lady's Realm* in 1904. 'So the average lady milliner takes an upstairs floor, furnishes it artistically, interviews and buys from the travelling salesmen, whose business it is to scent out ladies setting up in business, trims or causes to be trimmed a score of tempting headgear of all sorts and conditions, and waits with a certain degree of fear and trembling for the belated buyer.' Milliners' shops were often also those of dressmakers or costumiers, or they also sold scarves, lace, blouses, lingerie etc.

Girls could learn the trade by serving an apprenticeship, usually two years. Alternatively, there were plenty of opportunities to learn as a paying pupil with a 'lady milliner', usually on a year's course. At the peak of the profession was the Court milliner, a high class and high cost milliner making hats for society ladies and debutantes. Few reached the heights of Miss Jane Clarke, 'the celebrated Court Milliner' who died in 1859 – she left an estate of £80,000, most of it to charities, as well as 'several fine pictures to the National Gallery'. A little below this level were middle or upper class women like Lilian Clapham who opened 'Dolly Vardon's' in London's West End in 1901, or the many single women or widows who turned a talent to advantage in shops in market towns all over the country.

Milliners were also employed behind the scenes in the large city drapers' and department stores: in Coventry in 1871 milliner Annie Percival, four assistant milliners and one apprentice were living in on the premises at Broadgate of Edward Bushill, draper and hatter. At the lower end of the scale were the women working in their own homes trimming hats to order or for a wholesaler milliner manufacturing in quantity for the retail trade. See also **hat maker, straw**.

Hats were so important to women's fashions that they are a subject in themselves – see *The Century of Hats*, Susie Hopkins (Aurum Press, 1999) or any fashion guides for the 19th and 20th centuries to get some idea of the huge range of styles and trimmings that milliners worked with. The website 'The Hat Bible' (www.hatsuk.com) has a glossary of hat terms and a section on the history of hats and hat making. At Wellington Mill, Wellington Road South, Stockport SK3 0EV is 'the only museum dedicated to the hat industry' and the website (www.hatworks.org.uk) includes an online tour.

■ MINE WORKER

In the 19th century what we know as coal mining was often called 'coal getting' (i.e. collieries), while the term 'mining' applied to 'the raising of ore', including copper, tin, lead, iron, zinc etc. However, they are dealt with together here because experiences for women workers were so similar in these industries – coalfields, indeed, often ran alongside iron mines – although women were not employed so extensively underground in the mines as they were in the collieries. The centres for 19th century mineral mines were in the West of England, the Midlands, Cumberland and parts of Wales, with some lead mined in East Scotland.

The 1842 Regulation of Mines and Collieries Act banned the employment underground of women and girls, and of boys under the age of ten, following horrific evidence given before a Royal Commission on working conditions, particularly from the collieries. Whole families were working underground, the men at the face and the women taking the coal up to the surface. In the hot atmosphere, men often worked naked and women stripped to the waist. The work the women were doing included three specific tasks. 'Bearing' was work underground, carrying on their backs baskets of coal weighing up to one and a half hundredweight away from the coalface. The tugs or straps of the basket were placed over the forehead, and the body had to be bent almost double to prevent the coals falling out, particularly when carrying up steps or ladders. 'Getting' was using a pick to work the coal at the coalface. 'Hurrying' and 'drawing' were also underground tasks, with the women engaged in loading small wagons, called corves, with coals at the coalface and pushing them along a passage to the shafts. Sometimes the women had to crawl on their hands and knees along narrow passageways and drag the loads – a chain was fastened around their waist and passed between their legs to the box or sledge behind – and it was known for them to work in this way when heavily pregnant.

The passing of the act did not stop women working underground and they continued to do so illegally for some time. Elizabeth Melling, who was interviewed by the *Morning Post* in 1936 when she was 88, had worked underground when she started work at the age of twelve at the Barsley Collieries at Holland Moor, Upholland: 'I went to work for my Uncle George, who was a contractor at the pit. Another girl and I acted as drawers to him, but there were times when I set to with a pick, and got the coal myself.'

Most women, however, either found themselves other work, usually in the rapidly expanding manufacturing industries, or graduated to working on the surface, where they became known as the 'pit brow lasses' or 'balmaidens'. They resisted government and trade union efforts to oust them completely from the mines over the succeeding century – there was a strong bond between the women, just as there was in any mining community. HM Inspector of Mines reported in 1898: 'Among miners proper there are no women working underground, and the number of those above ground is decreasing gradually. Their employment consists principally in "banking the tubs", that is to say, in drawing mine wagons from the cages, running these wagons to the weighing machines, screens and tips; in greasing the wagons, cleaning safety lamps, picking out any waste rock from the coal, separating ironstone from shale, attending to offices, and acting as messengers.'

'Screening', 'sorting', 'picking' and 'dressing' involved the women in sorting coal and other ore into sizes and removing dirt and rocks, and in the tin mines crushing ore into small pieces. Before conveyor belts came into operation, all sorting had to be done by hand with sieves. 'Tipping' meant pushing tubs full of coal or ore to raised areas for the contents to be tipped onto the screens; 'tip girls' in the iron mines also tipped molten slag and rubbish. Women would also clean the tubs and return them to the mines or furnaces. Not forgetting, too, that women were also employed to clean, cook and wash in the mine offices. In 1918 there were still over 11,000 women employed in manual work in the mining industry and the last two women to be employed in mining, in Cumbria, were made redundant in 1972.

Balmaidens: A Portrait of Women in Mining, Lynne Mayers (Patten Press, 2004) is written by an expert on the women who worked the mines and quarries of the West Country; see also the website www.balmaiden.co.uk, which has information about and pictures of women working in mines, clay works and related industries in Cornwall and West Devon, with a free searchable name database. *My Ancestor Was a Coalminer*, David Tonks (Society of Genealogists, 2003) is useful for general colliery sources.

The website 'Women and the Pits' (http://freepages.genealogy.rootsweb. com/~stenhouse/coal/coalmine.htm) has a name index to 'Female Mining Deaths 1851–1913'. The British Mining Database (www.ap.pwp.blueyonder. co.uk/bmd/bmd.htm) is a guide to related websites, organisations, museums etc. The National Archives also has research guides on coal mining records and sources for the history of mines and quarries. The Scottish Mining Museum is at Lady Victoria Colliery, Newtongrange, Midlothian (www. scottishminingmuseum.com); see also www.mining-villages.co.uk.

■ MINISTER OF RELIGION

Although women ministers were not accepted into the Church of England until the 1990s, there had been occasional lay-preachers in the nonconformist church since the 18th century. However, Gertrude von Petzold (1876–1952) broke new ground when she trained for the ministry at Manchester College, Oxford and was inducted as minister by the Unitarian church in Leicester in 1904. Within 20 years another seven women had joined her in the Unitarian ministry and women were also coming forward in the Baptist and Congregationalist churches, although the Methodists at first remained wary of the idea. By the 1950s every denomination had female ministers. See also **deaconess**.

One Congregationalist minister, Elsie Chamberlain (1910–1991), made regular radio broadcasts in the 1940s, becoming the first ordained woman on the BBC staff and also the first to present the *Daily Service* on radio, and in 1946 she was the first woman chaplain appointed to the forces (the WAAF) – see *First Lady of the Pulpit: A Biography of Elsie Chamberlain* by Janette Williams (Book Guild, 1993).

■ MISSIONARY

The keen public interest taken in missionary work – particularly in India, China and Africa, but also Asia, the Caribbean and the Pacific – was quite remarkable in the 19th and early 20th centuries. A missionary's wife played a considerable role in the success of a mission through the care and support of her husband, but there were also women who became missionaries in their own right. For women 'of intelligence, earnest religious opinions, and some enterprise, who have few home ties, and are quick at adapting themselves to new conditions', plus who possessed good health and an aptitude for languages, it was a life that many found attractive, though by the end of the 19th century a good education and professional training were also required.

Most female missionaries travelled as teachers, doctors or nurses, but if they did want to evangelise then by the early 1900s 'study of psychology, pedagogy and sociology' was thought of value, as was possession of the diploma awarded by the Archbishop of Canterbury of 'Student in Theology' (S.Th.), which prepared women to be teachers of theology. At this time the position of women as preachers or teachers in the Church and other denominations varied (see **deaconess; minister of religion**).

Missionary schoolteachers were required all over the world – 'Every kind of school is to be met with, from the village hut-school up to the university. . . . Perhaps even higher qualifications are necessary for those taking up work in the mission field than for those teaching at home, for the missionary has not only to teach scholars, but to train native teachers. The elementary schoolteacher, the high-school mistress, the lecturer on domestic economy are all needed,' was the 1911 view. In India, teachers were used not only in schools but also in the private apartments of local women ('zenanas') who would otherwise have been forbidden contact with the outside world. The first single woman accepted as a missionary by the Society for the Propagation of the Gospel in Foreign Parts (SPG) was Sarah Coombes, a schoolteacher in Borneo, in 1856.

Qualified doctors ('medical missionaries') and nurses were equally sought after. For female doctors, missionary work abroad was held up as not only rewarding but also an easier career path than in the male-dominated home profession: 'Medical men in India welcome their lady coadjutors – a fact that cannot always be asserted of doctors at home' (*Young Woman*, 1892). In 1881, when arguments were raging over whether or not women should be allowed to train as doctors in Britain, *The Times* had reported that the Maharanee of Punnah had sent a message to Queen Victoria telling her of the need for female doctors to treat Indian women who would otherwise receive little or no medical assistance, and beseeching her to help. The difficult situation of poor women in India continued to form the basis of articles in women's magazines into the 20th century, with often an appeal for female doctors – perhaps if a young woman doctor 'disappears' from the records at home, she might be found in India?

The Wellcome Library has a *Sources Guide for Medical Missionaries and Missionary Societies* (http://library.wellcome.ac.uk/doc_WTL039929. html). The internet 'Gateway to missionary collections in the UK' (www. mundus.ac.uk) can be used to locate material for British missionary societies overseas, provided by the archive department of the School for Oriental and African Studies, University of London; over 400 collections are held in the UK. The School's own holdings are also listed and catalogued online (http:// lib.soas.ac.uk). For South African missionaries, see Rosemary Dixon-Smith's website including bibliographies and links (www.genealogyworld. net/missionaries/missionaries_b.html).

References to a woman as a 'missionary' may occasionally relate to missions established within the UK by every religious denomination in the 19th and early 20th century. Investigations into urban slum life in the second half of the 19th century revealed a shocking ignorance of Christian values amongst the poor and uneducated, and led to the creation of a variety of religious and philanthropic missions, some evangelical, others practical – district nursing had its roots in one such society. See **bible woman**.

■ MODEL, ARTIST'S

'As a rule the model, nowadays, is a pretty girl, from about twelve to twenty-five years of age, who knows nothing about art, cares less, and is merely anxious to earn seven or eight shillings a day without much trouble', was the opinion of Oscar Wilde in 1889 (*English Illustrated Magazine*). Being an artist's model was a precarious existence, with work well paid but irregular, depending upon whether an artist wanted a particular 'type'.

'The work is both hard and easy. An intelligent model, of course, is more useful to an artist than one who has nothing but beauty to recommend her, but intellectual qualities are a secondary consideration. A model's chief duty is to stand or sit in perfect repose for a given length of time. The usual pay is a shilling an hour, and it is well worth it, but as a girl could not earn so much in any other merely mechanical way, the calling is naturally popular. The academy schools pay rather more for models than is paid at most private studios, but then the work is harder, for the students generally get as much as possible out of the sitter. The artist who hires a model on his own account has to be more careful, for he knows that he is at his model's mercy, for at any moment she might get tired of her work and desert him, and his picture or statue would have to remain unfinished.' (*Home Notes*, 1895.)

Charles Booth (*Life and Labour of the People in London*, 1902) thought that models led a pleasant life, 'and in the end often marry one or other of those to whom they have been sitting. Those of them who are not fortunate enough to do this not infrequently end by going on the stage.'

■ MODEL, FASHION

For as long as clothes have been for sale to the better off, there have been models to display them. Elizabeth L. Banks described the scene in a designer dressmaker's shop in *Living London* (1902) – 'we seem to be surrounded by duchesses – handsome, tall, graceful, stylish. They approach us, then float away. They toss their heads, move their arms and elbows aristocratically, look beautiful and self-possessed. . . . A wave of the hand and the duchesses disappear. They are but model-girls, employed by Mr Fitly to spend several hours a day in putting on and off his gowns for the inspection of his patrons.' In less exalted shops, the model might be the dressmaker's assistant, who spent the major part of her time working on the gowns themselves.

The word 'mannequin' has sometimes been used for a fashion model, though more often it refers to the dummy that appears in the shop window or displays. The 'catwalk' model has a history going back to the 1920s and the evolution of the great fashion houses – see *Catwalking: A History of the Fashion Model* by Harriet Quick (Hamlyn, 1997).

■ MUNITIONS WORKER

Women were no strangers to working with gunpowder and explosives before 1914 but the huge numbers who went into the munitions factories during the First World War were astounding – it is believed that by the last year of the war almost a million women were 'in munitions', many of them middle class and experiencing factory work for the first time.

A woman shell-turning in a First World War munitions factory, with shell cases piled up behind her.

The Munitions of War Act of 1915 had given the production of weapons and ammunition for the Front priority over other industries and, six months later, when male conscription was brought in, the government encouraged women to take up jobs in the munitions factories. It was dirty and often dangerous work. One well-known side effect was that certain chemicals turned their skin yellow, but it was the threat of explosion that was most worrying. The Barnbow factory at Leeds employed about 16,000 women, some of them putting the fuses in shells already packed with high explosive – the fuse was inserted by hand and the cap screwed down. On 5 December 1916, a huge explosion at the factory killed 35 women. (There is more about the 'Barnbow Lasses' at www.history-uk.com/HistoryUK/England-History/BarnbowLasses.htm.)

Munitions factories could be found all over the country, often in works taken over 'for the duration' for war work: e.g. at Dartford in Kent the Vickers works was making explosives, grenades and shells, and J. & E. Hall were employing over 300 women as crane drivers, lathe operators and acetylene welders making bombs, bullets and bomb-dropping equipment. One of the largest factories, purpose-built, was at Gretna and the women's work is now commemorated by a museum: Devil's Porridge Exhibition, Daleside, Eastriggs, Annan, Dumfries and Galloway (www.devilsporridge.co.uk) – the 'devil's porridge' was the lethal mix of explosive that the women had to prepare by hand. See also *On Her Their Lives Depend: Munitions Workers in the Great War*, Angela Woollacott (University of California Press, 1994).

During the Second World War women again filled the munitions factories, now known as Royal Ordnance factories, making anything from bullets to aircraft. In March 1942 all single women aged 20 to 31 became liable for military service, but they could choose between going into the services, Civil Defence or industry. Those who decided to work in the factories could be directed anywhere in the country. By the following April 90% of single women aged between 18 and 40 were either in industry or the services, and in May 1943 married women (except those with young children) were also directed into part-time work – 1943 was the peak year for the production of munitions, the women working twelve-hour shifts, seven days a week. All histories of the 'Home Front' include some mention of the factory workers, or see the very readable *How We Lived Then*, Norman Longmate (Arrow, 1977) – the author remembered his sister's hands 'pitted with sharp metal splinters and covered in oil sores'.

■ MUSICIAN

Playing a musical instrument of some sort was almost obligatory in many families in the 19th and early 20th centuries – even working class homes had a piano in the front room. For those women who wanted to take their talent further and make it their livelihood, colleges of music had been accepting pupils since the Royal Academy of Music was opened in 1822. By the 1880s musicians and singers might have attended one of a number of schools or colleges – for instance, Trinity College, the Guildhall School of Music (where 'Mrs Charles P. Smith' was the 'lady superintendent in charge of all the ladies attending the school'), or the Royal College of Music. The Royal Manchester College of Music was opened in 1893, and the Northern School of Music in 1920 (today they are amalgamated as the Royal Northern College of Music).

Any professional musician would have studied formally and college archives may reveal details of students and their subsequent careers. The archives of the Royal Northern College of Music, for instance, were described in 'Tune into the past', Mary Ann O'Kane (*Ancestors* magazine, March 2007). The RNCM Archives are at 124 Oxford Road, Manchester M13 9RD (www.rncm-archive.rncm.ac.uk). A teacher of music will also have followed this path, though in the days when every neighbourhood seemed to have at least one woman who gave music lessons in her own home, there was no guarantee that she was any more than self-taught. It is always a possibility, too, that some women students may have studied abroad. *The New Grove Dictionary of Music and Musicians*, ed. Stanley Sadie and John Tyrrell (Oxford University Press, 2004) – all 29 volumes – can sometimes be consulted through local library websites.

There is an interesting collection of women composers of the last 250 years on Diana Ambache's website: www.ambache.so.uk/wIndex.htm.

■ NAILMAKER

'The work is not one that is suitable for women,' wrote a commentator in 1876, but nearly 11,000 women were engaged in nailmaking in the Black Country, the main centre of the trade – 'that portion of the South Staffordshire and Worcestershire coalfield which borders Stourbridge, Dudley, Cradley, the Lye, Rowley and Halesowen, while a smaller detachment is found near Bromsgrove, and also at Belper in Derbyshire'. Nailmaking was a home industry with a long history, though by the early 19th century it was at the start of a long decline.

The work was carried out in small forges attached to the workers' cottages and there were thousands of these workshops in existence. Each had a forge and a bellows to heat the iron rods. 'The nailer has to find his own bench and set of tools, at an outlay of from five to ten pounds,' wrote Robert H. Sherard for *Pearson's Magazine* in 1896. 'The bench is fitted with a peg, or miniature anvil, on which the red hot iron is pointed, a hardy, or fixed chisel, over which the iron is bent and partially cut, and a bore into which the severed length is inserted previous to the fashioning of the head of the nail. This is effected by means of the Oliver, which is a heavy hammer worked by a treadle, and restored to its upright position by a simple system of leverage. The completed nail is ejected from the bore by means of a lever, operating on a tit or tiny steel rod, which, jerked upwards, expels the nail.'

In 1889, in evidence to the parliamentary enquiry into the sweated trades, Caroline Cox, 15 years old and one of a family of ten, said she 'pointed dog-head nails about three inches in length and half an inch square. She and her mother cut the nails. Her food consisted mostly of potatoes and bread, and occasionally bacon. She was glad of a bit of meat for dinner on Sundays. She could get plenty of work even if she was restricted to the smaller kind of nails.' According to a commercial dictionary of 1878 there were 'nearly 300 different sorts and sizes of nails, applicable to all the various purposes of the carpenter, joiner, shipbuilder, wheelwright etc'.

It was hard, dirty and monotonous work. It also became increasingly difficult to make a living wage, especially when the middlemen, or 'foggers' (who could be women), paid in kind with food or beer tokens rather than cash. Several nailers might work together in the same forge, renting a 'hearth' from the owner, so that each one was independent.

The women did most of the work, a clever nailer making an attractive proposition as a wife, but even if all the family worked they could still hardly rise above starvation wages. In the factories that began to take over the trade from the 1860s, mostly in Wolverhampton, Leeds, Newcastle and Newport (Wales), the machines could cut and fashion a more standard product, so that by the end of the 19th century the home forges were being used for specialised items only, such as brush nails. The nailers could never hope to match factory wages.

See 'Hard as nails', Sara Wilson (*Family History Monthly*, December 2005); there are also two articles on the nailmakers' workshops of Birmingham and Harborne on the website of the Birmingham and District Local History Association (www.bdlha.org). A rescued Bromsgrove nailshop is at the Avoncroft Museum of Historical Buildings, Stoke Heath, Bromsgrove B60 4JR (www.avoncroft.org.uk).

■ NANNY

Otherwise called the head nurse, the traditional nanny (often called 'Nurse') ruled the nursery in upper and middle class households. She was almost always working class herself, and rose to command through experience and ability. In a 'big house' she might have a whole suite of rooms: a day nursery, a night nursery, a pantry, and somewhere for the maid(s) to sleep – she herself would probably sleep in the night nursery with her young charges. There was a clear demarcation between her kingdom and the rest of the household servants and she could wield a great deal of power and influence, answering to no one but the mistress of the house.

She was in effect a surrogate mother, and in some cases raised the children with very little input from the parents. 'As the hopes of families, and the comfort and happiness of parents are confided to the charge of females who superintend nurseries of children, no duties are more important, and none require more incessant and unremitting care and anxiety,' said *The Complete Servant* in 1825. The influence of the nanny on generations of children was immense and the demise of the old-style nanny did not come about until after the Second World War. From the end of the 19th century, however, college-trained nannies were increasingly common (see **nursery nurse**).

Read *The Rise and Fall of the British Nanny*, Jonathan Gathorne-Hardy (Hodder and Stoughton, 1972) for the full story. See also **domestic servant.**

■ NEEDLEMAKER

The importance of needles, which came in all sizes from the finest domestic sewing needle to the huge and hefty sailmaker's needle, can be judged by the existence of the Company of Needlemakers, which was granted a charter of incorporation in 1656. Evidence of needlemaking exists from early times, therefore, in London and other places such as Chichester, but during the 19th century the manufacturing industry became firmly rooted in Redditch in Worcestershire. By 1912 it was estimated that about 20,000 people were employed in the process, and many of them were women. The manufacture of fish hooks and fishing tackle was an allied trade. Visitors to the mills in the 19th century commented on the attractiveness of the surroundings and the generally superior grade of worker employed there. To make such a seemingly simple item, there were over 20 separate processes, starting with coils of steel wire arriving from Sheffield.

In the 1870s women could earn from 8s to 15s a week in the factories. They were particularly concerned with certain parts of the process, including hammering the needles straight, checking for defects, and packing them in coloured paper, some of the women being able to count and paper 3,000 needles an hour. At one time a girl called a 'header' or 'ragger' was responsible for turning the needles so that all the heads were one way – she had a rag or 'dolly' on the forefinger of her right hand and with her left hand pressed the needles against it, so that the points stuck in the soft cotton. It was reckoned in 1912 that Messrs Milward had an output of seven to nine million needles a week.

The Forge Mill Needle Museum, Needle Mill Lane, Riverside, Redditch, Worcs B98 8HY (http://redditch.whub.org.uk/home/rbc-al-forge-mill.htm) is housed in a Victorian needle polishing mill. See *Needlemaking*, John G. Rollins (Shire Publications) and *The Worshipful Company of Needlemakers 1656–2006: A Commemoration of 250 Years*, David John de Courcy Henshaw (2006).

■ NEEDLEWOMAN

The term, as with 'seamstress', covers a wide range of female trades in the 19th and early 20th centuries, involving working at home as an

In the 1880s it was thought that the new sewing machines would make life easier for the women working in the 'sweated industries' such as dressmaking, tailoring, millinery etc – but the reality proved different. Outworkers rented machines from Singer, but any slump in the trade meant they lost not only their income but also their machine if they could not keep up with the weekly payments.

outworker or in factories; hand-sewing or using a sewing machine. After the 1870s when sewing machines became common the terms 'machinist' or 'sewing machinist' might be used. 'Sewing' involved far more than clothing, see also **bookbinder; boot and shoe stitcher; corsetmaker; dressmaker; glovemaker; hat maker; hosiery worker; mantua maker; military clothing maker; milliner; tailoress; upholsterer.**

N

■ NET MAKER

Net making, or braiding, was women's work all around the coast of Britain. At Fleetwood in Lancashire, for instance, they worked either in braiding rooms or at home, where they produced sections of net which were collected by the middlemen of the industry, the 'net-fixers'.

One woman who started work as a 14-year-old girl in a braiding room in Grimsby in the 1930s recalled that after the first day her hands were swollen and blistered – the girls rubbed Friar's Balsam into their fingers to harden them, and an ointment containing laudanum to take the pain away. A wrist strap was sometimes worn, as the work, holding the nets, was so heavy. For the first two years she worked as a needle filler, earning 10s 3d the first year and 12s 6d the second; when the girls reached 16 they were allowed to make the nets and she then earned about £2 a week, which was 'as much as some men were earning'. She continued working during the Second World War, making camouflage nets (*Lincolnshire Within Living Memory*, Lincolnshire Federation of WIs, Countryside Books, 1995).

Bridport in Dorset was a famous centre for ropemaking and braiding – the women made seine nets for fishing, nets for tennis courts, the small nets that go in the corners of billiard tables, and even bags for Brussels sprouts. Bridport Museum, The Coach House, Gundry Lane, Bridport DT6 3RJ (www.bridportmuseum.co.uk) has details; and the Bridport Museum Trust has an oral history project online (www.spinningyarns.co.uk).

■ NURSE

For much of the 19th century nursing was unskilled work carried out by women of little education or aptitude, castigated by Florence Nightingale as 'too old, too weak, too drunken, too stolid, or too bad to do anything else'. Efforts to improve standards in hospitals were being made by the 1840s, with the foundation of church-based 'sisterhoods', but it was Miss Nightingale who grasped the attention of the public and forced a re-evaluation of the care of the sick. Yet progress was exceedingly slow and, by the 1880s, it was still being said that changes needed to be made in hospitals before women 'of decency and refinement could study in them with much advantage or comfort', despite the 'advancing spirit of the day' which was bringing a better class of women to consider nursing as a career.

*Nurses attending an operation at the Charing Cross
Hospital in the early 1900s.*

In the 1880s many voluntary hospitals trained their own nurses (St Bartholomew's school opened in 1877), but some contracted with outside institutions to supply nursing staff. The Royal Free, for instance, got its nurses from the British Nursing Association, which also supplied other London hospitals, while at St Thomas's nurse training was undertaken by the Committee of the Nightingale Fund, founded by Florence Nightingale in 1860.

Entry qualifications, grading and salaries varied from place to place, as did the length of training, some hospitals offering two years, others three, as each hospital was autonomous, and the class structure further complicated the successful creation of an efficient nursing service. At St Thomas's, for instance, women entered as Nightingale probationers for one year, during which they received £10 and part of their uniform costs, on acceptance by Mrs Wardroper, the matron at the hospital. For the next three years they were bound to go wherever the Fund sent them to work, whether at St Thomas's or another hospital, as a nurse probationer with a salary starting at £20. After successfully completing their training, if they were taken on the staff at St Thomas's, they were known as staff nurses, working under the ward sister.

'Ladies' at St Thomas's (daughters of clergymen and other professional men) had a different career structure: they could enter as a Nightingale probationer for one year on payment of a premium of £30, after which they were immediately eligible to become ward sisters, or to leave the hospital to perhaps go into district nursing. At the London Hospital in Whitechapel Road, ladies entered as 'sister probationers' – sisters were exempt from menial duties and took their meals with the matron – while the nurses themselves were 'drawn from the class of domestic servants, wages being £12, £18, £21, and £23 16s per annum, with uniform'. Probationer nurses were normally housed by the hospital, under the supervision of a lady superintendent.

Anyone could call themselves a 'nurse', with or without training, but there were a number of forceful women who were determined to create a regulated and respected profession. One was Ethel Fenwick (née Manson), who started her nursing career as a probationer in Nottingham, and before her marriage was superintendent of nursing at St Bartholomew's in London. She headed a protracted campaign to create an official register of nurses and in 1887 founded the British Nurses' Association. The General Nursing Councils of England and Wales, Scotland, and Ireland were created in 1921 with responsibility for the training, examination and registration of nurses. A Register of Nurses was first published in 1922; however, state registration was not compulsory for a nurse until 1943.

The Royal College of Nurses was founded in 1916 as the nurses' professional association, later their trade union. They have an excellent range of aids for anyone interested in a nursing ancestor – see their website for a factsheet on 'Tracing Nurses' in England and Scotland (www.rcn. org.uk/resources/historyofnursing/factsheets-tracingnurses.php). They also have historical nursing journals online, fully searchable by name or subject, including the *Nursing Record* 1888–1956 (http://rcnarchive.rcn.org.uk/). *A History of the Nursing Profession*, Brian Abel-Smith (Heinemann, 1960) is a good introduction to the background.

Apart from the voluntary hospitals, nurses may have found employment in a wide range of places (see below). See also **Princess Mary's Royal Air Force Nursing Service; Queen Alexandra's Imperial Military Nursing Service; Queen Alexandra's Royal Naval Nursing Service; Voluntary Aid Detachments.**

■ NURSE, ASSISTANT

A new hospital grade that appeared in 1943, later to be known as the State Enrolled Nurse (SEN), which regularised the position of women who had been working for some time in hospitals or sanatoria who had not completed a recognised full course of training but were nevertheless useful members of staff. The General Nursing Council became responsible for supervising their training (two years) and examinations, and their names were recorded in the Roll of Assistant Nurses.

■ NURSE, COLONIAL

In 1896 the Colonial Nursing Association (CNA) became the recognised source from which the Colonial Office could supply nurses, in government employment, to the Crown Colonies; the first nurse was sent to Mauritius in that year. In 1902 a sick-pay fund committee was created to ensure that nurses who fell ill abroad should not be left to cope on their own. In most cases the nurses went to work in Government hospitals and cared for British expatriates ('pioneers of the Empire', as the *British Journal of Nursing* had it in 1913), but they were also supplied to local groups, such as the South African Church Railway Mission, which managed a nursing service for employees on the Cape to Cairo Railway.

Applicants had to be fully trained, including in midwifery (except, for some reason, if they were going to West Africa or Western Australia), and women aged over 27 years were preferred. Salaries began at £60 per annum for private nurses in the employ of local colony committees, while for government appointments they varied between £30 and £150. The usual term of engagement was three years. A spirit of adventure was an asset, as a colonial nurse could be sent anywhere, at any time. Perhaps there were other lures too: 'Doctors take good care that colonial nurses shall not suffer from homesickness and boredom, and they get up dances, dinners, and tennis parties, to which the nurses are invariably invited. Colonial life, moreover, as everyone knows, is very much more of a holiday than life over here.' However, it was impressed upon every applicant that she would be an ambassador of her country, and of her class. One colonial nurse was Mary Johnson, who trained at Manchester's St Mary's Hospital and had her first appointment in 1901 in Cyprus at the government hospital, before becoming a sister at the hospital in the Federated Malay States.

In 1919 the name of the CNA was changed to the Overseas Nursing Association (ONA) and between the wars there was a change in emphasis to training local people in nursing skills. Over 8,000 nurses went through the CNA/ONA's hands before it closed in 1966.

A useful article, with reference to the archives of the Association, is reproduced at www.historycooperative.org.uk/journals/hah/7.2/rafferty. html, 'The seductions of history and the nursing diaspora' by Anne Marie Rafferty, from *Health and History*. The National Archives also holds some records under the country in which nurses worked.

■ NURSE, COTTAGE

The Cottage Benefit Nursing Association (based at Denison House, Vauxhall Bridge Road, London) was founded by Bertha Marion Broadwood (1846–1935) in 1883 and was based upon the idea that people were often better nursed in their own homes than in hospitals. Her aim was to send 'working class nurses to country cottages', and the Association trained young women in basic nursing and midwifery, 'to visit the sick in the homes of labourers, artisans, small farmers, tradespeople, and others'; they usually lived in and would also help with looking after the home if the mother was ill. The Association preferred to appoint country women, and training was given free on condition that the nurse stayed with them for up to four years; in 1911 salaries started at £16 a year in the first year after training. By 1906 there were 200 branches around the country, employing over 500 nurses.

Miss Broadwood's papers, diaries etc are held at the Surrey History Centre, 130 Goldsworth Road, Woking GU21 6ND (www.surreycc.gov. uk/surreyhistoryservice).

■ NURSE, DISTRICT

The district nurse on her bicycle (or latterly in her little car) was a familiar sight in both town and country in the earlier 20th century. Many of them became much loved members of the local community, seeing people into and out of the world and caring for them in between. District nursing had its roots in 19th century philanthropy and was supported by voluntary contributions until well into the 20th century.

There were a number of charitable organisations in the second half of the 1800s which existed to send nurses out into, particularly, the slum areas of cities to care for those who were sick but unable to afford any medical help. Some of them were also Christian missionaries, sent into 'darkest England' (see **nurse, Ranyard**). However, it is generally accepted that the origins of today's district nursing service lie in Liverpool in the 1860s, where a pioneering nursing scheme was started by William Rathbone. He was also instrumental in getting Florence Nightingale's support for a similar scheme in London, and the Metropolitan Nursing Association was founded in the 1870s, under Miss Florence Lees.

In 1889 money collected by 'the women of England' to mark Queen Victoria's Golden Jubilee was used to found the Queen Victoria Jubilee Institute for Nurses (from 1928 the Queen's Institute for District Nursing), and to extend district nursing schemes. One of the oldest was in Lancashire, for instance, at Garston and Grassendale, formed in 1893. People paid a subscription and were then able to call on the nurse if they needed help, and such schemes went on being funded locally right up to the 1940s and the start of the NHS, though local authorities were compelled to become involved in their support in the inter-war years. A 'Queen's nurse' was always fully trained, and some took on the supervision of village nurses and midwives. From 1919, state registration with the General Nursing Council was a requirement. 'District nursing is a branch of the profession which often attracts those who desire a more independent form of work,' advised a careers book in the 1930s.

See *A Hundred Years of District Nursing*, M. Stocks (Allen & Unwin, 1960) for background, and **nurse** for sources.

■ NURSE, HEAD

The title given to the traditional **nanny** in a large household. Later, may mean a ward sister, with permanent charge of a ward, or a staff nurse grade, with charge of a ward on a short-term basis in the third year of training. In 1910 at Guy's Hospital, Emily McManus was made head nurse, under a ward sister, in her third year; her status was marked by the addition of 'strings' to her cap – 'a little stiff white bow under your chin'.

N

■ Nurse, industrial

The first industrial nurse is thought to have been Philippa Flowerdew, who was employed by Colmans in Norwich in the 1870s. Neither industry nor government was quick to take up this specialism, and it was 1893 before the first female medical inspectors were appointed to inspect factories and industrial working conditions; they were trained district nurses. From the time it was created, the Royal College of Nursing was involved in preparing members for work in industry and in 1934 it set up an Industrial Nursing Course. In 1949 the Industrial Health Service was set up under the Ministry of Labour. 'Industrial nursing' became, of course, 'occupational health' from the 1950s. See **nurse** for sources.

■ Nurse, monthly

The monthly nurse was a familiar figure throughout the Victorian period and well into the 20th century – a woman who was employed to live in with a family for a month after the birth of a baby. Dickens' Sarah Gamp was not the only literary caricature of a monthly nurse of the 1840s and 1850s, which implies that they were commonly seen as despotic, ignorant, drunken and dirty. However, Queen Victoria had a 'monthly nurse' (Mrs Lilly) in attendance at the births of her children, and it was not only the upper classes who employed such women – the 1851 census for Hertfordshire records them in the households of a cooper, a police constable, a journeyman carpenter and a schoolteacher, for instance.

In 1860 Mrs Beeton recommended that a monthly nurse should be 'scrupulously clean and tidy . . . honest, sober and noiseless in her movements . . . possess a natural love for children, and have a strong nerve in case of emergencies'. The latter was particularly important, as she would be in charge of a birth and recovery that might at any time present life-threatening problems (hopefully with medical back-up if the family could afford it). Childbed was a hazardous time for women and their babies and a good monthly nurse must have been worth her weight in gold. Not all were good, of course, and they were sometimes blamed for carrying dangerous infections from one house to another. By the end of the 19th century calls for the training and registration of midwives were gathering steam, and after 1902 (see **midwife**) the women who made their living as monthly nurses were given a ten year period of grace to train and be certificated (either as midwives or as general nurses), or to cease their work. Other names: dry nurse, handy woman, untrained midwife, certificated monthly nurse, confinement nurse. See also **wetnurse**.

■ NURSE, NIGHTINGALE

A Nightingale nurse was one who had trained as a Nightingale probationer under the Nightingale Fund at St Thomas's Hospital (see **nurse**).

■ NURSE, PAUPER

see **nurse, workhouse**.

■ NURSE, PRIVATE

She might be employed through an agency, for a fee. Such nurses did not have to be registered, though obviously more reputable agencies would ensure their nurses were fully trained. An agency nurse might also be used in nursing or convalescent homes. See also **nurse, sick**.

■ NURSE, QUEEN'S

A nurse employed by the Queen Victoria Jubilee Institute for Nurses (Queen's Institute for District Nursing) – see **nurse, district**.

■ NURSE, RANYARD

A nurse working for the Biblewomen and Nurses Mission founded by Mrs Ellen Ranyard (d.1879). From 1868 trained nurses were being sent out into poor working class areas (usually near where they lived) to offer help and advice, and by the 1890s they were over 80 in number. Costs were all met by charitable donations. See *The Story of the Ranyard Mission 1857–1937*, E. Platt (Hodder & Stoughton, 1937). The Mission was still working up to the 1960s, in co-operation with the London County Council District Nursing Service. See also **bible woman**.

■ NURSE, RED CROSS

The British National Society for Aid to the Sick and Wounded in War was formed in 1870, and in 1905 became the British Red

Cross Society. Following the First World War the League of Red Cross Societies was formed to change the focus to 'the improvement of health, the prevention of disease, and the mitigation of suffering throughout the world'. In 1921, for instance, the first blood transfusion service in the UK began under the Red Cross, while overseas branches spread throughout the world. Today they continue to work wherever conflict or disaster strike.

During each world war the Red Cross and the St John Ambulance Brigade combined to support the services through the **Voluntary Aid Detachments** (**VADs**), but there were also many nurses who served with the Red Cross outside wartime. The British Red Cross Museum and Archives are at 44 Moorfields, London EC2Y 9AL (telephone: 020 7877 7058; www.redcross. org.uk). They have personnel indexes (extensive but incomplete) from both world wars but nothing for the pre- or inter-war years. However, there are county branch records that may be of help.

■ NURSE, REGISTERED GENERAL

Name in Scotland, originally, for a State Registered Nurse.

■ NURSE, SICK

A sick nurse can sometimes be found enumerated in a household at census time, and her inclusion points to someone in the family suffering either a short term illness or long term invalidism or disability, physical or mental. She was not necessarily a trained (or, later, registered) nurse, though her references would obviously have been key to her employment. In the 19th century she existed in something of a no-man's-land in a household, neither servant nor family, like the governess. By the 1880s it was being mooted that if she would only take recognised nursing training, she would be seen as 'a valued and respected member of every family she may enter, to be received on terms of an equal and familiar footing'.

■ NURSE, STAFF

Originally a nurse who had completed her training and been taken on the permanent staff of a hospital, reporting to the ward sister.

▪ NURSE, STATE ENROLLED (SEN)

The later name for an Assistant Nurse; not with the same level of qualification as a State Registered Nurse and with a different career structure within the National Health Service.

▪ NURSE, STATE REGISTERED (SRN)

It became compulsory to be state registered to be employed as a nurse in England after the 1943 Nurses Act.

▪ NURSE, UNDER

The second in command in the nursery of a big house, under the nanny and above the nursemaid.

▪ NURSE, WORKHOUSE

It had never been intended that workhouses would become hospitals, but that was precisely what happened over the 40 or so years after the passing of the New Poor Law Act in 1834 as it became common practice to admit sick paupers rather than leave them outside to die. Yet nursing was wholly inadequate to the task. Nurses in workhouse infirmaries were initially often drawn from the inmates themselves. They were not trained and had little interest in their work; stories of their harshness, idleness and thieving were rife. In 1844 at Liverpool Infirmary the nurses were said to leave patients to take their own medicines and to be entirely uninterested in cleanliness – most of them were over 60 and habitually drunk. Efforts were made to reform the system, and Liverpool opened its first training organisation in 1855, with the assistance of the Royal Infirmary.

In the 1860s there were inquiries into the state of workhouse nursing and the use of pauper nurses, revealing that outside London there were only six trained nurses employed in workhouses. In London, Florence Nightingale pressed for an inquiry into workhouse nursing after a particularly scandalous death occurred in Holborn Workhouse in 1864, and under her leadership the first poor law school of nursing was established at Highgate Infirmary, followed by a second at St Marylebone Infirmary. There were simply not the number of trained staff to go round at this time. Stories of terrible abuse continued to arise: in

1868 in Wigan a child died as a result of treatment at the hands of 'a batch of five nurses – two of whom are idiots, one paralytic 73-year-old, the fourth a feeble old woman of 79, and the fifth a pauper of 81 years' (*The Lancet*). Once improvements began to be made in nurse training in voluntary hospitals, it filtered down to the workhouses as well, although extremely slowly.

In 1913 the Poor Law Institutions (Nursing) Order required guardians to appoint trained nurses and the nursing of the sick by fellow inmates was forbidden. Larger institutions appointed a superintendent nurse to oversee the infirmary, while those with three or more staff appointed a head nurse (responsible to the Matron); both grades had to be qualified midwives. From 1930 until 1948, when many of them became general hospitals in the new National Health Service, workhouse hospitals were under the control of county or county borough councils. See **matron, workhouse** and **nurse**.

■ Nursery maid, nursemaid

The girl who carried out household duties in the children's nursery, as well as taking the children out for walks morning and afternoon. Because she, unlike the other servants, got out of the house for several hours a week, a pretty young nursery maid flirting with the soldiers in the park was a common theme in Victorian cartoons. In 1911 she might expect a salary of about £12 a year. She did not mix with the other servants but took her meals in the nursery – she would be under the direction of a nanny or head nurse in larger houses, where the nurseries might be an extensive suite of rooms including a day nursery and night nursery, a small kitchen and the servants' accommodation. She was up at 6 am to light the fire and clean the nursery before the children were up, took the nanny her tea, made the children's breakfast and had them out of the house by 10 am. After lunch another outing was taken, then it was time for nursery tea, and afterwards to dress the children to be taken downstairs to see their parents before baths and bedtime. See also **domestic servant; nanny**.

■ Nursery nurse

A nursery nurse might work as an assistant to a qualified teacher, employed in a day nursery or crèche, a hospital, school etc, or as a **nanny** in a private house. The difference between her and the traditional nanny was that she had a college-based training and qualification.

One of the greatest early influences on this professionalisation of the role was Emily Ward (née Lord, 1850–1930), who founded the Norland Institute in London in 1892 (www.norland.co.uk). She felt strongly that nurses held a great responsibility for their charges and should be educated and trained in their work, and the rules of her college forbade corporal punishment and followed her motto: 'Love never faileth'. Those accepted on her early courses were all middle class and educated women, some of them into middle age, and this aura of being well brought up and well connected stayed with the 'Norland nannies' into the 20th century.

In 1911 the training extended over a year, starting at the Institute in Pembridge Square, London. There the girls were instructed in domestic work ('cookery, laundrywork and housewifery'), needlework (making and mending children's clothes, dressmaking), hygiene and nursery management, how to manage sick or incurable children, and how to educate children. Then they went to the Norland Nurseries for hands-on training. After six months with a family, the nurse would be awarded the Institute's certificate. Other colleges had opened by this time, including the Princess Christian Nursery Training College in Manchester in 1901. By the 1920s these trained nannies were coming to dominate employment in the home nursery.

Elsewhere, recognition of the work done by nursery nurses and assistants – in day care crèches, for instance, was slow to come. It was not until 1945, when the increased number of women working outside the home made the provision of day nurseries essential, that the National Nursery Examination Board (NNEB) was created.

See *The Rise and Fall of the British Nanny*, Jonathan Gathorne-Hardy (Hodder and Stoughton, 1972).

■ NURSERY SUPERINTENDENT

A variation on the **nanny**, a lady with a middle class background, 'educated, intelligent and refined', who could take charge of the nursery and the children's upbringing and supervise the servants, especially for families living abroad. *Cassell's Household Guide* in the 1880s suggested that 'In India especially this plan has met with warm encouragement, Indian residents being only too delighted to treat the lady as an equal, and to be relieved from the infinite anxiety of trusting native servants to the extent they are compelled to do so at present'.

■ OCCUPATIONAL THERAPIST

Dorset House, in Bristol, was the first school of occupational therapy in the UK, established by Dr Elizabeth Casson (1881–1954) and opened in 1930. Giving those unfortunate enough to be incarcerated in mental asylums jobs such as weaving or tailoring had a long history, not as a treatment but simply to keep them busy and to produce items either for sale or for use within the hospital. In America and Canada the possibilities of also using occupation as therapy to rehabilitate wounded soldiers after the First World War, giving them the ability to cope with life and to develop new skills, had been fully grasped, but progress was slower in this country.

Dorset House was originally a nursing home dealing with mental disorders, but Dr Casson realised that the use of occupational therapy would also benefit those patients suffering or recovering from physical trauma. In the 1940s trained therapists from Dorset House ran the Allendale Curative Workshop, helping wounded servicemen and women, but bombing forced the school to move to Bromsgrove, where they struggled to provide enough trained therapists for hospitals and overseas.

The Oxford Brookes University website has cine film online of 1940s treatments and training, including students (www.brookes.ac.uk/library/specialcoll/dorset.html), and details of the Dorset House Archive. For a history, see *A journey from self health to prescription ('a history of occupational therapy from the earliest times to the end of the 19th century and a source book of writings')* and *A journey from prescription to self health ('a history of occupational therapy in the United Kingdom during the 20th century and a source book of archival material')*, both by Ann Wilcock (College of Occupational Therapists, 2001 and 2002).

■ OFFICE STAFF

Until the 1880s most company offices were very small affairs and staffed by male clerks who wrote and copied every document by hand. As the commercial and banking world, and the Civil Service (see **civil servant**), continued to grow, however, there was a huge expansion in the number of office staff required and women took to this new work with enthusiasm.

Life was speeding up, with the use of the telephone and telegram becoming commonplace and this was reflected in the office. Isaac Pitman had established the first schools for shorthand in the 1870s, and the first commercial typewriters, produced by Remington, were in use by the 1880s.

Middle class women, and clever girls from a working class background who were for the first time being given access to a basic education, found secretarial work, shorthand typing, clerical and book-keeping tasks in a clean, quiet, safe environment suited them: it was the 'white blouse' revolution. This was even reflected in late Victorian/Edwardian fashion, the women dressing in ready-made suits of long skirt and tailored jacket, over a white blouse and a tie, reflecting male office wear. The office also became a place of new freedoms and new social and romantic relationships for women. Unfortunately, as male workers gave ground to women in the office, so rates of pay went down, and female staff were paid less than men right into the last quarter of the 20th century. Women would be expected to leave if they got married. See also **secretary**; **typist**.

■ OPTICIAN

An 'optician' may indicate someone who tested sight, examined eyes, and prescribed and fitted spectacles (in other words, an ophthalmologist or optometrist), or a 'dispensing optician' or 'refractionist', who provided lenses and spectacles from a prescription made out by an ophthalmologist. Miss Adaliza Dunscombe, the 30-year-old daughter of a Bristol optician, seems to have been the first woman to sit and pass the examinations in ophthalmic optics of the British Optical Association (BOA), in February 1898. She subsequently worked with her father in Bristol, as a 'refractionist and optician'. The BOA had introduced examinations three years before, in 1895, and Adaliza was only allowed to enter for them because she was a close family relative of a male member of the Association and was able to undertake the required practical training.

Spectacle-making was for centuries controlled by the Worshipful Company of Spectacle Makers in London (www.spectaclemakers.com), and in the early 19th century there were a small number of female spectacle makers – such as Maryann Holmes, widow, who carried on her late husband's business in the 1830s. During the 19th century the Company was rather sidelined by the increased industrialisation of the craft, as well as by the growth of interest amongst the medical profession in ophthalmology – Moorfields Hospital in 1807 became the first exclusively ophthalmic hospital in the world, and was followed by others opening around the country, including at Exeter, Bristol and Manchester. In the 1890s the Company introduced its own examinations for opticians, followed in 1904 by examinations for sight testing. Until the later 1950s most practising opticians had taken the examinations of one of the four examining professional bodies – the Company, the BOA, the Association of Dispensing Opticians, or the Institute of Ophthalmic Opticians.

Until 1958, theoretically, anyone could set themselves up in business as an optician; the profession was voluntarily self-regulated from 1926, but in 1958 the Opticians Act made it a legal requirement to be professionally qualified and registered. The first Opticians' Register was published in 1960; at that time there were 137 female dispensing opticians and 276 optometrists. There is a history of ophthalmology online at the Royal College of Ophthalmologists' website (www.mrcophth.com /Historyofophthalmology/ introduction.htm). The British Optical Association Museum can be visited by appointment (College of Optometrists, 42 Craven Street, London WC2N 5NG; www. college-optometrists.org).

One of the street trades followed by women, orange selling was a seasonal option.

■ ORANGE SELLER

Costermongers of the 19th century rarely dealt in oranges, nuts or lemons and the trade was rather looked down on. Oranges had been sold in the streets since

Elizabethan times – hence Nell Gwynne – and in 1607 Ben Jonson had complained of the noisiness of the 'orange-wives', on a par with 'fish-wives'. At that time the oranges were carried in a basket supported on their heads, though by Henry Mayhew's time in the mid-1800s they were often displayed on a tray supported from the shoulders. Oranges came into the country from October to August. Many of the female orange sellers were Irish. Some hawked round the streets, selling in theatres etc as well as at the door, while others went out into the suburbs. Mayhew estimated that nearly 200 million oranges were imported each year, and that 15 million were sold by the street sellers. Orange sellers might also be nut sellers (described as 'often wretched', ill-fed and poor) or lemon sellers, though lemons were not much called for by Mayhew's time (since prices had gone up because 'the law required foreign-bound ships to be provided with lemon-juice'), or flower girls. See **flower girl; street seller.**

■ PAPERMAKER

Women **workers were** engaged in certain parts of the papermaking process. The rags that formed the main constituent of paper in the 19th century had to be sorted and cut up, with all buttons or other additions removed; the women in the rag room at a paper mill stood at long tables and worked either with scissors or with a curved knife set into the table. Rag rooms were liable to be full of dust, and the smell from the old rags must have been an added unpleasantness; later machinery treated the rags before they were sorted. Other ingredients were increasingly used as demand for paper increased, such as Esparto grass, and the women picked the bales over for roots or rubbish. In the 1870s rag sorters were paid about 10s a week.

Women also worked at the rolling machines that squeezed water from the paper pulp, and in the 'sizing' room, where the paper was laid on a moving belt of felt blanket to be carried through the glaze or size, which made the finished paper resistant to ink. Once the paper was made, it was sent to other parts of the factory or to other manufacturers to be made into, for example, envelopes, writing paper, notepads etc.

There were paper mills in many counties, including Buckinghamshire, Devon, Hertfordshire, Kent, Lancashire, Yorkshire, Lanarkshire, and also in Edinburgh; they tended to be situated in the country rather than in towns. There is a history of papermaking and a glossary of terms on the website of the British Association of Paper Historians (www.baph.org.uk); and the industrial processes involved can be seen on the Confederation of Paper Industries' website (www.paper.org.uk). There are pages on paper mills and papermakers of Wales 1700–1900 at www.genuki.org. uk/big/wal/Paper.html; and on the Hertfordshire mills of John Dickinson at www.thepapertrail.org.uk. See also local studies such as *Sheffield Papermakers: Three Centuries of Papermaking in the Sheffield Area*, Tanya Schmoller (Allenholme Press, 1992) or *The Endless Web: John Dickinson & Co Ltd 1804–1954*, Joan Evans (Jonathan Cape, 1955).

■ PARISH WORKER

'A small demand exists for Parish Workers,' said *Cassell's Household Guide* in the 1880s, 'to assist clergymen of the Established Church in the secular part of their duty – Evening Classes, Mothers' Meetings, Clothing Clubs, Bible Classes for Young Women, etc. This position would be a very happy one for many a clergyman's widow or daughter, and the salary of £30 or £50 she would obtain would keep the home together, while for the want of such work it might have to be broken up.'

■ PARLOURMAID

The parlourmaid was a later Victorian invention, meant to take the place of the increasingly rare manservant. If she worked alone she might be classed as a house-parlourmaid, and have all the cleaning tasks of a **housemaid**, but in any case her duties were more responsible than those of other maids and her pay correspondingly higher (about £18 to £30 p.a. in the early 1900s).

She answered the door to callers and announced them in the drawing room ('Unless already acquired, some slight drilling is often necessary to teach an inexperienced parlourmaid how to announce visitors, etc, in a clear, distinct, yet not loud voice'); by the 1920s she also answered the telephone. She brought up afternoon tea, and cleared it away, laid the table for lunch and dinner, and waited on family and guests. ('The appearance of a parlourmaid is of considerable importance, those possessing tall, trim figures being in far greater demand than

The parlourmaid always had to be dressed smartly in case she was called to answer the front door.

short, stout individuals on account of their more graceful movements when waiting at table.') Quiet shoes – no squeaking soles – were essential, and she was to take great care of her hands and not let them be roughened by manual work. She might assist either her mistress or master with laying out their clothes. All the less menial housework was hers where a housemaid was also kept – seeing to flowers and plants, for instance – and at night she locked up the house and put out the lights.

Her dress was similar to that of a housemaid – a print dress in the morning, a black dress in the afternoon, but in the mornings she did not wear the coarse apron needed for heavy work, only a white one so that she could go to the door quickly.

■ PEN MAKER

Birmingham was the centre of the steel pen making industry, employing about 2,000 women in the late 19th century – until the 1950s most of the pen nibs in use were still made in the city. The work was done in workshops or factories: steel or brass was pressed through rollers, cut into the required sizes, pierced and ground. The nibs were then heated, oiled, coloured, varnished and dried. Women were employed particularly on the presses and on sorting, counting and packing.

The Pen Room is a museum run by the Birmingham Pen Trade Heritage Association (Unit 3, The Argent Centre, 60 Frederick Street, Birmingham B1 3HS; www.penroom.co.uk), with some of the 100,000 varieties of nibs the women worked on; it has published *A Brief History of the Birmingham Pen Trade* (2000). See http://jquarter.members.beeb.net/walk9.htm for 'a walk through Birmingham's Jewellery Quarter' with a great deal of information about the pen making industry.

■ PERCUSSION CAP MAKER

At factories in Birmingham and London in the late 1800s women were employed making sporting and military percussion caps for firearms. Strips of copper were made into the shape of the cap, smoothed, cleaned, dried and then primed, i.e. charged with the detonating mixture (which was usually mixed away from the factory for safety). Even a tiny bit of grit on the iron charging plates could cause detonation and with something like 2,000 caps being done at a time, explosions were quite common: 'it is remarkable with what sangfroid the workers regard the constant popping off of stray dozens.' See also **munitions worker**.

■ PERSONNEL OFFICER

see **welfare worker**.

■ PEW OPENER

Awoman paid a small amount to look after the cleaning of the church and the pews, to keep all in order. In the 19th century many churches still had their boxed-in pews, allocated to specific individuals or families who paid pew rent, and the pew opener would also be on duty at service time to open the door to each pew and usher in the occupants. The women often did the work for many years and are mentioned in church records and histories. In 1882 Mrs Bates, for instance, had been pew opener at King's Cross Wesleyan church for 40 years, while Mrs Joanna Mott had been pew opener at Moulsham church in Essex for 30 years when she died in 1884, aged 77.

■ PHARMACIST

Achemist's shop has always been a staple of the high street, selling medicines, cosmetics and personal items. Working behind the counter was a sought after position for young women, and in fact having a bright, attractive assistant was a positive plus in a business where female customers were unlikely to have comfortably whispered their needs to a male assistant.

In addition to these counter assistants, many Victorian women took a more active role in the preparation of medicines and prescriptions, particularly in a family concern. Wives and daughters of local doctors, too, often helped dispense medicines. The familiarity of seeing women working with drugs, however, did not immediately translate into accepting them as fully qualified pharmacists.

In 1868 the Pharmacy Act stipulated that registration with the Pharmaceutical Society was necessary for anyone 'compounding and dispensing medicines and selling certain scheduled poisons' – those currently in business, which included over 200 women running high street shops, could register straight away, but in future passing the examinations of the Society would be necessary. The register has been produced annually since 1869. Since 1815 the Society of Apothecaries had been offering a short course of study and a certificate of 'Assistant to an Apothecary' (equivalent to a Pharmacy Technician), and many women chose to follow this route into the profession, even into the 20th century, although it did not hold the same standing as qualification under the Pharmaceutical Society.

In 1873 Alice Vickery was the first woman to pass the 'minor' examination of the Pharmaceutical Society to qualify as a 'chemist and druggist' – the 'minor' examination in 'prescriptions, practical dispensing, *materia medica*, pharmacy, botany and chemistry' qualified her as assistant to a pharmacist and enabled her to register with the Society. In 1875 Isabella Clarke passed the 'major' examination, which in theory allowed her to become a member of the Society and have her own business as a 'pharmaceutical chemist', but the Society took four years before it admitted her for membership, after a great deal of rancorous debate. Nonetheless, Isabella Clarke pre-empted them and opened her own shop in London in 1876 as a 'certified pharmaceutical chemist' and offered female apprenticeships at a premium of £100. She later, in 1905, became the first President of the Association of Women Pharmacists.

By then there were 195 female registered pharmacists, just over 1% of the total number (this had increased to 10% by 1945). A pharmaceutical career became an alternative to medicine or nursing for young women with a good education. As an article in *The Queen* put it in 1905, it was 'a suitable profession for the young woman who cannot afford to spend the requisite time and money to become a doctor, and yet is not without private means'.

The Museum and Library of the Royal Pharmaceutical Society of Great Britain (1 Lambeth High Street, London SE1 7JN) has a complete run of the Register of Pharmacists, and operates a search service; the library can be visited by appointment (fees payable). Their website (www.rpsgb.org) has an online exhibition celebrating the centenary of the National Association of Women Pharmacists, with a full history and photographs, and a useful research sheet on 'Tracing people and premises in pharmacy' (www.rpsgb. org/pdfs/tracing.pdf). See also *The Pharmaceutical Industry: A Guide to Historical Records*, Lesley Richmond, Julie Stevenson and Alison Turton (Manchester University Press, 2003).

■ PHOTOGRAPHER

Many early women photographers or photographic assistants have been concealed from posterity behind a husband, father or brother whose name appeared on the studio frontage, but their involvement in the profession is being increasingly acknowledged. By the 1850s most towns of any size had one or two photographic studios in the high street, and the appeal of dressing up for a studio portrait was beginning to spread across the classes, aided by increasingly cheaper processes, once cartes de visite and cabinet prints were available from the 1860s.

One of the first women professionals was Jane Nina Wigley, who purchased a licence from Richard Beard in 1845 to allow her to use the daguerrotype process 'in Newcastle upon Tyne, Gateshead and the surrounding area'. She moved to London in 1847 (see Michael Pritchard's *Directory of London Photographers 1841–1908*, online at www.photolondon.org.uk/directory.htm.) At this time, of course, no one could have predicted the enormous advances in photography that were about to take place, and in the 1851 census, Jane gives her occupation simply as 'artist'.

The very useful lists of local photographers being compiled and, often, put online are of great help in bringing professional female photographers to light:

Taken from the back of a carte de visite: Hannah Rogerson (later Hannah Jones) had a photographic studio in Newport for about 20 years from the late 1860s.
(Maureen Jones)

see for instance Staffordshire photographers 1861–1940 at www.genuki. org.uk/big/eng/STS/Stsphots.html; or Sussex studios at www.photohistory-sussex.co.uk. Some have also been published, e.g. *Lancashire Professional Photographers 1840–1940*, Gillian Jones (PhotoResearch, 2004). See also *A History of Women Photographers*, Naomi Rosenblum (Abbeville Press, 2nd edn, 2000) and *Victorian Photographers at Work*, John Hannavy (Shire Publications) for background. The National Media Museum in Bradford has a collection relating to photography (www.nationalmediamuseum.org.uk).

Women also worked behind the scenes in high-street photographic studios, developing prints and retouching and colouring portrait photographs (before the widespread use of colour film, colour was painted onto a black and white print with a small brush). One woman who worked for a time in a photographic studio in Chelmsford in the 1930s recalled that the girls used artistic licence on eye and hair colour according to their mood.

'Photographer' was a name also applied to those who administered the early X-rays ('Röntgen rays') in about 1900.

■ PHYSIOTHERAPIST

U ntil the Second World War, those who would today be called a physiotherapist were called a **masseuse** (or masseur for the men). In 1892 the *Young Woman* told its readers: 'The demand for masseurs and masseuses is very slight at the moment. I am quite sure no one could make a livelihood by it now. Massage was a fashionable medical fad some years ago, and it has had its day. Training may be had at the West End Hospital, 75 Welbeck Street, London.'

That rather terse advice was soon out of date, as in 1894 the Society of Trained Masseuses was formed by four nurses anxious to protect the professional evolution of their service – Lucy Robinson, Rosalind Paget, Elizabeth Manley and Margaret Palmer. It was incorporated in 1900 and in 1920 was granted a royal charter. The work done with injured servicemen by the **Almeric Paget Military Massage Corps** during the First World War had shown the wide range of mental and physical conditions that could be helped by qualified masseuses. Amalgamation with the Institute of Massage and Remedial Gymnastics followed.

By the 1930s the 'fad' had become a profession, the 18-month course of training for which included 'a study of anatomy, nerves and muscles' at a school recognised by the Chartered Society of Massage and Medical Gymnastics. 'The masseuse requires to be strong, for the work makes heavy demands upon the physical energy. It is also desirable to possess a knowledge of pathology and the causes and symptoms of disease.' Qualified masseuses might be employed by hospitals or nursing homes, or in hotels, or could work in private practice.

It was during the Second World War, in 1944, that the society became the Chartered Society of Physiotherapists – and only then did the now familiar name come into general use (the Society almost chose the name 'rehabilitant' instead). Massage was just one facet of the physiotherapist's work, involving also exercise, movement and manipulation, and electrotherapy, and again the dreadful injuries of battle provided the experience that moved the profession forward – the first spinal unit was opened at Stoke Mandeville Hospital in 1944. The Massage Corps had been founded to work with the services in 1936 and became the Physiotherapy Service in 1943, with corps members serving in Europe, Africa, India, Palestine and Egypt (those who were with the Army wore the Royal Army Medical Corps badge, and shoulder flashes). Women completing their training during the war years had to volunteer for either an Army hospital in the UK or to serve overseas.

See *In Good Hands: History of the Chartered Society of Physiotherapy 1894–1994*, (ed.) J. Barclay (Butterworth Heinemann, 1994). The Society's Library and Information Service, 14 Bedford Row, London WC1R 4ED, has a list of book and journal articles, and advice for family historians (www. csp.org.uk/director/about/thecsp/history/familyhistory.cfm).

■ PICKER OF FLOWERS, FRUIT, HERBS AND VEGETABLES

Until after the Second World War, every year country women spent weeks on farms or market gardens picking local produce, earning a welcome addition to the family income. This was casual labour and there will rarely be records of individual workers, but clues to the work women in a particular area may have undertaken can be found in local histories and surveys of agriculture.

In Herefordshire, for instance, picking cider apples for Bulmers paid £1 a ton (in 20-cwt bags) in the late 1940s. In the area around Market Drayton in Staffordshire in the 1930s women picked damsons every September

Picking tulips in Kent for the London markets in the 1950s.

for the dyeing industry in Sheffield. In the 1920s the 'lady pickers' of Devon picked tons of raspberries and other soft fruits for the jam making factories, at 3s 6d a day, working from 5 am to 3 pm. Mitcham in Surrey was famed for its flower and herb farms for much of the 19th century, with acres of lavender, roses, mint, poppies, sage, rosemary and much more scenting the air – Potter and Moore were a well known local firm. At Wallington Sarah Sprules (d.1912) carried on her father's growing and distillery business and was 'Purveyor of Lavender Essence to the Queen'. Some of these industries are well documented and will be included in local museum collections: e.g. see *The Story of Lavender*, Sally Festing (London Borough of Sutton, 1982).

■ PIN MAKER

Unlike **needlemaking, which** by the late 19th century was still a labour-intensive industry, pin making had been simplified in 1824 by the invention of the Wright pin machine. Whereas it once took 14 people to make a pin, now one woman could supervise the operation of three or four machines, the wire being fed in at one end and the complete pin emerging at the other at the rate of between 80 and 150 a minute (although in some factories women were still employed at mid-century fixing the heads onto pins, making from 12,000 to 15,000 pins a day). In the 1870s, pin factories were to be found mainly in Birmingham, and also in Stroud, Warrington, Bristol and Redditch.

'Pins' included hairpins and hatpins, and there was a strong hatpin making industry at Gloucester in the earlier 1800s; see the website of the Hatpin Society (www.hatpinsociety.org.uk/history.html) for more about the background. The industry is mentioned in local histories, such as *Warrington at Work*, Janice Hayes (Breedon Books, 2003).

■ POLICEWOMAN

Before the First World War, female involvement in the police forces throughout the country was restricted to an occasional quasi-official role in searching and supervising female and child suspects and criminals (see **matron, police; searcher**). This was often done by the wives or widows of police officers – marrying a police constable meant marrying the force, and especially in rural areas the policeman's wife acted as an unpaid helper to her husband.

The First World War brought women volunteers under the police umbrella for the first time, in response to a call by the Chief Commissioner of the Metropolitan Police. There were two main groups involved. One was organised by the National Union of Women Workers, the other was formed by Margaret Damer Dawson and Mary Allen and named initially the Women Police Volunteers, renamed the Women Police Service (WPS) in February 1915. By the end of the war there were hundreds of female police volunteers in cities and ports around the country; they were not sworn-in members of the constabulary and had no powers of arrest. They were used mostly in a welfare role, concerned with the problems of women,

Anything involving women or children was seen as the natural responsibility of a policewoman: here shepherding evacuees onto a train during the Second World War.

children, refugees and prostitutes. Occasionally there was something a little more exciting – in 1916 the Admiralty used a WPS volunteer to infiltrate the naval base at Scapa Flow to investigate claims of drug abuse and spying. Only in Grantham, which had a persistent problem with disorder and prostitution arising from the large army camp, were women sworn-in to the local force during the war, Mary Allen, Ellen Harburn and Edith Smith being the first 'official' women police constables. The WPS, in particular, was not universally popular and, in 1918, when recruitment began for policewomen to join the Metropolitan Police Force, Chief Commissioner Macready declined to make them a permanent part of the Met.

Regional police forces were not quick to employ policewomen – in Hertfordshire Annie and Margaret Johnson were the first, posted to Watford in 1928, and remained the only examples until 1941. The county's Chief Constable had in 1923 noted his reasons for objecting to women in the force. They included the lack of toilet facilities in stations, that women would be liable to talk too freely about their work and were not amenable to discipline, and that time spent training them would be wasted when they left to get married, as they inevitably would. In 1920, when the Baird Committee reported, some 43 police authorities in England and Wales were employing women constables, but by 1931 there were still 88 towns without a single policewoman. Essex was to be the last county force to recruit women, after the Second World War.

An applicant to the Met in 1934 would have to be single or widowed, aged between 24 and 35, and sit an examination in English, arithmetic, geography, general knowledge and 'intelligence'. Tests included writing a description of 'The attractions of a public park with which you are acquainted', and an essay on 'Street merchants and their ways'. Pay began at £3 16s a week. The whole question of what a policewoman was actually for was still perplexing the authorities and most senior officers thought they should only be employed on 'matters concerning their own sex'.

War in 1939 once again created a demand to fill posts left vacant as men went into the services, and the Women's Auxiliary Police Corps (WAPC) came into being for the duration. In that year there were 246 permanent women officers and by 1949 the number had quadrupled and the Police Federation was admitting them as members, albeit grudgingly. An account of a policewoman's life in Hereford in the 1940s is in *Herefordshire Within Living Memory*, Herefordshire Federation of WIs (Countryside Books, 1993); the first time women were taken into the force there was in 1941, under the WAPC. They were untrained and used as drivers, escorts and telephonists, but after the war three women stayed on to join the force.

My Ancestor Was a Policeman, Antony Shearman (Society of Genealogists, 2000) is a good place to start finding your way around the records of different forces and police authorities, although records for women will not start to appear until at least the 1920s. The history of the development of Scottish police forces and advice on research is online at www.scan.org.uk/familyhistory/myancestor/policeman.htm. *The British Policewoman*, Joan Lock (Robert Hale, 1979) tells the background story. The Imperial War Museum collections include material on First World War volunteers (www.iwm.org.uk), and the National Police Library (Centrex, Bramshill, Hook, Hampshire RG27 0JW; www.centrex.police.uk/business/police_library.html) may be able to help with publications.

■ POLITICIAN

Fifty years before women got the parliamentary franchise, in 1869, they were granted the borough vote, provided they were unmarried or widowed and had the equivalent rateable property qualification as men; by 1900 over a million women were eligible to vote in local elections. Not only that, but women became eligible to stand for election too and this 'domestic politics' was sometimes compared to an extension of women's natural duties in the spheres of education, poor law (workhouses and hospitals), public health and so on.

But it was politics for all that, and women who stood for election to school boards (from 1870), poor law boards of guardians (from 1875), parish councils (from 1894) and borough and county councils (from 1907) had to work within the political system and learn to canvass votes, organise their supporters, talk to public and press, and be accountable to the people who voted for them. Many of the women came from philanthropic backgrounds and used the system as an extension of the traditional duty of the better off to care for the poor, while others had a more purely political agenda and saw this as a route into trade union or parliamentary politics, allied to the suffragette cause that was to eventually come to the boil in the 1910s.

The influence exerted by female politicians should not be downplayed. As an active member of a local board they could play a direct role in the development of services that affected every resident's life, particularly schools, hospitals, workhouses, adoption and the care of children, clean water and better sanitary facilities. The first woman to be elected to a school board in London was Elizabeth Garrett (see **doctor**), following the passing of the Elementary Education Act in 1870, with three times more votes than her nearest male rival. And within 30 years there were women serving on school boards in every major town. Miss Martha Merrington was the first woman elected onto a poor law board, in 1875 in London, and again there was a rapid spread of female guardians.

Some of the women who stood for election to borough and county councils after 1907 used their experience as a springboard to Parliament. The parliamentary vote was extended to women over the age of 30 after the First World War, and the first woman MP to take her place in the House of Commons in 1919 was Lady Nancy Astor (1879–1964), who kept her seat for the Sutton division of Plymouth until 1945. Perhaps more representative of the women referred to above was Arabella Susan Lawrence (1871–1947), a solicitor's daughter, who was MP for North East Ham 1923–1924 and 1926–1931. She was a member of the London County Council (Poplar) from 1913 to 1927 and of Poplar Borough Council from 1919 to 1924, a member of the National Executive of the Labour Party, the Parliamentary Secretary Ministry of Health 1929–1931, and contested elections at East Ham, Camberwell and Stockton-on-Tees; she was also organiser for the

National Federation of Women Workers 1912–1921. From the late 1920s about 20 to 30 women were returned to Parliament at every election.

Local archives are the best source for background material on the women who served at local government level. In the first instance, a Kelly's Directory or similar is a good place to find lists of council and committee members: in 1937 in Southend-on-Sea, for instance, Mrs Constance Leyland of 17 Cotswold Road, Westcliff-on-Sea was serving for Milton Ward, while Mrs Harvey of 171 West Road, Southend was elected for All Saints Ward.

The *Who's Who of British Members of Parliament* in 4 volumes from 1832–1974, edited by M. Stenton and S. Lees (Harvester Press), or the far more detailed *History of Parliament* in 23 volumes published between 1965 and 1992 (now available in some archives and libraries on CD), give biographical information on MPs. For information about Parliament's own archives, see www.parliament.uk/parliamentary_publications_and_archives/ parliamentary_archives.cfm.

■ PORTERESS

Another name for an assistant matron in a workhouse. See **matron, workhouse**.

■ POST OFFICE

The **General Post** Office (GPO) was one of the few organisations to offer opportunities for employment to women from its earliest days, admittedly limited until the 20th century but still a source of pensionable and secure work that could be performed by intelligent women and girls. Its terms and conditions of work were those of the Civil Service. All applicants had to be single or widowed, and employment was terminated on marriage.

Postwomen: there were a few women employed as 'letter carriers', as postmen were called until 1883, when the parcel post started. One was Ann Carter, who, until she died in 1835, aged 77, delivered letters around Great Yarmouth, 'fortified by a glass of gin and with spectacles on her nose', according to the *Post Office Magazine* of 1937. She also had to collect money, as there were at that time no postage stamps and letters had to be paid for on delivery.

A surge in employment came nearly a century later during the First World War, when by 1915 women were replacing postmen called up for military service. For the first time they had a specific uniform, of a blue serge skirt and jacket and a blue straw hat with a detachable waterproof covering. The number of postal deliveries each day during the late 19th and early 20th centuries seems now quite utopian – in towns and cities there could be up to ten deliveries a day to homes and businesses, while in the suburbs that figure might drop to four a day; in rural areas it would of course be normally only one or two, particularly when in some areas postmen and women needed a whole day to get to all parts of their round.

Postmistress, sub-postmistress: postmistresses were full time, salaried staff, employed by the GPO to oversee mail distribution and take control of a designated post office. The first postmistress of Salcombe in Devon was Mrs Sarah (Sally) Stone, appointed in 1821 at a salary of £5 per annum, rising to £10, but there were few women in this position. By the 1880s they were paid from 14 shillings to 24 shillings a week.

Sub-postmistresses, on the other hand, were normally not employees but were paid according to the work they generated and they usually had another business, such as a village shop. They started simply as letter receivers, the shop being a convenient place for people to call in to leave their mail to be collected and sent; in later years the services they could offer increased, including savings, money orders, telephones and telegrams, and they became an indispensable cog in the local economy. Local trade directories are useful sources of information about these women and their businesses. White's 1874 directory for Suffolk, for instance, lists details for the village of Barrow, six miles west of Bury St Edmunds: 'Post Office at Mrs. M. Watson's. Letters arrive at 8.30 am from, and are despatched at 5 pm to Bury St Edmunds, which is the nearest Money Order Office.' Maria Watson was 'grocer, draper and postmistress, and agent for Liverpool and London and Globe Insurance Company'.

Post Office Savings Bank: clerkships in the Savings Bank (started in 1861 and by the 1880s handling accounts worth nearly £50 million) were considered amongst the best appointments for young women between 16 and 30 years of age, according to *Cassell's Household Guide*; second class clerks receiving from £40 to £75 a year, first class clerks £80 to £100, 'while principal and head-clerks get as much as from £110 to £150 yearly'. The examination for the Civil Service Commission included 'writing and orthography, grammar and composition, arithmetic, including both vulgar and decimal fractions, and geography'.

clerks, typists, and sorters were employed in large general post offices and in the cities. In 1892 the *Young Woman* advised its readers: 'The pay of post office female clerks begins at £65, and rises by £3 annually, till it reaches £100. Beyond that, special salaries reach £400 per annum sometimes, but £65 to £100 is the average. Each official is entitled to a Government pension when her term of service is over. Clerks are accorded a month's holiday in the year, and all Bank holidays. The subjects for the entrance examination do not cover a wide range, but competition is very keen, as there are usually four times as many candidates as vacancies, which the best qualified secure. Candidates for examination must not be under eighteen years of age. Female sorters enter the post office from fifteen years, and it is not very unusual for a sorter to qualify for a clerkship; but the combined work and study are too much for the strength of most girls, and therefore not to be advised.'

The telephone and telegraph services were open to women and some may have spent part of their working lives on the postal side and part in telecommunications. An example was Mrs Louisa Massey, who succeeded her father as sub-postmaster of Stonehouse, Plymouth and was later appointed a sorting clerk and telegraphist. As such she was salaried and entitled when she retired in 1897 to a government pension – which she was still collecting at the age of 100 in 1937.

The best place to start researching a postal ancestor is the British Postal Museum and Archive (Freeling House, Phoenix Place, London WC1 0DL; http://postalheritage.org.uk). The archives include employment records such as appointment books and details of pensions and gratuities (e.g. the marriage gratuity paid to women who left to get married). They also have a photograph collection. *Getting the Message: The Story of the British Post Office* by Christopher Browne (Alan Sutton, 1993) is a good general history. See **telegraphist** and **telephonist**.

■ POTTERY WORKER

In England the heart of the Potteries lay in north Staffordshire, in the area around the towns of Stoke-on-Trent, Burslem, Tunstall, Newcastle under

Lyne, Hanley, Shelton, Etruria, Longton, Cobridge etc, but there were also potteries, major and minor, in many other counties, such as Kent, Suffolk, Durham, Surrey, Sussex, Worcestershire, Yorkshire and London. The industry had come to prominence during the 18th century and many of the manufacturers are still household names – Minton, Copeland, Davenport, Wedgwood etc in Staffordshire, Coalport in Shropshire, Worcester in Worcestershire, Doulton in Lambeth, to name but a few. In 1871 there were nearly 16,000 female workers in the earthenware trade, the great majority of them in Staffordshire.

Women had certain jobs in the manufacturing process. A female 'baller' or 'handler' cut clay into pieces and weighed them ready to be handed to the potter to be thrown on the wheel. Before steam power, a girl was often employed to keep the potter's wheel turning, and another to take the piece off when it had been thrown. A turner, who operated on clay in much the same way as a turner of wood, also had a female assistant to hand him the clay and take away finished pieces. When the wares were dried and fired, they had to be sorted and stacked in warehouses, often women's work.

Now, if it was to be decorated the piece went to the printers. Women and young girls were employed in this department, as 'transferrers' and paper-cutters. In the 1880s at Minton's factory for instance, printing under the glaze was done with designs engraved upon copper plate. The women had to work quickly, transferring the design first to a piece of paper and then to the ware, which absorbed the colour – 'The work requires some little neatness of hand and quick rubbing down with a flannel roll. . . . Immediately the paper is washed off, leaving the design on the biscuit (ware) from which it will not wash off on account of its oily character.' The oil was got rid of by baking the ware, which then went to be dipped in glaze and fired again. If there was going to be overglaze work added, it was sent on to the painting department, where the women were 'of a much higher and more talented grade'.

These were all 'work women', not artists, merely filling in colours according to the design marked out for them. The work needed attention and neatness, but no particular skill in drawing or inventiveness. The 'artists' were those who hand-painted original designs. In 1876 an artist designer received pay of between £3 and £6 a week, while a female painter received 10–14 shillings, and a stenciller 21–23 shillings.

After this, the remaining areas in which women were employed were gilding, burnishing and scouring. The gilders completed the decoration before firing, and the gold had to be burnished using bloodstone or agate burnishers to bring out the brightness. Scouring with sandpaper to remove any trace of roughness was particularly injurious to health because the fine dust that came from the china was actually fine flint powder and a major cause of lung disease.

There are a multitude of books and websites about the individual pottery companies, their products and the famous artists and designers who worked for them. For an introduction to 'Clarice Cliff and her contemporaries', for instance, see the online exhibition at www.stoke.gov.uk/ccm/museums. *The Potteries*, David Sekers (Shire Publications) gives some background to the area. For Scottish potteries, the website of the Scottish Pottery Society (www.scottishpotterysociety.co.uk) has many links and bibliographies for the factories. The website www.thepotteries.org/jobs/index.htm has an alphabetical list of specific occupations and much more on methods of work, biographies and history, plus a family history index.

▪ PRINCESS MARY'S ROYAL AIR FORCE NURSING SERVICE (PMRAFNS)

The decision to create a nursing service for the newly formed Royal Air Force was taken early in 1918, to replace Army nursing sisters. It was to be run along the same lines as the Queen Alexandra's Imperial Military Nursing Service, but with sisters appointed on short-term contracts. By 1919 there were 130 qualified nurses in place. In line with post-war economies, when the RAF was reduced to a shadow of its wartime strength, the amalgamation of the service with QAIMNS was considered, but it was allowed to continue as a permanent service and in 1923 was renamed Princess Mary's RAF Nursing Service, under royal patronage – Princess Mary also equipped the RAF hospital at Halton.

On joining, a new recruit was sent to Halton or, after 1939, Ely or Wroughton, for instruction in service discipline and etiquette, though they remained specifically nurses rather than officers, and then drafted to an RAF hospital. The only overseas postings in the inter-war years were to Aden and Iraq, though during the Second World War they served in all fields of combat, including Burma, manning mobile field hospitals which moved up behind the lines as soon as airfields were in operation, casualties frequently being evacuated by air – in June 1944 they brought some 300,000 'casevacs' out following the D-Day landings.

The sisters held honorary military rank from the beginning, but after March 1943 held commissions, and wore the same badges of rank as men (on the shoulder of the cape, just as a male officer would wear it on his greatcoat). Their uniform was distinct from that of WAAF officers, with white shirt blouses and collars, and a black felt hat with four corners, the officer's hat badge worn at the front. On 1 February 1949 they were integrated into the RAF.

Equivalent ranks (RAF in brackets): Matron-in-Chief (Air Commodore), Chief Principal Matron (Group Captain), Principal Matron (Wing Commander), Matron (Squadron Leader), Senior Sister (Flight Lieutenant), Sister (Flying Officer).

There are no personnel records at The National Archives (apart from some relating to the very first intake in 1918/1919; see their leaflet 'Royal Air Force: Nurses and Nursing Services'), as these remain with the RAF (write to PMA (CS) 2a2, Building 248A, HQ RAF PTC, RAF Innsworth, Gloucestershire GL3 1EZ). See the website of the Royal Air Force Museum at Hendon (www.rafmuseum.org.uk) for information and history; and the website of the service (www.pmrafns.org) for history and photographs.

■ 'PRINCIPAL BOY'

During the Victorian period pantomime grew to be a hugely popular form of Christmas entertainment, so that by the late 19th century productions were lavish and intended for adult entertainment rather than for children. Early pantos were mostly vehicles for male performers, but the fairies were always female (see **ballet dancer**) and, from the 1800s, so was the 'principal boy', although the length of her skirts really began to rise only after the 1860s. The first principal boy may have made an appearance sometime in the early 1800s, although a Miss Ellington who appeared as the Prince in *The Good Woman* in 1852 at the Lyceum theatre 'has the strongest claim to be honoured as the first actual principal boy of pantomime' (*Pantomime Pageant*, A.E. Wilson, 1940s). Mr Wilson also described Harriett Vernon, a later and popular star of pantomime, who was 'a handsome, statuesque creature with a fine, ample presence and she was a sight for the gods when she took the stage, jewelled stick in hand and decked out with diamonds and ostrich plumes'. See **actress** for sources.

■ PRINTER, PUBLISHER

Women can be found running small printing businesses throughout the mid-19th and early 20th century, such as Harriett Welsford in Exeter in 1851, who was recorded as a printer employing two apprentices. She would probably have been a jobbing printer, producing letterheads, business stationery, fliers, posters, booklets etc.

Printers' offices tended to be badly ventilated and overcrowded, and the work highly pressurised, particularly in the newspaper and book trade, but women were finding work in the industry, particularly as readers, who corrected proofs for the press, and compositors. This latter was a skilled job in the printing trade, in the early days setting up the press by hand, inserting each letter of type individually by lines into frames to make up the pages. It required the ability to read upside down and right to left. From the 1920s machines took over the setting; they acted like a typewriter that the compositor tapped to put each letter into a mould, which was then filled with molten lead. When set, the blocks of type were put onto the bed of the press and inked, the paper pressed down firmly and the printed sheets peeled off. A disadvantage for women was that the Factory Acts prohibited night working, which was a necessity in many large companies, particularly newspapers. Books, magazines and newspapers then had to be collated, folded, sewn and bound (see **bookbinder**).

One woman who had an impact on the female printing and publishing trade was Emily Faithfull (1835–1895). In an interview in 1894 she recalled that she 'collected a band of women compositors in 1859 and started a regular typographic establishment' – this was the Victoria Press in London, which published the *English Woman's Journal* and, from 1863, the *Victoria Magazine*. In 1862 she was appointed Publisher and Printer-in-Ordinary to Queen Victoria. Her firm employed only women, except for machine hands. In the 1890s the Women's Printing Society Ltd at 21 Great College Street, Westminster was employing women as compositors, as were several large printing houses such as Messrs Hazell, Watson & Viney. Firms in Glasgow and Edinburgh also employed a considerable number. Fanny MacPherson, who was taken on as a compositor with other women in 1871 by the publishers R. & R. Clark of Edinburgh after a strike by the male staff, stayed with the company for the next 60 years!

Emily Faithfull's Victoria Press employed an all-woman staff of compositors from the 1860s.

From 1799, when the government was in the grip of fear following the French Revolution, all printing presses had had to be licensed by local magistrates in Quarter Sessions, so that records may exist locally of small businesses (after 1888 county councils took over the responsibility); local trade directories will also often be a good source of information. The St Bride Printing Library (Bride Lane, Fleet Street, London EC4Y 8EE; www. stbride.org/library) has a huge collection of books and archives relating to printing companies, though you would need to have an idea of the identity of the company you were interested in. Local museums may also have examples of the equipment used in the 19th and early 20th centuries: for instance, there is a collection of old printing presses at the Cockermouth Museum of Printing, 102 Main Street, Cockermouth CA13 9LX (www. visitcumbria.com/cm/printmuseum.htm).

■ PRISON STAFF

Nowadays a prison matron is concerned with prisoners' health but, in the 19th century, she was the chief female officer in the prison, or in charge of a women's prison. She should possess 'great judgement, sympathy and tact, not only because she has the care and superintendence of the prisoners, but also because the warders, servants, and all the female officials are under her charge, and she is responsible for the working and safe keeping of all beneath her sway'.

A matronship was seen as 'an excellent opening for educated women' in the 1880s (*Cassell's Household Magazine*): 'Matrons are elected by the magistrates in Quarter Sessions, or by a committee appointed by them; and the selection of the applicant is afterwards confirmed by the magistrates, in Quarter Sessions. In government convict prisons these appointments are made by the directors. The salaries vary in almost every prison, and pensions, or gratuities for length of service, are granted. Women of high principle and deep religious feeling are desired who unite kindness and firmness and have a great love of order, and a good judgement. The matron's salary varies from £100 per annum to £175, generally with furnished lodging, coals, gas and washing.' In 1881, the matron at Lincoln HM Prison was Ellen McGeoch, an unmarried woman of 42.

Just a few years before, in 1877, prisons had been brought under the central control of the Prison Commission (later, Prison Department) and this was a period when many smaller gaols were closed in favour of larger, purpose-built prisons. In 1919 prison warders, and wardesses, were renamed prison officers.

Finding the records of prison staff will depend on what has survived from the prison itself, often held now by the local record office. Search under the prison name at A2A (www.nationalarchives.gov.uk/a2a) and The National Archives' catalogue (www.nationalarchives.gov.uk). The Lincoln Prison matron's journals 1848–1878, for instance, are at Lincolnshire Archives. The Prison Service Museum and Collection is at the Galleries of Justice, High Pavement, Lace Market, Nottingham NG1 1HN (www.galleriesofjustice.org.uk). For background, try *Victorian and Edwardian Prisons*, Trevor May (Shire Publications, 2006), or *Prison Life in Victorian England*, Michelle Higgs (Tempus, 2007).

■ PUBLICAN, INNKEEPER

There can be few female publicans who could match the record of Margaret Tate, proprietress of the Boot and Shoe Inn at Ullerton, near

MRS. M. PRINCE,
Chairman, Birkenhead & District
Women's Licensed Trade Defence
Association.

MRS. H. BARNINGHAM,
President, Cambridge Licensed
Trade, Ladies' Auxiliary.

MRS. E. BEARD,
Hon. Secretary, Chester & District
Women's Licensed Trade Defence
Association.

MRS. L. K. KEEL,
Chairman, Eckington, Dronfield &
District Branch (Notts District)
Women's Licensed Trade Defence
Association.

MRS. S. E. EARNSHAW,
Vice-Chairman, Eckington, Dron-
field & District Branch (Notts Dist.)
Women's Licensed Trade Defence
Association.

MRS. N. GILLING,
Treasurer, Eckington, Dronfield &
District Branch (Notts & District)
Women's Licensed Trade Defence
Association.

MRS. M. WILLOUGHBY,
Secretary, Eckington, Dronfield &
District Branch (Notts District)
Women's Licensed Trade Defence
Association.

MRS. H. HARTLAND,
Chairman, Folkestone Women's
Auxiliary (Licensed Trade).

MRS. M. R. DONALD,
Secretary, Folkestone Women's
Auxiliary (Licensed Trade).

*Women publicans who belonged to the Women's Auxiliary
League of the Licensed Victuallers Association 1939–40.*

Selby, who died in 1910. As reported in the *Lancaster Mail*, 'The inn has been in her family for 300 years. Her father was 90 when he died. Mrs Tate was born in the house, and never slept a night away from home. It is the only public house in the village.' Many pubs were run by women, who often took over the licence on the death of their husband or father, subject to the consent of the local magistrates at licensing sessions. The terms 'inn' and 'public house' are roughly interchangeable today but an inn was legally defined as 'for the reception of travellers' and an innkeeper would be obliged to provide beds for them. The landlady of a public house, however, was under no such obligation and would only provide drink (and perhaps food) within normal licensing hours. See also **beerhouse keeper; hotel keeper.**

Because publicans had to apply for a licence, records can often be found at local record offices; see the finding aid *Victuallers' Licences*, Jeremy Gibson and Judith Hunter (Federation of Family History Societies, 1997). Sometimes a licence was refused or revoked, in which case it was often reported in the local newspaper, even if it was a small village pub. See also *Researching Brewery and Publican Ancestors*, Simon Fowler (Federation of Family History Societies, 2003), and his website (www.sfowler.force9.co.uk/page_12.htm) for pages about the history of pubs and tracing ancestors.

■ QUEEN ALEXANDRA'S IMPERIAL MILITARY NURSING SERVICE (QAIMNS)

The acorn that grew into the oak of the army nursing service was the arrival of 40 nurses in the Crimea in 1854, one of whom was Florence Nightingale. Wounded soldiers from the battlefields were in some cases brought back to Chatham, which was the first hospital to have nursing sisters in the wards. By 1861, six nurses and a superintendent had been employed at Woolwich and Netley by the Army Hospital Corps, and in 1881 the Army Nursing Service was formed. Three years later the regulations for a Female Nursing Service were laid down, to be followed in hospitals at Aldershot, Gosport, Portsmouth, Devonport, Dover, Shorncliffe, Canterbury, the Curragh in Ireland, Malta and Gibraltar. Army orders issued in 1889 required that sisters be employed in all military hospitals with more than 100 beds.

The sisters were to be responsible for administration and supervision on the wards and for training the male nursing assistants. Their uniform was the soon familiar grey dress and scarlet shoulder cape (exchanged for khaki during the Second World War), which led to them being known as the 'Ladies in Grey'. In 1897 the Reserve Service was formed and during the South African War of 1899–1902 some 1,400 nurses were sent to the Cape – they were awarded the Queen's and King's South African Medal and their names will appear on the Medal Rolls at The National Archives. In 1902, under the patronage of the Queen, the name of the service was changed to Queen Alexandra's Imperial Military Nursing Service.

For a woman who liked to travel and to enjoy a certain status (and earn more than her civilian counterparts), becoming a QAIMNS nurse in peacetime was extremely attractive. In 1911, before being accepted by the War Office, a nurse had to have served at least three years in a civil hospital with more than 100 beds. Once in the service, she could expect to be posted abroad – Egypt, Gibraltar, Malta, South Africa or Hong Kong – for a period of three to five years. Applicants for the post of staff nurse (between 25 and 35 years of age) were assessed at the end of six months and, if satisfactory, put on the establishment. A staff nurse in

1911 started at £40 per year, rising to £45, with generous allowances for board, fuel, uniform etc. A sister could expect a salary of between £50 and £65; a matron £75 to £150; a principal matron £175 to £205, and the matron-in-chief £305 to £350. They received a pension on retirement at age 55, or after ten years' service if they were rendered unfit for duty through illness or injury.

With the outbreak of war in 1914 the service was merged with the Territorial Force Nursing Service (TFNS). There had been only about 300 nurses in the QAIMNS pre-1914 but over 2,000 were quickly brought in from the Reserve. Just under 200 QAIMNS nurses died during the First World War, 36 of them drowned or killed in action.

Then it was back to peacetime nursing after demobilisation. In 1926 the service was amalgamated with Queen Alexandra's Military Nursing Service for India, and the following year absorbed Queen Alexandra's Military Families Nursing Service, so that now nurses might find themselves caring for not only soldiers, but also their families. There were military hospitals all over the country, including Queen Alexandra's Military Hospital at Millbank, London; the Cambridge Hospital, Aldershot; the Royal Herbert Hospital, Woolwich; the Royal Victoria Hospital, Netley; and Tidworth Military Hospital, as well as smaller family hospitals. Abroad, nurses might be sent to serve in China, India, Burma, Egypt, the Sudan, Malta or Gibraltar.

Since the beginning of the service, the sisters had had the status of officers, and in 1926 they were granted relative rank in King's Regulations. In 1940 they were authorised to wear relative rank badges, and the following year were recognised as commissioned officers of the armed forces, with equivalent rank as Army officers – so that they should salute and be saluted within mixed units.

With the outbreak of war again in 1939, the QAIMNS was merged with the Territorial Army Nursing Service 'for the duration', and served in all theatres of war over the next five years, culminating with the British Army of Liberation (later the Army of the Rhine). In 1949 the name of the service was changed, bearing in mind the demise of the British Empire, to Queen Alexandra's Royal Army Nursing Corps (QARANC).

Equivalent ranks (Army ranks in brackets): Matron-in-Chief (Brigadier), Chief Principal Matron (Colonel), Principal Matron (Lt-Colonel), Matron (Major), Sister with 10 years' service (Captain), Sister (1st Lieutenant).

The official website (www.qaranc.co.uk) has pages on history and information on nurses and hospitals. The National Archives' research guide 'British Army: Nursing and Nursing Services' also has a full history and information about the service records it holds. For nurses of the Second World War it will be necessary to contact the Ministry of Defence, Army Personnel Centre, Historical Disclosures, Mailpoint 400, Kentigern House, 65 Brown Street, Glasgow G2 8EX (telephone: 0141 224 3030; email: disc4. civsec@apc.army.mod.uk); records are only released to next of kin and there

Nurses on their way from Boulogne to pick up wounded soldiers being brought back from the trenches, during the First World War.

is a fee. See *Queen Alexandra's Royal Army Nursing Corps*, Juliet Piggott (Pen and Sword, 1975), or *Sisters in Arms: British Army Nurses Tell Their Story*, Nicola Tyrer (Weidenfeld and Nicholson, 2008). The QARANC museum is at the Army Medical Services Museum, Keogh Barracks, Ash Vale, Aldershot GU12 5RQ (www.ams-museum.org.uk).

■ QUEEN ALEXANDRA'S ROYAL ARMY NURSING CORPS (QARANC)

see Queen Alexandra's Imperial Military Nursing Service (QAIMNS).

■ QUEEN ALEXANDRA'S ROYAL NAVAL NURSING SERVICE (QARNNS)

The sick men of the Royal Navy were nursed by, mainly, untrained sailors' widows or male naval pensioners until the late 19th century, when the innovations begun in the Army nursing service provoked a similar reaction in the Senior Service. During the Crimean War, in 1854, six nurses had been taken out to the naval hospital at Therapia, near Constantinople, by Mrs Eliza Mackenzie, and much as Florence Nightingale's experiences influenced Army nursing, so Mrs Mackenzie's sisters were the pioneers of the Naval Nursing Service. In 1884 six sisters and four head nurses, under a matron, were appointed for the first time at the Royal Hospital for Sick and Hurt Seamen at Haslar, near Portsmouth, as Naval Nursing Sisters, and five started work at Plymouth.

The sisters were to supervise the nursing of injured and sick seamen, and to train the male sick berth attendants who assisted them. They did little hands-on nursing themselves, and apparently efforts were made to protect them from embarrassment at the display of the male body by shielding all except the patient's head, shoulders and feet from view – a Victorian nicety that would not survive long.

The uniform at first was a navy blue dress (replaced in summer by a blue skirt and white blouse) covered by a white apron, with a blue shoulder-cape and a white cap with frills and strings. Their badge was an Imperial crown with a double 'AA' (for Alexandra), over a naval anchor, with a red cross in a gold circle beneath, all on a black background. This stayed the same, but the uniform was changed after 1902 with red cuffs added to the blue dress and the frilled cap replaced by a white 'handkerchief' cap with a naval crown in the corner. The dress was also now linen, rather than the heavier serge used earlier.

In 1902 the service was renamed as Queen Alexandra's Royal Naval Nursing Service, in honour of its president. Applicants had to be trained nurses, between 25 and 48 years of age. Rates of pay in 1911 were £30 to £50 per annum for sisters, with varying rates for head sisters at each hospital – e.g. £40 to £60 at Chatham, £105 to £130 at Plymouth, £125 to £160 at Haslar. The nurses remained civilians and were never subject to naval discipline. At the end of their service they were eligible for a pension.

The QARNNS Reserve was first formed in 1910, creating a pool of nurses from civilian hospitals who were called on for service once the First World War started in 1914, and the much augmented QARNNS nurses served throughout the war. While only about 80 sisters remained on the strength in the inter-war years, the reserve again greatly expanded with the Second World War. Outside the UK the only naval hospitals were in Hong Kong and Malta, and the sisters in Malta endured the air bombardment that led to the whole island being awarded the George Cross for its endurance and courage.

In 1949, when a Medical Branch of the **Women's Royal Naval Service** was formed, female sick berth attendants were brought in for training, while women who had served as VADs were allowed to join a new QARNNS Auxiliary Branch as Naval Nurse ratings if they wished.

The QARNNS' official website (www.qarnns.co.uk) tells the story of the service.

■ QUEEN MARY'S ARMY AUXILIARY CORPS

see **Women's Army Auxiliary Corps.**

■ RAILWAY WORKER

Initially, **female railway** staff worked as either **telegraphists**, from the 1850s, or clerks. The first clerks seem to have been employed at King's Cross station in London in 1900. However, there were soon instances of women doing more responsible work – for instance as stationmistresses at Langford in Essex and Rosemount in Scotland, in 1906, or running the entire station, from selling tickets to changing the signals, as Elizabeth Davidson was doing at Dovenby. By 1911 there were over 3,000 women working for railway companies – office and booking clerks, ticket examiners and collectors – and this number had trebled by 1914. In the ensuing war years the staff shortages caused by men going into the services could only be filled by employing women in all station posts, including as porters, engine cleaners and labourers. Over 68,000 women were working in the railway industry by 1918. After the war many left, but there were still 9,000 by 1927. With the coming of the Second World War, women again appeared on stations and in signalboxes.

The records of the many railway companies of the 19th and 20th centuries are covered in the useful booklet *Was Your Grandfather a Railwayman?: A Directory of Railway Archive Sources for Family Historians,* Tom Richards (Federation of Family History Societies, 2002) – despite the title, female staff are included – and *Railway Records: A Guide to Sources,* Cliff Edwards (Public Record Office, 2001). The website of the Transport Salaried Staffs Association (www.tssa.org.uk) has a background article on 'RCA women and the railway industry'; see also *Railwaywomen: Exploitation, Betrayal and Triumph in the Workplace,* Helena Wojtczak (Hastings Press, 2005).

Company staff registers from four major railway companies, 1869 to early 1900s, are searchable online at the website of the Cheshire and Chester Archives (www.cheshire.gov.uk/recordoffice/railways/home.htm). The National Railway Museum, Leeman Road, York YO26 4XJ (www. nrm.org.uk) has a huge range of records and memorabilia. In both wars women were employed by railway companies to serve with the British Transport Police and there are photographs and background information on their website (www.btp.police.uk).

R

◼ REFRACTIONIST

see **optician**.

◼ REGISTRAR OF BIRTHS AND DEATHS

By 1910 there were some 130 women employed as registrars of births and deaths – the most famous must be Mrs Emmeline Pankhurst, who became registrar in Rusholme, Manchester, in 1898 after the death of her husband, and remained in the post until 1907.

The main part of the work was the registration of births and deaths, copies of which were forwarded to the Registrar General each quarter: an accurate knowledge of the boundaries of the sub-district was essential, and a willingness to 'adopt some measures by which knowledge can be gained of births and deaths in the sub-district – this is usually done by study of the local newspapers, and by inquiries of doctors, midwives, and people who come to give information of the births and deaths of their relatives'. In census years, enumerators would have to be appointed and their work supervised.

Registrars were appointed by the local board of guardians and were not paid a salary until 1929, but instead received fees for each of their duties, e.g. 2s 6d for each of the first 20 entries of birth or death registered in each quarter, 1s for every other entry, 2s 6d for registering a birth after three months and before twelve months, and 5s for registering a birth after twelve months. There would also be income from the sale of certificates under, for instance, the Factory and Workshops Act, and a fee for making out the quarterly returns. An average town might provide a registrar with an income of about £38 a quarter.

◼ ROYAL AIR FORCE (MEDICAL BRANCH)

Shortly after the start of the Second World War, in 1940, a small number of female doctors were appointed with responsibility for the WAAF, with recruitment expanded subsequently to include service in RAF hospitals, where only male service patients were nursed. At first holding relative rank with the men they had replaced, from 1942 they were granted commissions: Flying Officer, then Flight Lieutenant after one year's satisfactory service. They wore the WAAF officers' uniform, with collar badges of the RAF Medical Branch.

■ ROYAL AIR FORCE NURSING SERVICE

see **Princess Mary's Royal Air Force Nursing Service.**

■ ROYAL ARMY MEDICAL CORPS (RAMC)

During the First World War, when it was realised that there was a growing shortage of male doctors, about 80 women doctors were attached on short term contracts to the RAMC for service in Malta, Egypt and Salonika in 1916. They did not wear military uniform and were treated as volunteers rather than members of the Corps.

In the Second World War, about double that number served with the Corps and wore its badges and colours, receiving the same pay and allowances as the men and holding the same rank. Every entrant was commissioned as an officer, entering the Corps as a lieutenant and being promoted to captain after a year's service. A major had to be a specialist doctor – including physicians, anaesthetists, psychiatrists, oculists, and gynaecologists – and treated both men and women in the service. Most of the female doctors were medical officers for the Auxiliary Transport Service (ATS), while some acted as transfusion officers for the Army Blood Supply Depot. The RAMC is included in the Army Medical Services Museum, Keogh Barracks, Ash Vale, Aldershot, GU12 5RQ (www.ams-museum. org.uk).

■ ROYAL NAVY (MEDICAL BRANCH)

About 20 female doctors at any one time served with the Royal Navy during the Second World War, not exclusively for the WRNS. They were commissioned into the Navy, as surgeon-lieutenants, RNVR, with the most senior being a member of the staff of the Medical Director-General of the Navy. They wore the same uniform as a WRNS officer, with a badge of scarlet cloth between two 'wavy' gold stripes.

■ SANITARY INSPECTOR

Public health was a preoccupation of Victorian government, spurred on by recurrent epidemics and the huge problems of coping with a rapidly increasing and industrialised population. An act of 1855 empowered local authorities to appoint sanitary inspectors, who over the next few decades took under their wing the implementation of such diverse legislation as the Sale of Food and Drugs Act, the Pollution of Rivers Act and the Factories and Workshops Act. However, as well as sanitation and sewerage arrangements, one of their primary concerns was public health as it applied to people living in their own homes and it was in this sphere that women were seen as having something particular to contribute – a kind of extension of the home visiting amongst the poor that many ladies considered their responsibility. From the 1890s the post of sanitary (or public health) inspector was open to women; by the beginning of the 20th century they had been appointed in London, Liverpool and Birmingham. In some cases at this time they also had the title of **health visitor**, depending on the exact definition of their duties. The name was changed to public health inspector in 1956 (and then to environmental health officer).

In the *Lady's Realm* (1904), Rachel Montgomery described the printed instructions given by her local authority to each new 'lady inspector': 'The women health visitors are appointed to visit from house to house under the directions of the medical officer of health, calling attention to the necessity for cleanliness of the house and its surroundings, giving advice as to the rearing of children and the nursing of the sick, distributing and explaining handbills on the prevention of infectious diseases, and doing all they can in other directions to help the people whom they visit to keep their homes in as healthy a condition as possible.'

In addition, they were to make inspections of the houses – 'the house must be gone through from cellar to attic, the court and outhouses, including the drains, must be examined.' To this end, qualifications for the job included the certificate of the Sanitary Institute or the Sanitary Inspectors Examination Board, which involved study of mensuration, 'that is, the measuring and calculating the cubic space of different-shaped rooms, halls, workshops etc;

hygiene, including air, water, and ventilation; meat inspection; drainage and house construction; infectious diseases and methods of disinfection; and last, but by no means least, sanitary law'. Inspectors visited not only homes but also shops, lodging houses, schools and workplaces: Rose Squire, who later became an influential **factory inspector**, began her career as a Sanitary Inspector of Workshops and Laundries for the Kensington Vestry in 1893.

Records of female sanitary inspectors and their work as employees of county and borough councils, will be found in county record offices, within the archives of medical officers of health. See **health visitor** for details of the Women's Sanitary Inspectors Association.

■ SCAVENGER

Nothing was wasted in Victorian cities, including the dust and refuse from the streets and collected from houses. Great dust-yards of rubbish were picked over by men and women employed to sort and sift – the dust itself went for manure on the fields or for brickmaking, while cinders, wood, metal, pottery, vegetable waste, paper, glass or cloth could be salvaged and recycled.

A 'hill-woman' entered a contract with the owner of the yard to sift all the dust throughout the year, keeping for her own sale any rags, bones, metal, clothing etc as well as half of any money or valuables. She employed people to shovel the dust and to sift it. The 'sifters' were often women, paid about a shilling a day.

Henry Mayhew saw a group of sifters in a London dust-yard in the 1850s: 'Their coarse dirty cotton gowns were tucked up behind them, their arms were bared above their elbows, their black bonnets crushed and battered like those of fish-women; over their gowns they wore a strong leathern apron, extending from their necks to the extremities of their petticoats, while over this, again, was another leathern apron, shorter, thickly padded, and fastened by a stout string or strap round the waist. In the process of their work they pushed the sieve from them and drew it back again with apparent violence, striking it against the outer leathern apron with such force that it produced each time a hollow sound, like a blow on the tenor drum.'

Women sifting through the rubbish on a refuse site in the early 1900s.

■ SCHOOLMISTRESS, SCHOOLTEACHER

Teaching, **like nursing,** was a profession that attracted educated and dedicated women in their thousands from the late 19th century. And, as with nursing, in the early 19th century teaching was often undertaken by those who could get no other work, in particular elderly women. At Dagenham as late as 1851, for instance, Elizabeth Bennett, an 80-year-old widow, was recorded as 'schoolmistress' – in what was known as a 'dame school', run in the woman's cottage. In some areas these often overlapped with plait or lace schools (see **lacemaker; straw plaiter**).

In 1846 a government scheme for teacher training began, although there was no compulsion to join. At the age of 13 or upwards a bright student could apply to begin a five-year apprenticeship at an approved elementary school as a 'pupil teacher', during which she would teach in the school, under supervision, and also have daily tuition from the head teacher. (Several changes took place in the minimum age and length of apprenticeship over the next half century.) Success in the annual examinations would bring her a government grant to pay her way.

After the five years she could go on to a training college (by passing a Queen's scholarship examination) for two years to gain her teacher's certificate. Or she might simply stay on at the school as an unqualified assistant. The third option was to take the final, qualifying examinations while already working as a teacher rather than going to college. In this system, therefore, you could end up with trained and certificated teachers, untrained and certificated teachers, or simply untrained and uncertificated teachers, the differences between them being reflected in rates of pay and the status of the schools to which they could apply for work.

It was obviously a complicated and diverse system of education, very dependent on local conditions, with no central authority, and with a variety of schools: dame schools, factory schools, workhouse schools, ragged schools, industrial and reformatory schools, as well as the 'ordinary' schools, which themselves were divided on religious grounds between the nondenominational British and Foreign School Society ('British schools') and the Anglican National Society for Promoting the Education of the Poor ('National schools'), not to mention the many 'public' private schools and ancient grammar schools.

At the time of the 1870 Elementary Education Act, there were over 12,000 certificated teachers in England and Wales, and over 16,000 pupil teachers; within ten years, when education for children up to the age of ten was made compulsory, these figures had more than doubled. This was the beginning of the state system of education, with school boards financed by local ratepayers, and also the creation of one of the largest and most influential female-dominated careers.

In small country schools the pre-1846 'child monitor' system of training was still used into the 20th century, where an older pupil was used to teach classes under supervision – this was not only a cheaper option, as it saved on a teacher's wage, but it was also a reflection of the difficulty found in staffing remote areas. From the 1880s such schools were allowed to recruit 'supplementary' teachers, untrained and uncertificated and with a minimum age of 18. After 1902 pupil teachers were to be trained at secondary schools until they were 17 or 18, when they would go to a training college or work as a student teacher. In country areas, though, the problem of staffing meant that the Rural Pupil Teacher scheme, which ran on the same lines as that of 1846, continued until the Second World War.

A register of teachers was established in 1899 and in 1902 the Teachers' Registration Council was founded, although there was no great consistency in the system for a number of years. The registers for 1914 to 1947 (held by the Society of Genealogists) are searchable online, for a fee, at www. originsnetwork.com/help/popup-helpbo-teachers.htm.

The National Union of Elementary Teachers was formed in 1870 and became the National Union of Teachers (NUT) in 1889; the National Union of Women Teachers was formed in 1904 as the 'Equal Pay League' of the NUT and was an independent union from 1920 to 1961.

The National Archives has a Research Guide on *Education: Records of Teachers*, which relates the history of teacher training and the records held. For Scottish sources see the website of the National Archives of Scotland (www.nas.gov.uk/guides/education.asp); there is also very useful information at www.scan.org.uk/familyhistory/myancestor/schoolteacher. htm. School records will usually be found at county records offices, as will registers of training colleges based locally; many schools founded in the 19th century or before have had histories published and these should be available in local studies libraries. Directories will be valuable in finding the location of schools, both private and state.

For introductory background see *The Victorian Schoolroom*, Trevor May (Shire Publications), or *The Victorian and Edwardian Schoolchild*, Pamela Horn (Alan Sutton, 1989).

■ SCHOOLMISTRESS, WORKHOUSE

There were large numbers of orphaned and abandoned children in the workhouses before the development of child services by local authorities at the end of the 19th century, as well as those who had come in with their parents, and teachers were employed under the supervision of the workhouse master or matron to teach and discipline them. If there was also a schoolmaster, the mistress would teach the girls, otherwise she took charge of both boys and girls. Education was largely directed at making the girls suitable for employment and/or marriage, with an emphasis on the domestic arts. See **matron, workhouse** for sources.

■ SCHOOLROOM MAID

In a house large enough to have a schoolroom for the family's children, a maid might be specifically employed to look after it – cleaning the room, laying out meals, waiting at table, accompanying the children to and from lessons etc. At Hinchingbroke, Huntingdon, in 1861, Emma Hammond, aged 21, was a schoolroom maid. See **domestic servant**.

■ SCOTTISH WOMEN'S HOSPITALS

The War Office refused the medical assistance offered by Dr Elsie Inglis and other female doctors and surgeons at the beginning of the First World War, so they travelled to France on their own authority in November 1914 and initially treated victims of typhoid in Calais. By 1917 units of the SWH had hospitals in Serbia, in France (Royaumont, Villers Cotterets and Troyes), and in Salonika. Throughout the war, the organisation remained a voluntary one and was not officially recognised by the War Office, despite the vital work undertaken by the female doctors. See *The Women of Royaumont: A Scottish Women's Hospital on the Western Front*, Eileen Crofton (Tuckwell Press, 1997); *In the Service of Life: The Story of Elsie Inglis and the Scottish Women's Hospitals*, Leah Leneman (Mercat Press, 1994).

■ SCREW, NUT AND BOLT MAKER

Women were employed in factories and at home making screws, nuts and bolts, mostly in the Black Country or in Monmouthshire in Wales (1870s). One of their jobs was as a screw cutter – some made the notches in the heads, some the thread or spiral cut round the stem of the screw, some turned the heads on a lathe to 'give them a circular and smooth appearance'.

In 1892 there was an investigation into the work of the nut and bolt makers of Darlaston. A witness asserted: 'The work led to the demoralization of the women, as its tendency was to encourage a lowness of life. The mixing of the sexes too, in factories and workshops, had the same tendency. The hand hammers used weighed 2lb, and the Oliver hammer weighed 10lb to 20lb, entailing great physical labour. The women worked very scantily clothed, and in summer time the upper parts of their bodies were nearly nude. Married women brought their children to the factories and placed them in a box on the hearth, covering them sometimes to prevent accidents by burning. In other cases swings were suspended from the roof, and the children were placed in these and left swinging while their mothers were doing work more like that of a blacksmith than

Cutting the thread on screws by machine in 1844.

anything else. The women in the domestic workshops had to carry their bundles of iron, 56lb in weight, from the warehouse on their heads or shoulders, for a distance of half a mile. It was no uncommon sight to see a woman thus burdened suckling a child at the same time. With regard to the wages, although the standard was 30s per week, yet, owing to the depression, they did not make more than 20s a week.'

■ SCULLERY MAID, SCULLION

The maid who did the roughest work in the kitchen and the servants' quarters. She scoured and cleaned pots, pans and kettles – many of them extremely heavy – and did the hard cleaning in the kitchen, scullery (a small room off the kitchen with large sinks where washing up, and the cleaning of game, poultry, fish etc was done), servants' hall, outside steps etc. Her life consisted largely of fetching, carrying and cleaning at the beck and call of the cook and kitchenmaid. She was usually a young girl, in her first job, and was looked down on in the servant hierarchy as the very lowest form of life. See **domestic servant**.

■ SEAMSTRESS

A woman earning her living by sewing. See also **corsetmaker; dressmaker; needlewoman**.

■ SEARCHER

Before women came into the police force (see **matron, police**) a female searcher might be employed – in 1887 a Mrs Reynolds was employed as a female searcher at Highgate police station.

Searchers were also employed by the Customs service. In 1858 Ellen Casey was under suspicion of smuggling when she came ashore at St Katherine's Wharf in London and the local Tides Surveyor of Customs called in a female searcher – once stripped of her enormous crinoline, Ellen was found to have 22 lbs of cigars tucked into three separate petticoats. In 1870 Elizabeth Munro was prosecuted following a similar case but in this case the female searcher was named as a Mrs Mullett. It was always necessary to have a woman on call to search female suspects, and in 1940 during the Second World War the Liverpool Waterguard Superintendent made an official request to be able to employ a searcher, fearing that enemy agents were smuggling secrets out of Britain ('I have in mind an elderly, motherly sort of woman acquainted with, and able to handle, babies as well as women') and from 1942 to 1945 a Mrs Moneypenny was appointed full time searcher. Any surviving records will be with Customs and Excise documents at The National Archives (the case above is quoted from CUST 106/432) but many 'appointments' were ad hoc and informal.

■ SECRETARY

A secretary was originally a young man, usually working for a writer or a businessman, or perhaps for a man or woman with a high social position. However, with the expansion of **office staff** from the 1880s onwards it became a predominantly female occupation.

The role of 'private secretary' was described in the early 1900s as 'one of the most coveted positions for a woman to hold'. It was not only that it was a cut above the clerks and the typists in the office, but also that it could be a responsible and interesting job. Business training was advised, along with 'a knowledge of one or two languages'. Duties would vary with each job, but involved in great part organising the office and the boss's diary, and acting as intermediary between him, or her, and the staff and callers.

There has always been a sense in which the secretary looked after the businessman in the office as the wife did at home, and this domestic aspect to the job, so infuriating to later feminists, was clear in 1911: 'Men are proverbially careless and will sit with an open window, in a dangerous draught, or do other equally foolish things, and the secretary will earn the thanks of the wife at home if she can rectify quietly any oversights. If afternoon tea be served in the office she may be able to see that it is brought in punctually, and made properly, or, in the case of a threatened breakdown in health, will see that the doctor's orders are obeyed as to the taking of medicine, etc.'

■ SERVANTS' REGISTRY, EMPLOYMENT OFFICE

Domestic, office and teaching staff increasingly found employment through professional employment exchanges or servants' registries, which were overwhelmingly run by women as small businesses. Local newspapers and trade directories are good places to find advertisements.

Should you require a MAID, COOK, MANSERVANT, or DOMESTIC SERVANT *consult—*

The "Astoria"

Domestic and Hotel Servants Agency
Principal: Miss Dickie
ASTORIA HOUSE
(Adjoining Astoria Cinema)
21 Gloucester Place
Brighton
Phone: B'TON 4877

★

Every effort is made to supply clients with reliable servants—
MODERATE FEES
Maids of any capacity placed in good employment

A 1937 advertisement for Miss Dickie's agency in Brighton.

■ SHIRTMAKER

Shirtmaking was one of the sweated trades that produced such shocking revelations of starvation wages and overwork in the Victorian era, epitomised by Thomas Hood's *Song of the Shirt* in the 1840s. See military clothing maker; tailoress.

■ SHOP ASSISTANT

At the end of the 19th century shop assistants were amongst the employees with the longest working hours in the country. None of the reforming Acts of Parliament relating to hours of work applied to them, and despite persistent attempts to gain protection it was not until 1950 that shops were forced to close at 6 pm from November to February four days a week, with one late night (7.30 pm) and one half day to 1 pm. Shop assistants had to wait until 1963 before they were given equivalent protection to factory workers under health and safety laws. Even the right to a meal-time break was not compulsory until 1912. The reason why shopkeepers resisted restrictions on their employees' hours was simply that commercial competition was so fierce on the high street that shops stayed open for as long as they could reasonably expect to attract customers, sometimes until 10 pm or 11 pm.

Shop assistants were rather looked down upon by both their working class and middle class customers but young women frequently preferred it to domestic service or factory work, especially if they were relatively uneducated. This was despite the autocratic way they were often treated – in some large shops persistent failure to secure a sale could lead to dismissal and Whiteley's department store, for instance, had a list of some 200 rules that staff were expected to obey and they were fined if they transgressed, e.g. for being late, or untidy, or making a mistake at the till. In some instances, especially with these large department stores, staff lived in on the premises or nearby, so that their lives were under scrutiny 24 hours a day.

Female assistants were not usually employed in shops or departments dealing with heavy or rough work, such as ironmongery, butchery etc, or in those that involved selling to men, such as tailoring. Sainsbury's, for instance, was largely staffed by men until the First World War, when it was discovered that women too could prepare, weigh, cut and sell bacon, cheese, butter etc. Most female assistants were to be found in department stores, milliners' and dressmakers', confectioners', fancy goods shops and so on. In a chemist's shop, an attractive and sympathetic female assistant who would not frighten away female customers was positively sought after.

Without background sources, finding out where an assistant worked will usually be impossible, unless they appear in the census as living on the premises. Many of the bigger shops and chains have published histories which give an insight into working conditions – such as *The Best Butter in the World: A History of Sainsbury's*, Bridget Williams (Ebury Press, 1994) – or have information on their websites. *Shops and Shopping 1800–1914*,

Alison Adburgham (George Allen & Unwin, 2nd edn, 1981) is a very readable introduction to the world of commerce.

■ SHOPKEEPER

A glance at any trade directory will show that women were running a wide range of shops in village high streets and city centres from the 1850s onwards – butchers, bakers, booksellers, stationers, fishmongers, grocers, greengrocers, drapers, furniture dealers, glass and china dealers, haberdashers, and the list goes on. It's safe to say that whatever the product, somewhere there was a woman running a shop selling it.

One very familiar place associated with women proprietors was the village shop/corner shop, run by widows, spinsters or married women bolstering the wage of their labourer or tradesman husband. Village shops were a new development from the 1850s and continued to increase in number throughout the 19th and early 20th century, varying greatly in size and scope. Many started off in the front or back room of a cottage, and perhaps then grew to take over the whole of the ground floor while the shopkeeper and her family moved upstairs over the shop. What epitomised the village store was the wide variety of goods that it carried, which was a necessity if the shopkeeper wanted to protect her business from the services increasingly offered in the 20th century by larger town shops with transport and the capacity to deliver over a wide area.

Shopkeepers of all kinds can be traced in local directories, and also in local authority rate books and other town records. Unmarried or widowed female shopkeepers were among the first women to get the vote, because as local ratepayers they were eligible to be entered on the municipal electoral roll from 1868 onwards. For background see *The Village Shop*, Lin Bensley (Shire Publications, 2008); or see *The Shopkeeper's World 1830–1914*, Michael Winstanley (Manchester University Press, 1983).

■ SILK SPINNER, SILK WEAVER

Raw silk imported into this country had to be prepared for weaving in the same way as cotton fibres and there were silk throwing (spinning) mills in several counties – Hertfordshire had seven such mills in the late 19th century, for instance. It was an industry heavily dependent on the labour of women and children.

Female designers at work in the Manningham silk mills in Yorkshire in the early 1900s.

The silk usually arrived on skeins, having been teased from the silk cocoons before export. When it arrived at the mill it was first graded and washed, then placed on winding frames ('swifts'). This part of the process usually took place on the top floor of the mill because the machinery required little power to turn the frames. The silk was then cleaned, spun by twisting the filaments together to strengthen them, doubled by bringing two or four filaments together, and thrown – twisting the doubled threads, again by machine, but in the opposite direction this time, to make the thread strong and pliable. The finished silk yarn was then ready to be sold on to the weaving mills.

Powerlooms did not have so overpowering an impact on the industry as they did on cotton weavers, and the Spitalfields weavers using handlooms were still in business in the late 19th century, albeit dying out (from tens of thousands employed at the height of the industry in the 17th century, the figure had fallen to only 500 or so by 1900). Although this was a male-dominated environment, women did work at the looms alongside husbands and fathers. There is a detailed history of the Spitalfields weavers in Volume 2 of the *Victoria County History of Middlesex* (see also online at www.british-history.ac.uk/report.aspx?compid=22161).

There was also a certain amount of weaving done by outworkers or in small workshops, especially of coarser silk used in linings and items as diverse as hatbands, fringes and garters. Mostly weaving took place in factories by the 19th century, especially following introduction of the Jacquard loom which could produce figured and intricate designs. By the end of the 19th century, however, the industry as a whole was in decline. The firm of Courtauld's, which was founded in Essex as a silk weaving business and made its fortune in the production of mourning crepe, only ensured its survival by obtaining the rights from 1904 to weave rayon, 'artificial silk'.

Other manufacturers were based around the country, including Norwich, Manchester, Paisley, etc. Coventry was already famous for the weaving of silk ribbons by the 1840s when Cash's firm was founded. From employing weavers as outworkers, it built workshops over their cottages so that several could work together – the 'topshops'. In the 1870s it began manufacturing woven nametapes, still familiar today. There is a great deal of information about the Hillfields area of the city and ribbon weaving online (www. hillfields.org.uk/History/Weaving.htm).

Macclesfield, however, was the main centre of the silk-weaving industry in England, with over 100 mills in business. The last working handloom-weaving mill, dating from 1862, is today open as the Paradise Mill museum (Park Lane, Macclesfield; telephone: 01625 618228) and the town also has the Silk Museum Heritage Centre (Roe Street, Macclesfield; telephone: 01625 613210) – see the website at www.macclesfield.silk.museum.

Archive union material is held by the Working Class Memorial Library, 51 The Crescent, Salford M5 4WX (www.wcml.org.uk/holdings/ silkworkers). For general background try *The Silk Industry*, Sarah Bush (Shire Publications); *The Story of Silk*, John Feltwell (Alan Sutton, 1990); or *Under Control: Life in a 19th Century Silk Factory*, Carol Adams, Paula Bartley, Judy Lown and Cathy Loxton (Cambridge University Press, 1983). There is a dictionary of silk fibres at www.ntgi.net/ICCF&D/silk.htm.

■ SLATE PACKER

About 70 women were employed at the Delabole slate quarry in Cornwall in the mid-19th century, earning about 6s a week. Women were also employed as packers of slate until the last decade of the 19th century – wagonloads of slate were hauled six miles from the important Delabole quarry to the nearest harbour at Port Gaverne and loaded onto waiting ships for carriage around the country and abroad. The women received the slates on board and packed them into the hold; about 30 wagonloads were needed to load a 60-ton ship. Delabole was an important local industry employing over a thousand people in the 1850s. See the website of the Delabole Quarry (www.delaboleslate.co.uk); Lynne Mayers wrote about 'The women slate-packers of Port Gaverne' in the journal of the Cornwall Family History Society in September 2002.

■ SLOPWORKER

A maker of cheap ready-made working garments for the poor, usually on piece work at home at very low rates of pay. See **dressmaker; tailoress.**

■ SOCIAL WORKER

see **almoner.**

■ SPECIAL OPERATIONS EXECUTIVE (SOE)

The SOE was created in July 1940 in response to Winston Churchill's demand to 'set Europe ablaze' – an underground army that supported local resistance groups, sabotage and subversion. About 3,000 women served in the SOE during the Second World War – in Europe, the Middle and Far East, and Africa, acting as couriers and radio operators – and unlike those in the rest of the armed services they were expected to be combatants if necessary. If caught behind enemy lines they faced interrogation, torture, imprisonment and possibly execution. To try to protect them as far as possible under the Geneva Convention, female SOE agents held commissions in either the **WAAF** or **FANY**, the latter predominating. Many of these tremendously brave women received the MBE in recognition, and one a George Medal (Christina Granville). Three Victoria Crosses were awarded (Odette Sanson, Violette Szabo and Noor Inayat Khan, the latter two posthumously).

The National Archives has a research guide, *Intelligence Records in TNA*, which details its holdings; unfortunately some 80% of the records are believed to have perished through fire or housekeeping. *The Women Who Lived For Danger: The Women Agents of SOE in the Second World War*, Marcus Binney (Hodder and Stoughton, 2002) tells their story and includes a good bibliography and notes on sources. There is a fascinating website about the women of SOE at www.64-baker-street.org.

■ STAYMAKER

An older term for a **corsetmaker**. It was still in common use in the later 19th century, and even in the 20th century women occasionally referred to wearing 'stays'. It tended in later years to refer more to the heavily boned type of corset.

■ STEWARDESS

Women acted as stewardesses of women's clubs and friendly societies from the early 1800s. They would be expected to keep records of members and of finances. The term was also used for women acting as domestic administrators: in 1860 the obituary of Sgt John Rowley mentioned that his widow had been for 23 years 'matron and stewardess of the Ordnance Hospital at Portsmouth'.

■ STEWARDESS, AIR

Little girls in the 1950s believed the job of air stewardess was one of the most glamorous they could aspire to – beautifully groomed, smartly dressed, accomplished and unflappable, they were the catwalk models of the skies.

Employing women to look after passengers aboard civil aeroplanes was a natural progression from the stewardess of the ocean liner. In the US the first air stewardess, Ellen Church, was employed by United Airlines in 1930, and six years later in England Air Despatch took on Daphne Kearley to fly on their Avro 642 'Dawn Express', which carried mostly businessmen from Croydon to Le Bourget (Imperial Airways had tried out young 'cabin boys' in the 1920s). A combination of waitress, cook (though meals consisted mostly of smoked salmon and caviar), and secretary, she spoke fluent French, took dictation and had letters typed up ready for when they landed. She was paid £12 a month. The war interrupted the civil development of the role for a while, but it took off again in the late 1940s and 1950s.

Daphne is believed to have been the only pre-war stewardess, but to find out more about civil airlines in general in this period, see the website of the Croydon Airport Society, www.croydonairport.org.uk (Secretary: 68 Colston Ave, Carshalton, Surrey SM5 2NU) or investigate British Airways – they have records relating to BOAC, Imperial Airways, BEA and other companies: www.bamuseum.com (BA Archive and Museum Collection, Building 387 (E121), PO Box 10, Heathrow Airport, Hounslow, Middx TW6 2JA).

■ STEWARDESS, SHIP'S

As soon as women began to emigrate in large numbers, or to take long sea voyages, the benefits of having females on board ship to offer passengers a combination of waitress, nurse and chambermaid services became apparent to shipowners. As early as 1828 an advertisement appeared in *The Times*: 'Wanted, for a first-rate Steamer, a Cook and Stewardess. The stewardess must be a respectable middle-aged woman, of good address, and one who will not be above her business. Apply at 18, John-street, Crutchedfriars.' Sometimes the job was divided between a conductress (for better class passengers) and ship's matron. By 1840 the P&O Line had stewardesses sailing to Australia, India, the West Indies and South America.

Stewardesses were employed at both the luxury end of the long-distance market and on cross-channel, coastal and river ferries. In 1829 the *George the Fourth* steam packet from Southampton to Havre-de-Grace was able to promise that 'a stewardess will attend on the ladies', while in 1860 the *Mermaid* clipper bound for Australia advertised its 'large and handsomely furnished' saloons, complete with 'piano, library etc', and its ability to provide a cow for fresh milk, an experienced surgeon, and 'a stewardess to wait on saloon passengers'. Less pleasant work awaited the ferry stewardesses charged with keeping an eye on Irish paupers being sent home under the settlement laws.

Women working in the mainly male environment on board ship, away from home for weeks or months at a time, risked being considered little better than the prostitutes with whom the sailors mingled when on shore, particularly by wives left at home. The job also had its dangers. One was the very real risk of shipwreck. In the 1860s alone, stewardesses who went down with their ships included Christina Wyness of the *Lifeguard* off Flamborough Head, Margaret Duncan of the *Stanley* at Tynemouth, Grace Logan of the *London* in the Bay of Biscay, Kate Crozier of the *Cawarra* off Newcastle (Australia), and Mary Ann Jewell of the *General Grant* off Australia. One shipwreck in particular captured the public imagination in 1899, when the courage displayed by Mrs Mary Rogers of the *Stella* led to the starting of the 'Stella Stewardess Memorial Fund' and the eventual raising of a memorial at Southampton; see www.jakesimpkin.org.

Trying to trace the career of a stewardess will be difficult without knowing for which shipping line she worked: see www.red-duster.co.uk for details of the many merchant lines. *My Ancestor Was a Merchant Seaman*, Christopher Watts and Michael Watts (Society of Genealogists, 2007) is a comprehensive guide to research and records.

■ STILLROOM MAID

The stillroom in a big house was where wines, jellies, preserves, cosmetics, perfumes and medicines were made, and where aromatic waters and oils were distilled, so that it must always have had a delicious aroma of spices, flowers and herbs, as well as of the tea and coffee which were kept and made there. A stillroom maid would assist, and wait on, the **housekeeper**. In 1851 Mary Ann Duncombe, aged 19, was the 'still room maid' under housekeeper Mary Dawkins at Sudbrooke Holme, in Lincolnshire. She would be responsible for cleaning the housekeeper's room and making up her fire, and for waiting on the senior servants when they ate in the housekeeper's room. She helped the housekeeper to wash the china, bake pastries and fine cakes, and make ice creams and dainty sandwiches for afternoon tea upstairs. See **domestic servant**.

■ STRAW PLAITER

The straw hat and bonnet industry had a history going back to the 17th century, but it was immensely successful in the 19th century before succumbing to foreign imports. Its raw material was woven straw plait, produced as a cottage industry by female workers and children (usually the families of agricultural labourers) in certain parts of the country, especially Bedfordshire, Hertfordshire and Buckinghamshire around the factories in the towns of Luton and Dunstable, but also in parts of Essex, Devon, Wiltshire, Dorset, Suffolk, Northamptonshire, and even for a time in the Orkneys.

The straw was sorted and cleaned, stripped of leaves and ears. The best stalks were the longest and straightest. The straw might be bleached or dyed, and graded by thickness using a straw-sorter. Then, tied into bundles, it could be sold to the plaiters at market or by a dealer, the middleman, travelling door to door.

The plaiters worked by holding a bundle under their arm and drawing out the straws one at a time to be moistened between their lips before being twisted into plait. There is an old story that in these areas the local men preferred a 'lace gal' to a 'straw gal' because the constant drawing of the treated straw through the lips often caused small cuts, which hardened and thickened with time – making them not so sweet to kiss as those of a lacemaker. Even very young children could plait, and 'plait schools' acted as a kind of industrial crèche in villages where almost every woman was plaiting from morning to night. The money they earned made a valuable contribution to a family's income – some commentators remarked that these women had developed a disquieting independence from their regular income.

There was a great variety of design in plaiting and the women would work to order, depending on what was fashionable and what the hat factories wanted. The finished plait was pressed through a mill to make it pliable. Once complete, it was made into bundles of lengths, to be sold back to the dealers, or sometimes to be sold at market by the women themselves.

Children of Straw, Laszlo L. Grof (Barracuda Books, 1988) is full of information for the industry around Luton, and *Straw Plait*, Jean Davis (Shire Publications, 1981) covers the processes and products around the country – see also the Guild of Straw Craftsmen (www.strawcraftsmen. co.uk). Several villages whose women engaged in straw plaiting have information on their websites; e.g. for Wing in Buckinghamshire (www. wing-ops.org.uk/straw.html), or the Leighton Buzzard area (www.leighton-museum.org.uk/gallery/strawplaiting.index.html). See **hat maker, straw** for more sources.

▨ STREET SELLER

Every town and city had its small army of street sellers in the 19th century, and such traders could still be found up to the Second World War. Many of them were women. While it was a family lifestyle for some (the daughters, wives or widows of traders), for others selling on the streets was done in desperation to help out the family budget and keep out of the workhouse. What they sold might vary through the year, as they took advantage of each season's produce or what they could buy or make cheaply enough to be able to realise a small profit. In the mid-1800s, for instance, some women sold culinary and medicinal herbs during the autumn and winter and anything they could get, such as soft fruits, during the rest of the year. Other women sold crockery and glassware, their baskets so heavy that they developed a permanent bend to one side, or boot and stay laces in working class districts.

Henry Mayhew and Charles Booth give many such examples of street sellers and their lives, and Mayhew goes into some detail about the female street sellers in mid-Victorian London: 'The sales in which they are principally concerned are in fish (including shrimps and oysters), fruit and vegetables (widows selling on their own account), fire-screens and ornaments, laces, millinery, artificial flowers, cut flowers, boot and stay-laces and small wares, wash-leathers, towels, burnt linen, combs, bonnets, pin-cushions, tea and coffee, rice-milk, curds and whey, sheep's-trotters, and dressed and undressed dolls.' See **coster girl/woman**. For a great deal more about street sellers, see Mayhew, *London Labour and the London Poor*, vol 1 (Dover Publications, 1968).

▨ SUPERINTENDENT, LADY

A woman in authority, she might be found in a hospital, school, or nursery/crèche in the late 19th century. The word 'lady' attached to an occupation in the 1800s usually denoted a woman from a middle or upper class background who had undergone training for which she had paid her own fees; at this time superintendent posts were rarely occupied by working class women who had 'come up through the ranks'.

A lady superintendent of nurses was employed to manage the nursing staff in larger hospitals from the late 1860s, and she was at the forefront of the drive to professionalise nursing: 'On them depends the care of the nurses, their well-being and moral tone; and this of itself requires much firmness and determination,' said *Cassell's Household Guide* in the 1880s. 'The salaries attached to this position vary greatly at present, being from £30 to £100 per annum, with board and lodging. . . . The same rules hold good in cases of Superintendents of Cottage Hospitals. Of course, in this case, there is a greater measure of responsibility, as the superintendent has no resident medical officer always at hand to refer to, and accordingly must use her own best judgement in difficult cases. The salaries vary from £20 to £50, with board and lodging.' Her duties as a trained nurse, dovetailed with those of the hospital **matron**. Miss Maria Machin, for instance, from the Florence Nightingale School at St Thomas's Hospital was appointed 'Matron and Superintendent of Nurses' at St Bartholomew's in 1878.

■ SURVEYOR

In 1922 **Irene Barclay** (1894–1989) qualified as the first female chartered surveyor and went on to run her own business for over 50 years in the Somers Town area of London. The Royal Institute of Chartered Surveyors (RICS) had resisted accepting female candidates for the compulsory qualifying examinations, but in 1919 had been forced to open a separate 'housing manager' section for women; Irene Barclay, however, insisted on full qualification and others followed.

See *Surveying Sisters: Women in a Traditional Male Profession*, Clara Greed (1990). RICS (www.rics.org.uk) has a help page for family historians trying to trace surveyor ancestors (and also chartered auctioneers, estates agents, land agents and valuers) and a query form can be downloaded; their libraries are at 12 Great George Street, London SW1P 3DD, and 9 Manor Place, Edinburgh EH3 7DN.

■ SWEET MAKER/CHOCOLATE MAKER

Our **national sweet** tooth ensured a thriving confectionery industry and hundreds of women worked in factories producing sweets of all kinds, many of which would end up in jars on shop counters.

In Hackney Wick the factory of Messrs Clarke, Nicholls & Coombs was visited in the early 1900s by C. Duncan Lewis for the *Living London* series of articles. The company, he noted, supplied 2,000 varieties of sweets, 'and so agreeable is the stuff that in the course of twelve months from fifteen to twenty tons of it are consumed by the employees themselves'.

BOURNEVILLE - GIRLS IN DINING ROOM

Women made up a large part of the workforce in sweet and chocolate production – this postcard shows the dining room at Cadbury's Bournville factory in about 1908.

He went on to describe the scene in the factory: 'Some are boiling sugar in great pans; some are kneading a thick, jelly-like, transparent substance that we have never seen before. It is sugar and water. One woman is especially vigorous, and we admire her biceps. Presently she flings her jelly on to an iron peg and proceeds to pull it about with the strength of a Sandow [a contemporary strong man]. In two or three minutes it resembles a beautiful skein of silk. Later on it will go through a rolling machine, from which it will emerge a delicious sweetmeat.' That pulling of the mixture to make it smooth and pliable would also have been seen on street markets in the 19th and early 20th centuries, when sweets were often made on the spot by specialist traders.

Lewis noticed one oddity: the way the ingredients affected the women working on them. In the fondant room, they were all grey-haired and grey-faced from the starch used in making the fondant moulds, while upstairs in the chocolate room, they were 'brown as a berry'. Yet Clarke, Nicholls & Coombs were good employers, who provided their workers with facilities such as spacious dining rooms and subsidised food. In 1890 the girls at Messrs Allen's Chocolate Works went on strike because they were so hemmed about by rules and regulations, including being forbidden to go outside the factory during their dinner hour in case they ended up in the pub.

There is a fascinating film online which shows women working at Fry's chocolate factory in Bristol in the 1930s – 'Life inside the Fry's factory' (www.bbc.co.uk/bristol/content/articles/2007/10/09/frys_archive_feature. shtml). Fry's was one of the oldest chocolate-making companies, formed in 1728 and merged with Cadbury's in 1919; by the late 19th century it employed over 4,000 workers at its Keynsham works. There is some information about the history of Cadbury's at www.birminghamuk.com/cadburyhistory.htm and on their own website (www.cadbury.co.uk). You can, of course, visit 'Cadbury World' in Bournville to see more of the sweet-making process. See also *The Cadbury Story: A Short History*, Carl Chinn (Brewin Books, 1998).

■ Tailoress

A 'tailoress' might be a specialist in the making of women's tailored clothing, such as riding outfits, outdoor cloaks etc. The advent of the 'tailor-made' from the late 1870s – a costume for women that was more severe and masculine than had been seen up till then and which was ideal for the New Woman to wear to the office or other work – meant that the line between dressmaking and tailoring became more blurred.

Tailoresses were also employed in 'steam tailoring', mass producing men's ready-made clothing in factories, from the late 19th century. David Paton visited Leeds in 1893 for *Good Words*, finding that a single factory could turn out over a million garments – coats, jackets, waistcoats and trousers – a year. Some of the factories were huge, employing over a thousand workers, while smaller concerns used outworkers. Women worked as pressers and machinists, making up clothes on treadle machines driven by steam power, and each specialising in one task: some only did button-holes, making about 1,500 a day. They were paid by the piece and wages were anything from 15s to 30s a week. For better quality clothing, hand-sewing was still common.

Robert H. Sherard also went to Leeds in 1896, but he saw the 'sweating dens', where women worked in terrible conditions for up to 17 hours a day. Miss Clowes was a young girl he met who had 'broken down in health, after trying for years to maintain her mother, three brothers, and herself on the 15s a week which she was earning', out of which she had to pay 1s 3d for her thread and machine needles (the 'sewings').

A woman listed as a 'tailoress' in the census may, therefore, also have been one of the army of sweated workers who worked on shirts, trousers and other men's garments in small workshops or their own homes. The select committee that investigated the Sweating System 1888–1890 interviewed several of these women in London. One was Mrs Lavinia Casey, who was making shirts at 7d the dozen, working from seven in the morning to eleven at night as well as looking after her children, and from her low weekly earnings she had to deduct 2s 6d for the hire of a Singer sewing machine and about 1s for machine oil and thread.

See also **dressmaker** for fashion sources.

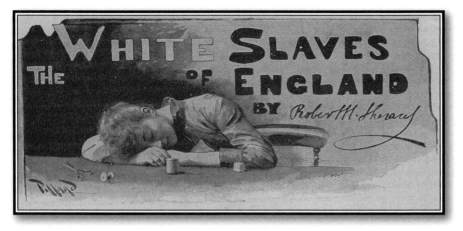

The heading from Robert H. Sherard's series in Pearson's Magazine *1896.*

■ TAMBOURER

A **tambour was** a frame on which cloth, particularly muslin, could be stretched so that the tambourer could embroider with a needle from both top and bottom – just as tapestry frames or needlework hoops work: 'It consists simply in drawing the loop of a thread successively through other loops, in such a manner as to allow the thread to stand out prominently on the muslin, to form a pattern, and yet to adhere durably to it' (*Penny Magazine*, 1844). The frame could be quite large, so that several people could work at the same time, and in the early 19th century this was a female home industry, very common in Scotland. The women were supplied with the muslin by a middleman, who purchased from them the finished product, often used for collars or cuffs. By the mid-1800s, a machine had been invented which could be worked by three women yet do the work of dozens, but the hand craft continued in some areas.

■ TELEGRAM GIRL

S **ometimes girls rather** than boys were employed to deliver telegrams – one woman recalled being paid 5s a week at the West Malvern post office in 1919: 'While I waited for the telegrams I did housework and mending for the postmistress.' See **Post Office.**

T

■ TELEGRAPHIST

The electric telegraph was first used commercially in 1843 and its importance grew alongside the railway system, promoted particularly by Brunel's Great Western Railway in Bristol. By 1854 the Electric Telegraph Company was employing female clerks to work the telegraph (which *Punch* greeted as a 'happy idea', given the ladies' 'love of rapid talking'). In February 1870 the government took over all the private telegraph companies and gave this new state service to the Post Office to run. The impact of the telegraph on communications in the 19th century has been likened to that of the e-mail in the 21st century – it must have seemed like a minor miracle to have a message arrive at its destination almost instantaneously by means of wires strung across the country, not to mention being able to send words across the oceans of the world.

Anyone who wanted to send a telegram (or a 'wire', as it was sometimes called) went to a post office and wrote out their message on a special form, which they handed over the counter. Payment was according to the number of words, so messages tended to be brief and to the point. In large post offices the form would then be rolled up into a little box, placed in a pneumatic tube and sent by means of compressed air to the operator. She worked at a keyboard, using a knob or 'key' to tap out the message letter by letter in Morse code. It would be decoded at the receiving office, and the message delivered in person in the form of a telegram by one of the Post Office's small army of telegram boys (or girls). That was the system at its simplest, though technological advances were as keen in the telegraph industry as they were everywhere in the Victorian era.

Some telegraphists worked at 'receiving houses' – shops that acted as agents for the Post Office – but were poorly paid. Far better to work for the Post Office at any of the provincial telegraph stations, or at the Central Telegraph Station at Blackfriars in London. The pay was slightly higher (though not generous), overtime was paid, there was scope for promotion to supervisor, and, as civil servants, the women would qualify for a pension after 25 years (if they did not marry, when they would have to give up their job). Girls aged 14 to 18 were allowed to take the Civil Service examination, entering as probationary clerks. A good basic education would see them through, and knowledge of a foreign language was an advantage in the larger stations.

Women telegraphists at the Metropolitan Gallery of the Telegraph Office in 1871, soon after the service had been taken over by the Post Office – 'lady-like labour' that opened up new employment possibilities for middle class girls.

By the late 1880s over 30 million telegrams were being sent each year – the introduction of the 'sixpenny telegram' in 1885 brought a sharp rise in demand. Over 700 women were employed in the main London station alone. The busiest times for the girls were said to be from 10 am to 1 pm, when the Stock Exchange and the betting world were busy, and after 6 pm when the wires hummed with Press reports for the next day's newspapers. In London they were linked also to the foreign cable companies, and to the House of Commons by two miles of pneumatic tube.

The telephone would eventually supersede the telegram. Perhaps the most evocative use of the latter was during the two world wars, when the arrival of a telegram at the front door was usually the dreaded prelude to tragic news. See **Post Office**.

■ Telephonist, telephone operator

When Alexander Graham Bell demonstrated his new invention to Queen Victoria in 1877, no one could have foreseen that in 50 years time over one and a half billion telephone calls would be made in one year in the UK alone. The number of telephones in private homes and in offices grew steadily, from a slow start when the telegraph still held the ascendancy, and by 1912 there were nearly 3,000 telephone exchanges and over 700,000 telephones already in the system. There was no direct dialling and every call had to go through a local switchboard exchange until automated exchanges gradually replaced them between the wars.

Thousands of women were employed as telephonists – until the end of 1911 – by the National Telephone Company (which had itself merged in 1889 with other early pioneers such as the United Telephone Company and the Lancashire and Cheshire Telephone Company) and the Post Office (GPO). On 1 January 1912 the GPO took over the entire telephone system and all the exchanges; by 1981 the telecommunications section had become so vast that it was made into a separate public corporation by the government and British Telecom became a private company in 1984.

It was a job that seemed especially suitable for women – clean, sociable, and with 'prospects' for a career if necessary and a pension at the end of it. 'The National Telephone Company recruit their operators from the ranks of bright, well-educated, intelligent girls, who are, in many cases, the daughters of professional men, doctors, barristers, clergymen and others,' wrote Henry Thompson in 1902 (*Living London*). From the callers' point of view, the pleasant and friendly voices, calm and reassuring manner, and helpfulness of the girls made a big impression. When they picked up their telephone in their home or office and dialled for the operator, a light came up on the switchboard in front of the telephonist. She plugged into the number, received the order, and made the connection. The exchanges eventually varied in size from the large and bustling hall-like rooms of the cities, to the small village exchange run in her own front room by the local postmistress.

Both the NTC and GPO employed girls from the age of 16, of a minimum height (5 ft 3 ins for the NTC, 5 ft 2 ins for the GPO) and in good health – any girl taken on by the GPO was 'examined by a lady physician, her eyesight tested, her teeth put in order – to avoid absence through toothache

– and, if considered necessary, revaccination follows'. Girls were employed first as learners on about 10 shillings a week, with a probationary period of two to three months, and pay then rose annually to £1 a week; promotion was also a possibility, to swupervisor, or to clerk-in-charge (at £85 to £170 per annum in 1910). The NTC allowed the girls to wear gloves, 'to better maintain the contour and complexion of their busily worked fingers', and to cover their dresses with 'a loose kind of graduate's gown in dark material' so as to 'shield a sensitive and modestly-garbed operator from being distracted by an extra smart frock on either side of her'. The GPO must have believed their girls were made of sterner stuff and had no such dress sensibilities.

If a girl married, she was expected to leave her employment. Perhaps there were some compensations, though: one commentator in 1910 wrote that 'the work of the telephone operator is healthy, and the action of stretching her arms up above her head, and to the right and left of her, develops the chest and arms, and turns thin and weedy girls, after a few months' work

Telephonists working at the Central Telephone Exchange, St Paul's Churchyard in the early 1900s.

in the operating room, into strong ones. There are no anaemic, unhealthy-looking girls in the operating rooms'.

It was a responsible job, especially in time of emergency or danger. Telephonists were essential workers during both world wars and many put their lives at risk by working on during air raids to keep the lines open. Lilian Ada Bostock, for instance, was awarded the BEM in 1918 for 'displaying great courage and devotion to duty during air raids'. The GPO took over the staff of the NTC in 1912 and the records relating to telephonists who left before 1959 are still in the archives (see **Post Office**).

■ TOBACCO WORKER

Female labour was used to a great extent in the tobacco industry 'whatever form it takes, cake or flake, Cavendish or bird's eye, snuff, cigar or cigarette'. Loose tobacco had been profitable since the 17th century, most usually smoked by all classes of society in the ubiquitous clay pipe, or chewed, while taking snuff (finely ground tobacco, blended with perfume or herbs) was mostly an upper class habit. Cigars (or 'seegars', as the first Cuban imports were called) became popular with the upper classes during the early years of the 19th century, and cigarettes were a French innovation that reached Britain in the mid-1800s – the first cigarette factory was opened at Walworth in 1856.

At that time, too, new companies were established to feed the demand, many of them still familiar names such as W.D. & H.O. Wills in Bristol (1830) or Ogdens in Liverpool (1860). By 1900 smoking was such an established part of life that smoking jackets and hats had become popular for the aspiring middle class man, as well as the after-dinner cigar. Many large towns and cities had their own tobacco factories, such as Chester, which in 1910 had five manufacturers. From 1900, faced with aggressive competition from America, the major manufacturers banded together to form the Imperial Tobacco Company, beginning a process that saw the gradual reduction of the number of individual companies to three by 1980.

In some cases in the 19th century girls were employed from a young age as apprentices in the factories, hand-making cigarettes. Later, women were employed as low-paid machine operatives, once the larger companies began to install cigarette-making machinery from the 1880s.

In the early 1900s, for *Living London*, C. Duncan Lewis visited 'the great tobacco factory belonging to Messrs Salmon and Gluckstein, Clarence Works, City Road'. In one room he watched men making cigars. 'In the next room women are just as busy. These are stripping the stalks from the leaves; those are sorting the leaves for quality; to the right, men are employed in preparing the leaf for the cigar maker. In other rooms you find girls busily engaged in banding, bundling, and boxing cigars, which are then passed on for maturing. In an adjoining department cigarette making is in progress on a colossal scale, and many machines are here running at a high rate of speed, producing

A girl at Messrs Cope's factory at Liverpool in 1896, sorting the leaves taken from a hogshead of tobacco.

huge quantities of cigarettes hourly. Apart from these machines, very large numbers of men and women are engaged in making cigarettes by hand.'

Some companies have produced their own histories, e.g. *John Player & Sons: Centenary 1877–1977* (John Player & Sons, 1977). There is a tobacco museum at Sutton Windmill and Broads Museum, New Road, Sutton Vale, Norwich, NR12 9RZ (www.yesterdaysworld.co.uk). Papers of the Tobacco Workers' Union are held at Warwick University (www.warwick.ac.uk/services/library/mrc/ead/101tw.htm). See www.history-of-tobacco.com for background on tobacco and smoking.

■ TRACER

'**A** n office has** lately been established in London by ladies for tracing the plans of architects and engineers, a new branch of art-work, which has been found a successful opening. Lady-apprentices must, however, give three months' work without wages, and even at the end of the first three months the earnings are but small; the inducements held out are not, therefore, very great.' (*Cassell's Household Guide*, 1880s.) However, tracing maps and plans became a female branch of employment, working with male draughtsmen or cartographers. In 1902, for instance, the Ordnance Survey employed women for the first time, to mount and colour maps.

Women were employed particularly in the engineering industry to make draughtsmen's plans into production drawings ready for the factory, often working with Indian ink on linen. An all-female trade union was formed – the Tracers' Association – which, in 1922, amalgamated with the Association of Engineering and Shipbuilding Draughtsmen. By the time of the Second World War, the trade of Tracer was held by members of the **Women's Auxiliary Air Force** (WAAF) and the **Auxiliary Territorial Service** (ATS), the latter working with the Royal Army Ordnance Corps to produce drawings of new designs for tools and parts for tanks and lorries.

▦ TRADE UNIONIST

From the 1880s women's trade unions or associations were being formed and many women were taking an active part in political activity for the first time. Mark Crail's website (www.unionancestors.co.uk) lists some of the thousands of trade unions that have been in existence since then and is an excellent starting point for pinning down which ones would have been active in an industry at a particular time.

A few women found paid employment with their union. Anne Godwin (1897–1992), for instance, the daughter of a draper, trained as a shorthand typist when she left school in 1912. After the First World War she joined the Association of Women Clerks and Secretaries (AWCS) and in 1925 began working in their offices, becoming a full time union official in the 1930s. She successfully negotiated an amalgamation with the male National Union of Clerks in 1940 and in 1956 became General Secretary of the union; in 1961/2 she was only the third woman to be President of the Trades Union Congress (TUC) and was made a Dame of the British Empire. (Her predecessors at the TUC were Anne Loughlin of the Tailors and Garment Workers Union in 1943 and Florence Hancock of the Transport Workers Union in 1948.)

For an introduction to the subject see the online exhibition 'From kitchen table to conference table' at www.politicalwomen.org.uk. This was put together by the Working Class Movement Library (51 The Crescent, Salford M5 4WX; www.wcml.org.uk) and their archives include biographical material. Today's trade unions' websites are also useful in disentangling their sometimes complicated life stories, e.g. www.tssa.org.uk for railway workers.

■ TRIMMING MAKER

see **hat maker; milliner.**

■ TROTTER SELLER, TROTTER SCRAPER

Sheep's **trotters were** a form of fast food available on the streets of London, Liverpool, Newcastle upon Tyne and other cities in the Victorian period. They were a by-product of the leather industry and had originally been sold wholesale for use in glue manufacture but by the 1850s there was more profit in selling them for food. Henry Mayhew describes one establishment in Bermondsey where women were employed to scrape the hair off the trotters 'quickly but softly, so that the skin should not be injured, and after that the trotters are boiled for about four hours, and they are then ready for market. . . . One of the best of these workwomen can scrape 150 sets, or 600 feet, in a day, but the average of the work is 500 sets a week, including women and girls. . . . they were exceedingly merry, laughing and chatting . . .'. Those who sold on the streets were mainly elderly women, with a hand-basket and a white cloth on which to display the trotters (see **street seller**).

■ TYPIST, TYPEWRITER

The original name for a woman (or man) who used one of the new office machines in the 1880s was a 'typewriter', becoming the modern 'typist' by the 1900s. A copy typist simply typed up letters and other documents, while a shorthand typist, on a higher wage, would be required to type up from dictation, and both occupations grew hugely in number from the late 19th century (see **office staff**); either might work for an individual or be in the typing pool and on call for a number of men. By the 1930s there were some 200,000 women typists in Britain

An article in *Woman's Life* in 1896 described the foundation of the 'shorthand and typewriting office' in the Houses of Parliament, opened 18 months before for the convenience of MPs and under the direction

A warning to enamoured businessmen, dating from 1908.

of Miss May H. Ashworth, a rector's daughter, who also 'manages, and has done so for many years, a large office in Victoria Street'. Her girls had been given apartments adjoining the House of Lords, complete with 'electric light and every modern convenience', under the supervision of the Sergeant-at-Arms. Miss Ashworth, who is a good example of the kind of female businesswoman taking advantage of the new opportunities for educated women in the late 19th century, trained the girls herself in 'a school which I have established in connection with my business . . . all of them are able to write 120 words a minute, or more, in shorthand, and an average speed of 80 words a minute on the typewriter'. This was at the higher level of expertise; Civil Service examinations for shorthand typists in the early 1900s required only up to 100 words a minute shorthand and '1,000 words an hour' on the typewriter. Their starting salary was 25 shillings a week, rising with experience.

■ UPHOLSTERER

Upholstery was another trade that could be plied by a needlewoman. One woman who was apprenticed to an upholsterer in the 1930s for five years described her job in *Cheshire Within Living Memory*, Cheshire Federation of WIs (Countryside Books, 1994). For the first year she did little other than sweep up, shop, cook and clean at the beck and call of the other women in the workroom. In the second year she still had to clean up when everyone else had gone home, but she was also taught how to sew carpets: 'In those days, carpets were all sewn by hand, seamed together and cross stitched all round with steel rings sewn on every six inches apart. There was a two inch turn-under all round too.' From the third year, she was taught how to make loose covers, curtains and bedspreads, and to repair table linen and bed linen, as much of the work was for shipping lines; even sewing up '500 or 600' feather pillows at a time was part of her duties.

■ VETERINARY SURGEON

The first veterinary school (now the Royal Veterinary College) was founded in 1792 and the Royal College of Veterinary Surgeons created in 1844, but it was 1922 before the first woman was admitted as a member of the professional body.

Aleen Isabel Cust (1868–1937) was the eldest daughter of Sir Leopold Cust and had the appropriate upbringing of a wealthy young aristocrat, being presented at Court in 1886. What she really wanted, however, was to be a vet and she pursued her dream. She attended the New Veterinary College in Edinburgh and in her first year was awarded the first prize medals, but then was barred from taking the professional examinations because the authorities decided that the word 'student' in this context meant 'male student'. Nonetheless, she finished the course and went off to practise in Ireland, her birthplace, where she won the approval of local farmers and even held the post of Veterinary Inspector to the Galway County Council – the most vociferous opposition came from the parish priest, who was won over when she managed to save the life of his cow. By 1901 she was living in Northumberland, at Falloden Kennels. The First World War saw her volunteer to serve with the veterinary hospitals in France. She had continued her fight for professional recognition and registration, and finally the RCVS allowed her to sit a practical examination, which of course she sailed through, and admitted her to their number (see *Aleen Cust, Veterinary Surgeon: Britain's First Woman Vet*, Connie M. Ford, Biopress, 1990).

Until the 20th century the great part of a vet's practice was made up of farm animals, particularly horses and cattle. Much of the popular prejudice against women vets arose because they were seen as too weak to be able to control large animals, not to mention the impropriety of a woman undertaking tasks such as castration and insemination. The growing popularity of small pets opened up new opportunities for employment and although a woman would still have had a hard time convincing a rural practice of her competence, before her death in 1937 over 60 women had followed Aleen Cust into the RCVS and demand for places at the College was such that the number of women students had had to be limited to 50.

In 1934 Olga Uvarov qualified from the College – forty-two years later, as Dame Olga (DBE, DSc, HonCBiol, FIBiol, FRCS), she became the first woman President of the Royal College of Veterinary Surgeons.

Although vets in large practices would have had auxiliary staff, the position of veterinary nurse did not gain official approval until after the scope of this book, in the 1960s – see the website of the British Veterinary Nursing Association (www.bvna.org.uk).

It is only since 1948 that all vets have had to hold qualifications approved by the RCVS, though the majority of vets after 1844 were registered. The RCVS has a library and archive (Belgravia House, 62–64 Horseferry Road, London SW1P 2AF; www.rcvs.org.uk), and so has the Royal Veterinary College (Royal College Street, London NW1 0TU; www.rvc.org.uk). The latter is the principal college but there are others associated with different universities (the Society of Genealogists has a good collection of published lists of university alumni). The veterinary school of the University of Edinburgh is the Royal (Dick) School of Veterinary Studies (www.vet. ed.ac.uk/History.htm).

■ VOLUNTARY AID DETACHMENTS (VADs)

The origins of the VADs lay with the formation of the medical service of the Territorial Force (in 1901 in England and Wales, 1910 in Scotland) and they were intended only as home defence units. From the beginning, recruitment was carried out with the support of the British Red Cross and the Order of St John, but the women's detachments were always seen as nursing assistants rather than fully trained professionals, and as cooks, domestics etc. All VADs – which was also the name given to members of the detachments – were required to gain certificates in first aid and home nursing.

Once the First World War began volunteers flooded into the VADs; the value of using the detachments overseas in France and Belgium was immediately recognised and the first units left England in August and September 1914. At this point their most important task was to staff rest stations, providing food and comfort to wounded servicemen, but within six months VADs were being sent to military hospitals in the UK and at the Front – in the Mediterranean, Egypt and Mesopotamia as well as France. Here they worked under the supervision of **QAIMNS** nurses;

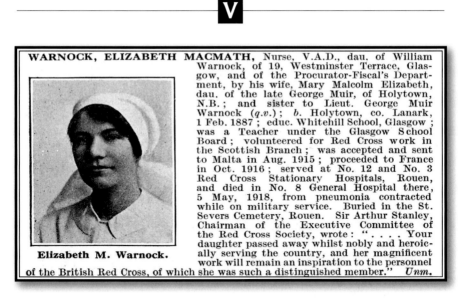

WARNOCK, ELIZABETH MACMATH, Nurse, V.A.D., dau. of William Warnock, of 19, Westminster Terrace, Glasgow, and of the Procurator-Fiscal's Department, by his wife, Mary Malcolm Elizabeth, dau. of the late George Muir, of Holytown, N.B.; and sister to Lieut. George Muir Warnock (*q.v.*); *b.* Holytown, co. Lanark, 1 Feb. 1887; educ. Whitehill School, Glasgow; was a Teacher under the Glasgow School Board; volunteered for Red Cross work in the Scottish Branch; was accepted and sent to Malta in Aug. 1915; proceeded to France in Oct. 1916; served at No. 12 and No. 3 Red Cross Stationary Hospitals, Rouen, and died in No. 8 General Hospital there, 5 May, 1918, from pneumonia contracted while on military service. Buried in the St. Severs Cemetery, Rouen. Sir Arthur Stanley, Chairman of the Executive Committee of the Red Cross Society, wrote: " . . . . Your daughter passed away whilst nobly and heroically serving the country, and her magnificent work will remain an inspiration to the personnel of the British Red Cross, of which she was such a distinguished member." *Unm.*

Elizabeth M. Warnock.

An entry from Volume IV of the Roll of Honour, published after the First World War.

the age limit was set at 23 to 38 years, and they were paid £20 a year plus board, lodging and travelling expenses. VADs also worked with the American Army and in hospitals administered by the Australian, Canadian and South African services.

Not every VAD was a nurse. Apart from acting as nursing assistants and ambulance drivers, as 'general service members' they provided clerical, cooking, laboratory, laundry, telephone, pharmaceutical and X-ray support. From 1917 these general service members also served overseas. VADs of all kinds also continued to serve after the war, particularly with the Army of Occupation in Germany.

The future of VADs was considered in the inter-war years, in collaboration with the British Red Cross, the St John Ambulance Brigade and the St Andrew's Ambulance Association, and it was decided that in future they would support the armed services anywhere in the world and that members would be asked to formally sign up and give an undertaking to serve in the event of war, as if they were a member of the Territorials. Women aged 21 to 40 (later, 19 to 45) would be considered 'mobile', while the age limits for 'immobile' VADs were 18 to 65 years – and as well as nurses, once again pharmacists, dispensers, radiographers, cooks, clerks, masseuses, opticians and laboratory assistants would be encouraged to join. When war was declared in September 1939, mobile VADs were called up immediately to military hospitals under the control of the Joint War Organisation, and many 'immobile' VADs transferred to the new Civil Nursing Reserve to enable them to work at Emergency Services Hospitals (civilian hospitals).

Every 'mobile' VAD wore on her left arm 'a Red Cross brassard stamped by the competent authority', which gave her protection under the Geneva Convention. Those serving with the Royal Navy also had a blue anchor flash on their left arm; with the RAF a pair of golden eagles on their collar; with the Army the RAMC badge on their left breast; and for India VADs had a pair of red enamel Tudor roses on their collar. VADs in the Second World War served in military hospitals, auxiliary hospitals and convalescent homes, in the blood transfusion service and first aid posts and mobile units during the Blitz, and on ambulance trains and hospital ships.

There is quite a lot of background information available about the VADs, particularly during the First World War. The classic account of personal service is *Testament of Youth*, Vera Brittain (first published 1920 and reprinted many times since); see also *The Roses of No Man's Land*, Lyn Macdonald (Penguin, 1993) and its bibliography.

The British Red Cross Museum and Archives (44 Moorfields, London EC2Y 9AL) has indexes of service details for VADs of both world wars, although they may be incomplete: they include dates and place of service, nature of duties, detachments, honours etc. See their website (www.redcross. org.uk/standard.asp?id=3423) or write to the address above for details. The Museum of the Order of St John is at St John's Gate, St John's Lane, London EC1M 4DA (www.sja.org.uk). The Imperial War Museum has a very useful guide to 'Voluntary Aid Detachments in the First World War' (Information Sheet 40) online at www.iwm.org.uk/upload/pdf/Info40.pdf. A listing of auxiliary hospitals, which could help to point the way to finding local records, is online at www.juroch.demon.co.uk/kentvad.htm.

■ WAITING MAID

Very wealthy households might employ a waiting maid for every grown-up daughter, to keep her rooms in order and act as a fledgling **lady's maid**. See **domestic servant**.

■ WAITRESS

Waitressing was an option by the late 19th century for young women who did not want to go into domestic service, though the uniform was often similar to that of a **parlourmaid** – black dress, white apron, cuffs and collar, and a neat cap (and often had to be provided by the girl herself). While male waiters might be more common in restaurants and large hotels, waitresses would invariably serve in teashops and the new chains of tea houses cum restaurants founded in the 1880s and beyond, such as the Aerated Bread Company (ABC) and the British Tea Table Company (BTT) – which makes tracing a waitress to a particular employer almost impossible without supporting evidence.

The most famous, right into the 1950s, must be the 'Nippys' of the Lyons tea houses, so named because, as 97-year-old Ena Norris recalled in an interview in the *Guardian* (12 September 2004), 'we nipped about all the time'. It is delightful to learn that in the 1880s the common name for a Lyons' waitress was a 'Gladys'. The girls worked in shifts, taking orders, delivering to the table and clearing away; Ena remembered that most of their customers were regulars, some coming in at every mealtime. Employment was terminated when a girl married. For a history of J. Lyons & Co and the Nippys, see www.kzwp.com/lyons.

■ WARD MAID

A maid employed in a hospital to clean the ward, make the patients' beds etc (they later became known as domestic assistants).

■ WARDROBE DEALER

A dealer in second-hand clothes, to be found in every city and large town in the country. Mrs Millest, for instance, of 164 Whippendell

Road, Watford, advertised in 1911 'Every description of Ladies' and Gents' Cast-off Wearing Apparel and Household Linen bought for Cash. Fair prices given'. In some cases these women may also have acted as unofficial pawnbrokers, lending money on clothing, or as dressmakers, turning old clothes into new. In 1845 *The Times* commented that a wardrobe dealer was 'a new name for a dealer in old clothes'.

■ WEAVER

Women were traditionally hand-spinners, but in the factory system of the 19th century they were particularly important in the weaving of cloth – see the entries for workers in the **cotton, linen, silk** and **wool** industries.

The website of the Worshipful Company of Weavers (www.weavers.org.uk) has a useful alphabetical glossary of textile terms. *Looms and Weaving*, Anna Benson and Neil Warburton (Shire Publications, 1986) is a good introduction to the development of the loom, and mentions the 20th century revival of the craft of handloom weaving in which women were prominent – Elizabeth Peacock, who founded the Guild of Weavers, Spinners and Dyers with Mabel Dawson, for instance, and Ethel Mairet, called 'one of the most influential weavers of the 20th century'.

Some women worked at home, on handlooms, into the 1900s; at Glemsford in Suffolk, for example, there was a cottage industry for women weaving cotton and horsehair cloth for railway carriage blinds and upholstery. Horsehair was an important Victorian commodity – see www.johnboydtextiles.co.uk/history.html for more about horsehair weaving.

There are useful articles online at www.origins.net/help/resarticle-so-weaving.htm ('Weaving and the Textile Industry' in Scotland), and http://scottishtextileheritage.org.uk/onlineResources/articles.

■ WELFARE WORKER

The Welfare Workers' Association was founded in 1913, with 29 of its 34 founding members being women engaged in welfare work in factories belonging to companies such as Rowntree & Co, Cadbury's, Boots, Robertson's, and W.D. & H.O. Wills. When Seebohm Rowntree was appointed wartime Director of Welfare at the Ministry of Munitions in 1916, the appointment of welfare workers was made compulsory in government controlled factories, many of them with female workforces, so that by 1918 their numbers had risen to over 1,000. At the same time, 'labour officers' (usually men) were appointed for the 'hiring and firing' side of labour relations.

Membership of the professional body declined along with demand from industry during the 1920s, but remained mainly female. From 1924 it was called the Institute of Industrial Welfare Workers. In 1931 welfare workers and labour officers combined in the Institute of Labour Management, with the female-dominated welfare side the junior partner. In the US 'personnel management' had long been accepted as a blanket term and by the late 1930s was in use here. After the Second World War, in 1946, it became officially the Institute of Personnel Management (changing to the Institute of Personnel and Development in 1994).

The website of the Chartered Institute of Personnel and Development describes the history of the profession – www.cipd.co.uk/about/history.htm; and a history of the Institute is given in *Personnel Management 1913–1963*, Margaret Niven (Institute of Personnel Management, 1967).

■ WETNURSE

A wetnurse was employed specifically to care for a baby, as opposed to a monthly nurse who looked after the mother after birth. It was often necessary to find a woman to breastfeed the baby because the mother was ill or had died in childbirth, a too common occurrence throughout the 19th century, although some wealthy women simply preferred to pass the task of breastfeeding to a substitute because of the perceived effect nursing a baby would have on their figures.

It would probably be a private arrangement between the wetnurse and the family, and she might live in at the house for a while or simply come in to perform her duties. Some women made a career out of breastfeeding a 'nurse child' – parish babies and foundlings were frequently 'farmed out' to such women, sometimes a long way from their home parish – and it could be a welcome source of income for rural families. On the other hand, single mothers who had been forced to seek shelter in the workhouse while they gave birth were sometimes found places as wetnurses by the board of guardians, as they were in Shrewsbury in 1837.

Mrs Beeton in the 1860s recommended seeking a woman aged between 20 and 30, of sound health and 'free from all eruptive disease or local blemish. The best evidence of a sound state of health will be found in the woman's clear open countenance, the ruddy tone of the skin, the full, round and elastic state of the breasts, and especially of the erectile, firm, condition of the nipple, which, in all unhealthy states of the body, is pendulous, flabby and relaxed'. The interview must have involved the prospective nurse exposing all.

■ WHITE LEAD WORKER

White lead was carbonate of lead, which produced the pigments used in paint (and was only banned in 1988). Its manufacture was important, but also highly dangerous.

In Newcastle, at least, in the mid-19th century most of the processes at the Gallowgate lead works were performed by women. They melted pigs of lead in cauldrons, heated by fires beneath, and poured the molten metal into flat iron moulds to form sheets. The thin pieces of now solid lead were taken to form stacks – layers of ash, spent tanner's bark, earthen pots containing vinegar, and lead were built up until they filled the room, set aside, and then left for several weeks. The bark fermented, giving off enough heat to slowly evaporate the vinegar, which in turn acted on the sheets of lead to transform it into white lead. The stack was then dismantled;

Women wearing the rudimentary masks that were all they had to protect them from the effects of the lead in 1896.

any lead that had not been carbonated was collected and taken back to the beginning of the process. The white lead was ground finely in water to a paste, and dried. It was sold either dry or mixed with linseed oil.

The dangers of working with white lead were well known: exposure could cause sickness and might bring on miscarriages; long term it could cause convulsions, blindness, paralysis and brain damage. In 1878 women and children were banned from working with the substance (see also **enameller; pottery worker**).

■ WOMEN'S ARMY AUXILIARY CORPS (WAAC)

By 1916, two years into the First World War and after the slaughter on the Somme, the shortage of manpower in the Army was becoming increasingly worrying for the military establishment. An obvious source of extra troops was the large number of men serving in non-combatant roles in France, particularly on communications, and it was decided that they could be replaced by women. By this time, female participation in the **Women's Legion** at home, and in military nursing and war work generally, and sheer necessity, had begun to break down the prejudice against employing women.

Mrs Chalmers Watson, a doctor and the sister of the Director General of National Service, was asked to report on the concept of the enlistment of women into the Army, and Sir Douglas Haig, Commander-in-Chief of the British Army, finally agreed to the formation of a new military unit, though not without reservations: one was that women would not act as clothing storekeepers because they could not assist the men trying on their clothes. Mrs Chalmers Watson became the first Chief Controller of the newly formed Women's Army Auxiliary Corps in March 1917, with Mrs Gwynne-Vaughan the Chief Controller Overseas, and the first WAACs were soon being sent out to France, though not without much chuntering about the problems of admitting women to military discipline. It was also decided to recruit women for service at home. They were to serve with the Army in clerical and telegraphic work, as well as cooking, carpentry and driving, releasing men for active service (the four sections of the Corps were Clerical, Cookery, Mechanical and Miscellaneous). Recruitment went so well that fears were expressed in some quarters that too many women from the cotton mills were leaving their jobs. The women who joined were predominantly working class, which led to them gaining an unfortunate and uncalled for reputation for being 'common' and promiscuous.

Because there was no precedent for women to receive commissions in the British Army, their ranks have a civilian ring to them – controllers, administrators and forewomen. Even though they worked behind the lines, they still lived under conditions of danger from shell fire; nine WAACs were killed at Abbeville in May 1918 by a long-distance shell. Women whose husbands were serving at the Front were not sent overseas, and single women were not allowed to get married within six months of their date of enlistment.

It is said that over 100 women went out to France each week; some 57,000 women served in the WAAC and over 10,000 served on the Western Front. In April 1918, the Corps was renamed Queen Mary's Army Auxiliary Corps. By 1 May 1920 it had been disbanded and when an equivalent service was created for the Second World War, it was under another name – the **Auxiliary Territorial Service** (ATS).

The war records for women who served in the WAAC from 1917 to 1921 are held at The National Archives; many were destroyed by bombing during the Second World War but those that survive (about 9,000 of them) are now available to search online (www.nationalarchives.gov.uk/documentsonline/waac.asp). There are also other relevant records at Kew on the history and organisation of the WAAC: consult the leaflet on 'Women's Services, First World War; Military Records Information 74'. *Women at War 1914–1918*, Arthur Marwick (Fontana, 1977) includes a transcript of Mrs Elsie Cooper's memories of life in the WAAC, and the Imperial War Museum has further oral, manuscript and photographic archives.

■ WOMEN'S AUXILIARY AIR FORCE (WAAF)

Formed on **28** June 1939, when war was inevitable, and mobilised on 28 August, the Women's Auxiliary Air Force was rapidly staffed by voluntary transfers from the RAF companies of the **Auxiliary Territorial Service** (ATS). As with the WRAF in the First World War, the intention was to free men for active service from any post that could equally well be filled by a woman.

It was from the beginning an integral part of the Royal Air Force, and the WAAF officer in charge of a detachment reported to and was responsible to the relevant RAF officer. Initially women only substituted for code, cypher and administrative duties, but WAAFs were soon employed in the Accountant, Equipment, and Administrative and Special Duties branches. Their work covered a huge range, from clerks, cooks and hairdressers to flight mechanics, acetylene welders, bomb and aircraft plotters, photographers, and balloon and parachute packers. The original five trades had increased to over 70 by 1944, when WAAFs were serving in every RAF Command and all over the world, including the Middle East, Malta, Italy, India, Canada, the USA and Africa.

The WAAFs may not have been combatants but like all the women's services they faced danger in their everyday duties. The first woman in the services to receive the George Cross came from the WAAF – Flight Officer Daphne Pearson, who in May 1940 risked her life to rescue an injured pilot from a burning plane, finally throwing herself on top to protect him when a 120 lb bomb exploded only 30 yards away.

From April 1941 WAAF officers were granted commissions as full members of the Armed Forces. The uniform was the same colour and style as that of the RAF, and identical badges of rank were worn. Before 1941 the ages for enlistment had been restricted to between 18 to 43, and that year they were extended by a few months (though apparently Flight Sergeant Stalker was almost 70 when she was allowed to serve, as she had been an officer in the WRAF during the First World War!).

Equivalent ranks (RAF ranks in brackets): Air Chief Commandant (Air Vice-Marshal); Air Commandant (Air Commodore); Group Officer (Group Captain); Wing Officer (Wing Commander); Squadron Officer (Squadron Leader); Flight Officer (Flight Lieutenant); Section Officer (Flying Officer); Assistant Section Officer (Pilot Officer); Warrant Officer (same); Flight Sergeant (same); Sergeant (same); Corporal (same); Leading Aircraftwoman (Leading Aircraftman); Aircraftwoman 1st or 2nd class (Aircraftman 1st or 2nd class).

The history of the WAAF is told online at www.raf.mod.uk/history_old/wraf.html, or see *The WAAF*, Beryl Escott (Shire Publications, 2003). The RAF Museum at Hendon has downloadable guides for 'Researching RAF, RAFVR, RAuxAF, WRAF and WAAF Personnel' (www.rafmuseum.org.uk). Service records are only available to next of kin, from PMA IM1b (RAF), Room 5, Building 248A, RAF Personnel Management Agency, RAF Innsworth, Gloucestershire GL3 1EZ. The WAAF Association website (www.waafassociation.org.uk) has a bibliography and list of 'useful sources'. Some women have written about their experiences, e.g. *Sand in My Shoes: Wartime Diaries of a WAAF*, Joan Rice (HarperCollins, 2006).

■ WOMEN'S FORAGE CORPS

The importance of finding forage for the thousands of horses used by the military during the First World War cannot be overestimated. Some of the members of the Women's Land Army were detailed for this, and from 1915 there was also a small corps of women under the Forage Purchasing Department of the Army Service Corps, who supervised the movement of hay and straw. Some later in the war were employed as Forage Guards, with the responsibility of guarding valuable storage sites.

■ WOMEN'S FORESTRY SERVICE

Formed during the First World War under the Board of Trade, and employing about 2,000 women. They carried out the same kind of work as the Second World War **Women's Timber Corps.**

■ WOMEN'S HOSPITAL CORPS

Formed by Dr Louisa Garrett Anderson (daughter of Dr Elizabeth Garrett Anderson) and Dr Flora Murray in response to the outbreak of the First World War, in August 1914, who took an all-female surgical unit to France to work with the French Red Cross and set up hospitals in Paris and at Wimereux. From March 1915, with the approval of the War Office, they also ran a hospital in London which was attached to the Royal Army Medical Corps. See *Women as Army Surgeons*, Flora Murray (Hodder & Stoughton, 1920).

■ WOMEN'S IMPERIAL SERVICE LEAGUE

A small unofficial voluntary mission of female doctors, created at the beginning of the First World War by Mrs Muriel St Clair Stobart (who had gained experience in the 1912 conflict in the Balkans with the Women's Convoy Corps, a small group of women doctors who went to Bulgaria to care for the Serbian troops). They went first to Antwerp, but were forced to leave when the Germans advanced, then to France and in April 1915 to Serbia for a few months before that country was invaded by Bulgaria. They treated not only wounded soldiers but also the civilian population. See *The Quality of Mercy: Women at War, Serbia 1915–18*, Monica Krippner (David & Charles, 1980).

■ WOMEN'S LAND ARMY

Although it is the Women's Land Army (WLA) of the Second World War that is usually referred to, there was a similar organisation in existence from March 1917, during the First World War, when British food reserves were becoming low and it was essential to get extra hands onto the farms to replace male labourers. In both wars, the women remained civilians and these were never 'armies' in any military sense. They took on every aspect of farm work – milking cows, driving tractors and operating farm machinery, ploughing, working in the fields sowing and planting crops, hoeing, weeding, manuring, harvesting, carting crops and muck, and caring for livestock.

A land girl of the First World War.

Women had been encouraged to help on the land, particularly at harvest time, from the start of the First World War, for instance under the Women's Land Service Corps from 1916. That year the Rector of Great Leighs in Essex recorded his reaction to seeing two young women working on the land who 'looked as if they had gone astray, out of a comic opera' in their riding-breeches and overalls (*Echoes of the Great War: The Diary of the Reverend Andrew Clark 1914–1919*, ed. James Munson, Oxford University Press, 1988). The WLA, officially formed under the Ministry of Agriculture and Fisheries in 1917, gave the movement far greater emphasis, and recruitment brought in several thousand more women. The number, though, was never great, perhaps adding about 16,000 to the agricultural workforce after 18 months. The women wore a uniform of an overall smock, breeches, boots and gaiters, and a hat. They signed a contract for six months or a year and were employed by the farmer for whom they worked; there were three departments within which they were organised – agriculture, timber and forage (some women worked for the **Women's Forestry Service** or the **Women's Forage Corps**). The first WLA was disbanded with the end of the war in 1918.

In June 1939, with the threat of war, the WLA was re-formed and began recruitment, so that there were some 17,000 women registered for service by the time war was declared in September. The age limits were roughly 17 to 50, but don't seem to have been too strictly kept. For the first year or so the land girls, as they came to be known, who were drawn from all walks of life, often with no knowledge of agriculture or animals, were sent to farms with little preparation or training. Later, courses were provided on general farm work or specialised jobs such as thatching or rat catching. As before, they were employed and paid by the farmers, but in 1942 the War Agricultural Executive Committee ('War Ag') in each county took over responsibility for their employment and efforts were made to force farmers to regulate their hours to 48 a week in winter and 50 a week in summer and to pay a minimum wage (advances that benefited regular male farm workers as well). The uniform has become famous – fawn breeches and matching shirt, green pullover, brown trilby-style hat, long woollen socks, leather boots; in summer dungarees that were often rolled up or cut to shorts length.

The WLA continued to operate after the end of the war in 1945 and was only disbanded in 1950. The women who served received little recognition for their efforts until belatedly, in December 2007, it was announced that surviving members of the WLA could apply to the government for a commemorative badge.

The service records of individuals have not survived but there are index cards to the records, held at the Imperial War Museum and available to search on microfiche at The National Archives. The Imperial War Museum also has a full bibliography of works relating to the WLA of both wars. Little has been written about the first WLA but try *Rural Life in England in the First World War*, Pamela Horn (Gill and Macmillan, 1985). There is much more on the land girls of the 1940s and a good start is

They Fought in the Fields, Nicola Tyrer (Sinclair Stevenson, 1996) or see www.myweb.tiscali.co.uk/homefront/womenatwar/landarmy/landarmy. html. Museums too have material, for instance at the Women's Land Army Museum at Little Farthingloe Farm, Folkestone Road, Dover (telephone: 01304 212040), which celebrates the work of the Kentish land girls in what became known as 'Hellfire Corner' because it came under attack so often from the Luftwaffe. See also **Women's Timber Corps.**

■ WOMEN'S LEGION

Founded in December 1914 and intended to offer support to the Army. In February 1915 its Cookery Section began providing Army cooks (see **cook, Army**), first in convalescent camps and subsequently throughout Army camps in Britain. In 1917 this section, by now several thousand strong, formed the core of the new **Women's Army Auxiliary Corps.** The Mechanical Transport Section was formed in 1916 and attached to the Royal Army Service Corps (RASC), providing despatch riders and chauffeurs; if they served in France they were seconded to the QMAAC. Drivers working with the Royal Flying Corps were taken into the new **Women's Royal Air Force** in 1918.

Between the wars the Women's Legion Reserve continued to provide a focus for women willing to form a pool of trained personnel for military support and civil defence duties. Just as sections had been used during the First World War to form the nuclei of the WAAC and the WRAF, so during the Second World War its younger members were recruited en bloc for the new **Auxiliary Territorial Service** (ATS). The Women's Legion itself continued to serve on the Home Front all through the war, particularly concerned with mobile canteens, evacuation, air raid casualties and shelters.

■ WOMEN'S ROYAL AIR FORCE (WRAF)

On 1 April 1918, during the First World War, the Royal Air Force was formed from an amalgamation of the Royal Flying Corps (RFC) and Royal Naval Air Service (RNAS), and included drivers from the **Women's Legion.** The same month, the Women's Royal Air Force was created, initially transferring volunteers from the **Women's Army Auxiliary Corps** and **Women's Royal Naval Service.** In the next few months the service grew to over 20,000 strong. From March to May 1919, about 500 women were sent abroad to France and Germany to bolster the occupying forces.

It was the intention that women be trained to take the place of home-based clerks and mechanics and free the men for active service. They signed up for at least one year, at a minimum age of 18. They were counted either as 'mobile' (serving anywhere in the UK) or 'immobile' (living at home and serving within travelling distance). The jobs that they undertook included riggers, fitters, painters and dopers (reassembling engines, repairing, cleaning, and maintaining aircraft), and signwriters (painting the aircraft with RAF markings, roundels etc); pay clerks, store clerks and typists; and despatch riders and motor drivers. There were even 'pigeon women' who looked after the messenger pigeons at Pulham St Mary airship base.

The uniform in the first days was a scratch issue of QMAAC uniforms with the simple addition of the words 'Royal Flying Corps' on the sleeve. Then they were issued with a khaki tunic and skirt, with the RAF badge on the cap, tunic and greatcoat sleeves. After a few months, in November 1918, they received a new blue RAF-type uniform. The WRAF was demobilised after the war, on 1 April 1920, and the equivalent service from 1939 was the **Women's Auxiliary Air Force (WAAF)**.

No officers' records have survived from the WRAF, but airwomen's records are at The National Archives and may include enrolment forms with personal information: see the research guide *Women's Services, First World War*. The RAF Museum has a downloadable guide to 'Researching First World War personnel: RFC, RNAS, RAF, WRAF' (www.rafmuseum.org.uk). There is more about the history of the service at www.raf.mod.uk/history/wraf.html. *From the Ground Up: A History of RAF Ground Crew* by F.J. Adkin (Airlife, 1983) puts the women's service in the context of RAF history.

■ WOMEN'S ROYAL ARMY CORPS (WRAC)

see Auxiliary Territorial Service (ATS).

■ WOMEN'S ROYAL NAVAL SERVICE (WRNS)

The **Women's Royal** Naval Service was formed in November 1917, disbanded on 1 October 1919 after the First World War, and re-formed in April 1939. In 1993 it was integrated into the Royal Navy.

New recruits to the WRNS learning to cook under difficult conditions, 1942.

The loss of men in the Navy during the First World War, and the success of the Women's Army Auxiliary Corps in supporting the Army, prompted the Admiralty to consider the recruitment of women to 'free a man for sea service'. Theirs was to be a shore service and originally was intended to be 'immobile', i.e. the Wrens would be recruited to work close to where they lived. Applications came in from all over the country, however, not just around the naval ports, and 'mobile' officers and ratings were soon commonplace. By March 1918 one division had even been formed overseas, employing Wrens in Malta, Gibraltar and Genoa, mainly on cypher and coding work. At its maximum strength, the WRNS had over 400 officers and nearly 6,000 ratings. They filled any role needed – including cooks, stewards, waitresses, clerks, telephonists, despatch riders, wireless operators, fitters, motor drivers, sailmakers and mine cleaners. About 2,000 Wrens were based at air stations and were eventually transferred to the newly formed **Women's Royal Air Force**.

Between the wars former Wrens kept in touch through the Association of Wrens, formed in 1920 'to maintain the esprit de corps'. When in April 1939 Mrs Vera Laughton Matthews was appointed Director of WRNS and recruitment for the re-formed service began, some of the applicants were veterans of the first conflict. There were over 3,000 Wrens in place by December 1939.

It was intended to repeat the success of the First World War by replacing men at Naval shore establishments, but from 1941 there was a vast increase in the range of duties, including on submarines, torpedoes, the Fleet Air

Arm, and at Bletchley 'Station X' working on, amongst other things, the top secret Enigma decoding. Some Wrens worked aboard ship on transatlantic convoys as code-breakers; there were even female stokers and coxswains. Boats' crews were based at south coast ports from 1940, with Wrens crossing the Channel to bring back damaged boats during the Normandy landings in 1944. Wrens served overseas, but only on a voluntary basis until 1943.

By late 1944 there were over 74,000 women in the WRNS. In 1946 the Board of Admiralty announced that the WRNS was to be retained, and from 1 February 1949 it was 'a permanent and integral part of the Naval Service and is regarded, in all respects, other than its subjection to a separate disciplinary code, as part of the Royal Navy itself'.

The uniform was a navy blue double-breasted jacket and skirt, shirt and tie. Officers wore a tricorne hat in black velour felt, with a hat badge similar to that of RN officers except that it had blue leaves instead of gold. Chief Wrens and petty officers also wore a tricorne hat, with a white waterproof cover, while ratings wore a blue cloth cap similar to that of RN ratings.

Equivalent ranks (Royal Navy in brackets) from 1939 to 1993: Director (Rear Admiral); Deputy Director (Captain); Superintendent (Captain); Chief Officer (Commander); First Officer (Lieutenant-Commander); Second Officer (Lieutenant); Third Officer (Sub-Lieutenant); Chief Wren (Chief Petty Officer); Petty Officer Wren (Petty Officer); Leading Wren (Leading Seaman); Wren (Able Seaman); Ordinary Wren (Ordinary Seaman).

The National Archives holds records for WRNS officers and ratings from 1917 to 1919, and these are available to search online (www.nationalarchives. gov.uk/documentsonline/wrns.asp). Those for Wrens who served during the Second World War (and up to 1955) will only be released to next of kin (The Directorate of Personnel Support (Navy), Navy Search, TNT Archive Services, Tetron Point, William Nadin Way, Swadlincote, Derbyshire DE11 0BB; telephone: 01283 227913; e-mail: navysearchpgrc@tnt.co.uk).

The Royal Naval Museum (HM Naval Base (PP66), Portsmouth, PO1 3NH) holds no Naval service records but does have a library, photographs etc; see their website (www.royalnavalmuseum.org/info_sheets_WRNS.htm) and Information Sheet 86. There is also a history of the WRNS at www. seayourhistory.org.uk. *The WRNS: A History of the Women's Royal Naval Service*, M.H. Fletcher (Batsford, 1989) has a wealth of information and pictures.

■ WOMEN'S TIMBER CORPS

Formed in April 1942 as a specialised branch of the **Women's Land Army**, which had been carrying out timber work. (Scotland had a Forestry Service of its own from 1941.) It was disbanded in August 1946. The women did general forestry (felling trees, clearing brush and undergrowth, charcoal burning), sawmill work (sorting, cutting and stacking timber), or measuring (travelling, often alone, to select trees for felling, etc). They were often known as 'Timber Jills' or 'Lumber Jills' and wore the same uniform as the Women's Land Army, except that the hat was replaced by a beret and their badge had a crown over a fir tree.

Gwen Magor worked in the Women's Timber Corps during the Second World War as a measurer. (Barbara Clarke)

■ WOMEN'S TRANSPORT SERVICE (FANY)

see **First Aid Nursing Yeomanry.**

■ WOOL SPINNERS AND WEAVERS

The 'woollen industry' covers a wide range of jobs and products, and was the most important in the country from the 16th to the 18th centuries. Women had traditionally been the spinners of wool ('spinsters') when cloth was made on home handlooms, but it was common in woollen cloth factory production for the spinning and weaving to be carried out by the same firm, and women came to dominate the work by the beginning of the 20th century.

In some areas women still did the spinning at home as they had done for centuries, but increasingly outworkers were provided with yarn by

Women working in the unbearable heat and dust of a Bradford woolcomber's factory, where the raw wool was cleaned and prepared for spinning, stripped to the waist for comfort.

the mills and either wove or knitted as required. In Cumbria they knitted woollen stockings, gloves, hats and sweaters for the local mills (see www.fellsanddales.org.uk/trails/woollen_ways.php for the Cumbrian industry). There was a distinction between 'wool' and 'worsted' in production – woollen cloth was woven from a softer, short-staple, carded wool yarn, which could be felted for some processes, while worsted cloth used the strong, long-staple, combed yarn. There is a dictionary of standard worsted and wool fibres at www.ntgi.net/ICCF&D/wool.htm.

Yorkshire was, of course, the 'Wool County' and there is background information at the Bradford Industrial Museum, Moorside Mills, Moorside Road, Eccleshill, Bradford BD2 3HP (www.bradfordmuseums.org).

The area around Bradford, Leeds, Wakefield, Dewsbury, Huddersfield, Halifax and Keighley was thronged with woollen cloth manufacturers, woollen and worsted printers, woolstaplers, worsted spinners, stuff manufacturers ('stuff' was a very old name for worsted cloth without any nap or pile), 'fancy goods' manufacturers (such as worsted and silk mixed in 'waistcoatings'), woollen millers, cloth dressers, flannel manufacturers, blanket manufacturers, baize manufacturers and so on. There were even 'shoddy mills', which turned woollen rags into new cloth.

Woollen mills were in production in many counties up to the early 19th century. In some areas, such as Devon, Somerset and Wiltshire,

*Drawing 'slivers', or continuous ribbons of fibres, using a machine
for combing the wool in 1844.*

the industry then declined in importance, while in others it continued
and prospered. In the Cotswolds there were about 150 mills active in
the 1850s, but only 20 or so by 1900, while in Carmarthenshire factory
production took over from handlooms and made a thriving business from
blankets, knitting wool and flannel. The National Wool Museum is based
there (Dre-Fach Felindre, Llandysul, Carmarthenshire SA44 5UP; www.
museumwales.ac.uk/en/wool).

Blankets were also the basis for the Oxfordshire industry, with six major
blanket manufacturers based in Witney in the mid-19th century. William
Smith, who set up his business in 1851, introduced the first steam power
to Witney in 1857 and the industry flourished (the last mill only closed
in 2002). See www.witneyblanketstory.org for an excellent background

to wool spinning and weaving in the area, with a glossary of terms and links to other sites (this is useful for all woollen cloth, not just blankets). A visit to the Witney and District Museum (Gloucester Court Mews, High Street, Witney, OX28 6JF; telephone: 01993 775915) can also help to bring the industry to life. See also the *Victoria County History of Oxfordshire*, volume XIV.

The *Woollen Industry*, Chris Aspin (Shire Publications, 2006) is a good general introduction to the subject. Books about particular areas of the country include *Warp and Weft: The Somerset and Wiltshire Woollen Industry*, Ken Rogers (Barracuda Books, 1986); *The Tweedmakers: A History of the Scottish Fancy Woollen Industry 1600–1914*, C. Gulvin (David and Charles, 1973); *The Flannelmakers: A Brief History of the Welsh Woollen Industry*, J. Geraint Jenkins (Gwasg Carreg Gwalch, 2005). See also **carpet maker; weaver.**

Finding out more about your female ancestors' working lives is a fascinating extension of family history. Perhaps reading through the dictionary has inspired you to investigate further? The suggestions given below for background research are intended to supplement those included with the occupations listed in the dictionary, and to give ideas for possible progress with the many entries that have no obvious 'next step'.

Records – of companies, trade unions, associations, individuals – can turn up at surprisingly long distances from where you might expect, and in the past might have been undiscovered. However, searches can now be easily made through the websites below, as well as through local record offices (see 'Useful Addresses'). Records of town and city life are sometimes of great help in tracing businesses and the owners of premises, through local rates books for instance. Other **property records** such as deeds, estate records, business papers, apprenticeships, licensing records, tax records can all prove useful.

A2A, short for Access to Archives (www.nationalarchives.gov.uk/a2a), is a searchable catalogue of archives held locally in England and Wales, in record offices, libraries, universities and museums. There are currently over 10 million references to records on the database and it is regularly updated. This is a great starting point, though obviously not everything is here.

The **National Register of Archives** (www.nationalarchives.gov.uk/nra/default.asp) has information on the location of manuscript and historical records, which you can search by company, personal, family or place name.

The **Women's Library** (www.londonmet.ac.uk/thewomenslibrary) has an extensive collection of archives connected with women's history.

The **Scottish Archive Network** (www.scan.org.uk) is an online catalogue of historical records held in Scottish archives, and the **National Register of Archives for Scotland** (www.nas.gov.uk/onlineRegister/) lists private collections registered with the National Archives of Scotland.

Many businesses over the years have run into difficulties and gone **bankrupt**. If your ancestor ran her own business for a time, it is always worth checking these records. The National Archives (see

An example of what might be found in family papers. Clues to women's working lives may be discovered in birth, marriage and death certificates, census returns, parish records, and family stories and heirlooms.

'Useful Addresses') has a research guide detailing their relevant holdings. Bankruptcies were also listed regularly in the *London Gazette* and its sister publications in Edinburgh and Belfast. These can be searched online (www.gazettes-online.co.uk). There may also be reports in local newspapers.

The Business Archives Council (www.businessarchivescouncil.org.uk) is dedicated to preserving 'business records of historical importance', and, although it holds no archives itself, it suggests, amongst other things, using *A Guide to Tracing the History of a Business*, Dr John Orbell (Gower, 1987) for sources and ideas. Most small companies' records, it warns, were destroyed in the past unless they were kept in the family. **Companies House** (www.companieshouse.gov.uk) is the place to go to trace a current company. The National Archives holds a variety of company records (see contact details in 'Useful Addresses'; they have a range of relevant research guides available through the website or at Kew). See also *Company and Business Records for Family Historians*, Eric Probert (Bury, 1994).

In Scotland, the **British Archives Council of Scotland** (13 Thurso Street, University of Glasgow, Glasgow G11 6PE) fulfils a similar role. See their website (www.gla.ac.uk/services/archives/scottishbusinessarchive/) for business records since the 18th century, advice on sources for specific industries, and an online catalogue.

Trade and town **directories** are very useful aids, which developed from the late 18th century to fill the need for quick access to commercial information and were well established by the 1850s. Kelly's is a well-known name but there are many others, and they include listings of businesses and prominent local residents. Some were very local, targeting visitors to spa and seaside resorts. Good runs of locally important directories are usually held by the local record office or main libraries (see above); most were published regularly, if not annually, and can help to trace a business or individual through several decades. They will not identify individual wage-earners, but will include anyone with a shop or business in the area.

By courtesy *"Doncaster Chronicle"*

Assistant P.M.G. greets Miss E. Ely, Doncaster's first telephonist, at opening of new automatic exchange

From a Post Office Magazine *of 1937 – company journals can be a mine of information about staff.*

Some directories can be searched online. The major website is that of the **Historical Directories Library** of the University of Leicester (www.historicaldirectories.org), and other examples can be found by using a search engine, with the word 'directory' and a county or city. Many have now been published on CD by various suppliers, for instance S&N Genealogy Supplies (www.genealogysupplies.com; telephone: 01722 716121).

There is a huge archive of advice on researching occupations for family historians in the back copies of the major **family history magazines**. For *Ancestors*, see the website www.ancestorsmagazine.co.uk – go to 'Search Issues'; for *Family History Monthly* go to www.familyhistoryonline.com and click on 'Back Issues'.

Businesses that have been in existence long enough to have an anniversary often publish a **company history** describing the development of the firm and including photographs and perhaps details of long-serving employees. Their websites, too, have a certain amount of historical information. **Histories** of towns and villages, and of particular crafts, trades and industries are common. **Autobiographies** written by local people may also help you by describing what local people did for a living.

Many of the books mentioned in the dictionary are out of print, but should be available through your local library and the inter-library loan scheme. Sale catalogues of **secondhand book dealers** are easily available and searchable online (eg, www.abebooks.co.uk and www.addall.com, but there are many more – simply type 'secondhand books' into a search engine). Support your local bookshop for books in print, and a website such as www.amazon.co.uk will also produce a list of available books, both in print and out of print, for whatever subject you desire. The catalogue of the British Library (see 'Useful Addresses') lists every book published.

For background information, advertisements and news stories there is nothing like a contemporary **newspaper**. Unfortunately there are few indexes to local newspapers and going through them is time-consuming unless you have a specific date or event in mind. The local record office should know if there is an index to any newspapers in their area. Copies of county newspapers, usually on microfilm, will be found at the record office or library.

The Newspaper Library of the **British Library** (see 'Useful Addresses') holds copies of every newspaper and magazine published in this country. There is an exciting development online with the 19th Century British Library Newspapers website, currently available at the British Library itself and at further education and higher education institutions; this has examples of Victorian newspapers from around the country, searchable by keyword. Also available online and a tremendous source is *The Times* digital index, fully searchable from the 1780s; this is available at many libraries and record offices.

Many professional bodies, large companies, trade associations etc had, and have, their own regular **journals**, which list staff news such as promotions, retirements, awards and so on as well as items of interest – the *Post Office Magazine*, for instance. Some of these are mentioned in the dictionary, but it is always worth finding out if there is anything relevant to your search: you could enquire from the company, association etc direct, or the Newspaper Library at the British Library. Copies relating to local industries may also be found at record offices or museums.

Telephone directories have been in existence since the 1880s and there are examples now available to search online at www.ancestry.co.uk (fee payable). Shops, companies, tradeswomen and professionals may all be found here and traced to an address in much the same way as trade and street directories.

The Modern Records Centre at Warwick University has links to occupational sources, including the trade unions associated with them. It also has some trade union archives, as well as employer or trade associations and business records. It gives advice for family historians on its website (www2.warwick.ac.uk/services/library.mrc).

Museum collections are indispensable for getting the feel of an industry or craft, and for bringing to life the local working community. Addresses of museums across the UK are available online (www.24hourmuseum.org. uk; or see ARCHON below).

See *Family History on the Net*, Colin Waters (Countryside Books, 2008) for more suggestions for searching the internet.

There are many suggestions for further reading or research throughout the book, but two Victorian writers deserve a special mention. Henry Maythew (1812–1887) wrote a series of articles on *London Labour and the London Poor* which first appeared in the *Morning Chronicle* between 1849 and 1850, and were published in four volumes in 1861–2; there have been many edited versions since then, but Dover Publications reprinted the full text in 1968. Similarly, Charles Booth (1840–1916) wrote a massively important study of the *Life and Labour of the People of London*, which first began appearing in 1889 and was finally published in 17 volumes from 1902 to 1903 (see the website http:///booth. lse.ac.uk for more information). I also find the website www.victorianlondon.org full of wonderful things.

Useful Addresses

To find what record offices, museums, libraries etc exist in the area you are interested in, throughout the UK (and some abroad), go to the ARCHON website (www.nationalarchives.gov.uk/archon/). This gives contact details, including addresses, telephone numbers and websites, for all record repositories, and is very useful to browse.

British Library, St Pancras, 96 Euston Road, London NW1 2DB; telephone: 0870 444 1500; www.bl.uk.

British Library Newspaper Library, Colindale Avenue, London NW9 5HE; telephone: 020 7412 7353; www.bl.uk/collections/newspapers.html.

Federation of Family History Societies, PO Box 8857, Lutterworth LE17 9BJ; telephone: 01455 203133; www.ffhs.org.uk.

Imperial War Museum, Lambeth Road, London SE1 6HZ; telephone: 020 7416 5320; www.iwm.org.uk.

The National Archives, Kew, Richmond, Surrey TW9 4DU; telephone: 020 8876 3444; www.nationalarchives.gov.uk (click on 'Research' to see the list of guides).

The National Archives of Scotland, HM General Register House, 2 Princes Street, Edinburgh EH1 3YY; telephone: 0131 535 1314; www.nas.gov.uk.

The Society of Genealogists, 14 Charterhouse Buildings, Goswell Road, London EC1M 7BA; telephone: 020 7251 8799; www.sog.org.uk.